BEHAVIORAL, HUMANISTIC-EXISTENTIAL, AND PSYCHODYNAMIC APPROACHES TO COUPLES COUNSELING

Couples counseling is distinct from individual and family therapy and, while ideas from these other formats may be overlapping, applying theoretical concepts to couples has distinctive challenges. *Behavioral, Humanistic-Existential, and Psychodynamic Approaches to Couples Counseling* is unique in that it addresses how to conceptualize various theories around a single case. By discussing only one case, the reader is more readily able to compare and contrast the theoretical ideas of each theory, as well as the pragmatics of techniques. Five theories are discussed around four consistent parts: history, theory of problem formation, theory of problem resolution, and case transcript.

Michael D. Reiter, PhD, LMFT, is a Professor in the Department of Family Therapy at Nova Southeastern University.

Ronald J. Chenail, PhD, is Associate Provost and Professor in the Department of Family Therapy at Nova Southeastern University. He is the current Editor of *Journal of Divorce and Remarriage*. He also served as Editor-in-Chief of the *Journal of Marital and Family Therapy*, the flagship research journal of the American Association for Marriage and Family Therapy (AAMFT).

BEHAVIORAL, HUMANISTIC-EXISTENTIAL, AND PSYCHODYNAMIC APPROACHES TO COUPLES COUNSELING

Edited by Michael D. Reiter and Ronald J. Chenail

Routledge
Taylor & Francis Group
NEW YORK AND LONDON

First published 2017
by Routledge
605 Third Avenue, New York, NY 10017
4 Park Square, Milton Park, Abingdon, Oxon OX14 4RN

Routledge is an imprint of the Taylor & Francis Group, an informa business

Library of Congress Cataloging in Publication Data
Names: Reiter, Michael D., editor. | Chenail, Ronald J., editor.
Title: Behavioral, humanistic-existential, and psychodynamic approaches to couples counseling / edited by Michael D. Reiter & Ronald J. Chenail.
Description: New York, NY : Routledge, 2016. |
Includes bibliographical references and index.
Identifiers: LCCN 2016030423 | ISBN 9781138936409 (hardback : alk. paper) | ISBN 9781138936430 (pbk. : alk. paper) | ISBN 9781315676869 (ebook)
Subjects: | MESH: Couples Therapy–methods
Classification: LCC RC488.5 | NLM WM 430.5.M3 |
DDC 616.89/1562–dc23
LC record available at https://lccn.loc.gov/2016030423

ISBN: 978-1-138-93640-9 (hbk)
ISBN: 978-1-138-93643-0 (pbk)
ISBN: 978-1-315-67686-9 (ebk)

Typeset in Bembo
by Out of House Publishing

MDR: To Patricia and Salvador Minuchin—two people who came together to become an amazing couple and who helped countless couples and families through their work.

RC: To Paula—this is our first book and first year of marriage—may we have many more of both.

CONTENTS

About the Editors viii
About the Chapter Contributors ix
Preface xi

1 Couples Counseling 1
Michael D. Reiter

2 The Case: David and Natalie Johnson 9
Michael D. Reiter

3 Psychodynamic Couples Counseling 15
Albert J. Brok

4 Adlerian Couples Therapy 51
Jon Carlson, Leigh Johnson-Migalski, and Ebony Spriggs

5 Cognitive Behavioral Couple Therapy 87
Terence Patterson

6 Gottman Method Couples Therapy 113
Vagdevi Meunier

7 Imago Relationship Therapy 148
Wade Luquet

Index 178

ABOUT THE EDITORS

Michael D. Reiter, PhD, LMFT, is a licensed Marriage and Family Therapist, Clinical Fellow of the American Association of Family Therapists (AAMFT), and a state and AAMFT Approved Supervisor. Currently, Michael is Professor of Family Therapy at Nova Southeastern University. He has written four textbooks on therapy and family therapy and has written many journal articles and book chapters on Solution-Focused Brief Therapy. Michael was able to obtain training from Insoo Kim Berg and Steve de Shazer, the founders of Solution-Focused Brief Therapy, and has provided Solution-Focused Brief Therapy trainings and conference presentations nationally and internationally.

Ronald J. Chenail, PhD, is Associate Provost and Professor of Family Therapy at Nova Southeastern University (NSU). Since 1990, he has published over 120 publications including five books and given more than 180 formal academic presentations at conferences and meetings. He also served as Editor-in-Chief of the *Journal of Marital and Family Therapy* (*JMFT*), the flagship research journal of the American Association for Marriage and Family Therapy (AAMFT). In addition, he is an editorial board member of *Qualitative Research in Psychology*, *American Journal of Family Therapy*, *Contemporary Family Therapy*, *Qualitative Social Work*, *Counselling, Psychotherapy, and Health*, *JMFT*, and *Sistemas Familiares*.

ABOUT THE CHAPTER CONTRIBUTORS

Albert Brok, PhD, is Director of Couple Training at the Training Institute for Mental Health in NY and Faculty of Derner Institute, Adelphi University. He serves on the Board of the Division of Psychoanalysis, APA, and is former Professor of Education and Supervisor of Clinical Psychology, TC Columbia University, and Director of Clinical Psychology, New School for Social Research. He is bilingual in Spanish and is guest Presenter at the Argentine Psychoanalitic Association, and the Asociacion Psicoanalitica de Madrid.

Jon Carlson, Psy.D., Ed.D. ABPP, is Distinguished Professor of Adlerian psychology at Adler University, Chicago, Illinois and a psychologist with the Wellness Clinic in Lake Geneva, Wisconsin. Jon is the author of more than 60 books in many areas and has also produced 300 video programs that feature the most prominent leaders in the field demonstrating their theories in actions. These videos are used to train the next generation of practitioners. He has received lifetime achievement awards from several professional associations including the American Psychological Association, the American Counseling Association and the North American Society of Adlerian Psychology.

Leigh Johnson-Migalski, PsyD, is an Associate Professor in the Department of Psychology at the Adler University. She teaches all of the Adlerian core courses in the curriculum and coordinates the Advanced Adlerian Psychotherapy Emphasis for students enrolled in the Doctorate in Clinical Psychology. She is interested in research on Adlerian theory and therapy, women's issues, and mood disorders. The North American Society of Adlerian Psychology conferred Leigh with Diplomate status last year.

Wade Luquet, MSW, PhD, is Associate Professor of human services at Gwynedd Mercy University in suburban Philadelphia. He is the author of *Short-term couples therapy: The Imago model in action* and co-editor of *Healing in the relational paradigm: The Imago relationship therapy casebook* and *Imago relationship therapy: Perspectives on theory*. He is also the author of numerous book chapters and articles on IRT and couples therapy and on the academic faculty of Imago Relationships International. He has a private practice in North Wales, Pennsylvania.

Vagdevi Meunier, PsyD, is a licensed clinical psychologist and a Clinical Assistant Professor in the Clinical Psychology doctoral program at the University of Texas in Austin. She has a private clinical and consulting practice in Austin where she specializes in couples and family therapy, couples workshops, training and supervision, and organizational consultation. Vagdevi is the founder and Executive Director of The Center for Relationships, a wellness center that specializes in counseling, outreach, education, and research based on relationship science. She has also been a certified Gottman Couples Therapist and a certified Gottman Workshop Leader since 2006.

Terence Patterson, EdD, ABPP, is a licensed psychologist and Professor at the University of San Francisco. He also practices independently, specializing in couple and family therapy and individual behavior disorders. He is past president of the APA Society for Couple & Family Psychology and the Association of Family Therapists of Northern California, and currently serves on the American Board of Couple & Family Therapy (ABPP). His scholarly endeavors focus on professional ethics and competence to practice in specialty areas.

Ebony Spriggs is a current doctoral student in clinical psychology at Adler University. She received her Bachelors in psychology from Roanoke College and her Masters in clinical psychology from Adler University. Her clinical and research interests include working with couples and families.

PREFACE

This book was born from our work as family therapy teachers, supervisors, therapists, and researchers. In working with students, we saw that they usually tended to have an individualistic orientation and that learning to think systemically and relationally could sometimes be difficult for them. Further, we realized that in many family therapy graduate programs, students are taught family therapy approaches in many different classes, but may only have one course in couples therapy. While we see family therapy and couple therapy as siblings—since they both are predicated on understanding problems from a relational perspective—we also know that many couples therapy approaches are not given the exposure they deserve.

In thinking about how to present many of the most utilized and significant contemporary couples approaches, we wanted readers not only to understand the key concepts, but most importantly learn how to apply the ideas to an actual case. We found in many handbooks and case study collectives of couples therapy, there may have been a wide range of approaches presented; however, each chapter presented worked with distinct and different cases. While the reader may be able to learn about the model, the distinctions between models may not come through as well as they might. This is why we decided to have one case that is used in every chapter. This way, the reader is able to compare and contrast how the various models conceptualize why the same couple is having difficulties (the theory of problem formation) and what the therapist might do with the couple in therapy (the theory of problem resolution). This format of presentation of various models using a single case was utilized in my (Michael D. Reiter) previous book, *Case conceptualization in family therapy* (Reiter, 2014). Based on the positive responses from students and readers of that book, we utilized again this same format. This book has a companion (Reiter & Chenail, 2017)—each book presenting five different couples theories and using the same case. This way, you can compare and contrast models in that book and across books. This current book explores what we are classifying as behavioral, humanistic-existential, and psychodynamic approaches. The companion book highlights constructivist, critical, and integrative approaches.

We want to thank a few people who helped out in various areas of making this book come together: Alexandra Alfaro, Paula Boros, Clint Lambert, and Melissa Rosen for genogram and chapter reviews. Christopher Burnett, our friend and colleague, who let us use one of his amazing photographs for the cover of the book. This book would not have been possible without the contributions of all of the chapter authors: Albert Brok, Jon Carlson, Leigh Johnson-Migalski, Wade Luquet, Vagdevi Meunier, Terence Patterson, and Ebony Spriggs. We would also like to thank Elizabeth Graber, Associate Editor at Routledge, who helped us bring this book to fruition.

References

Reiter, M. D. (2014). *Case conceptualization in family therapy*. Upper Saddle River, NJ: Pearson.

Reiter, M. D., & Chenail, R. J. (Eds.). (2017). *Constructivist, critical, and integrative approaches to couples counseling*. New York, NY: Routledge.

1

COUPLES COUNSELING

Michael D. Reiter

When two people enter into a romantic relationship, they usually do so with hopes that they will have a positive and enriching relationship. However, as we know, all relationships are fraught with periodic disagreements, difficulties, and problems. Sometimes the members of the dyad are able to resolve these conflicts in a mutually satisfying manner. However, sometimes they are not and seek outside pathways for resolution. One means of resolution is through couples counseling.

Couples

This book, and its companion (see Reiter & Chenail, 2017), are about conducting psychotherapy with two people who are in a romantic relationship. While we can conduct couples therapy with just one member of the couple (using a systemic perspective), in this book we will be exploring what occurs when they both come together—what was classically called conjoint therapy. There are many terms that can be used for the dyad that is coming for change as well as the change process. The two people in therapy may be called spouses, marital partners, partners, significant others, boyfriend/girlfriend, or other such terms. They may be of different sexes, the same sex, different or same religion, race, educational background, socioeconomic background or may vary in age.

According to the US Census, in 2010, there were approximately 60 million married couples in the United States. This does not take into account the amount of unmarried cohabitating couples as well as noncohabitating couples. These couples may have recently come together or have been together for many decades. However, couples have been changing in various ways over the last century—with the Supreme Court's ruling that anti-miscegenation laws were unconstitutional in 1967, the Supreme Court ruling in 2015 that same-sex marriage is a right, the influx of immigrants interculturally marrying, as well as people altering the timing of relationship formation and marriage. As an example, for married couples, both men and women are marrying for the first time later in life than in previous generations, with the median age for women at first marriage being 25.8 and 28.3 for men (Copen, Daniels, Vespa, & Mosher, 2012).

One of the reasons for the later age of first marriage is the increase in cohabitation (Copen et al., 2012). For instance, in 1982, approximately 3 percent of women cohabitated while 11 percent of women cohabitated in 2006–2010. This increase in cohabitation is related to an inverse trend in marriage. The marriage rate in the Western world has been decreasing in the last part of the twentieth century and into the twenty-first century (Pinsof, 2002). Sixty years ago, cohabitation was not as prominent as it is today, but has now become either a pathway toward marriage or an alternative to marriage. Between 2006 and 2010, for first premarital cohabitation for women, 40 percent transitioned into marriage by three years, 32 percent continued to cohabitate, and 27 percent of the couples ended their relationship (Copen, Daniels, & Mosher, 2013). While primarily utilized as a union of choice for younger couples, older couples—especially those who had previously been married to someone else—are deciding to cohabitate rather than marry (Noack, Bernhardt, & Wiik, 2014). The type of residence coupling is important as it may impact relationship happiness. For instance, married couples tend to be with one another for longer periods of time and stay together at higher levels, even in instances of couple distress (Moore, McCabe, & Brink, 2001).

It is important for therapists to be cognizant of the changing trends in couplehood as this impacts the internal and external dynamics of the couple. For instance, a cohabiting couple who come from one or more very religious families may experience social disapproval for their living situation. Or a same-sex couple or a couple with one or more transgendered members may experience discrimination from friends, family, or others in society.

A couple can be considered a family—even if there are no children involved (Del Rio & Mieling, 2010). While most people consider a family to be at least one parent and one child, couples, especially those that are married or in long-term committed relationships, function as the spousal subsystem of families. But the couple is also a subsystem of at least two larger families—that of each partner's extended family. As such, the couple attempts to distinguish itself as separate but still connected to each partner's family-of-origin. This is where the dyad has developed some type of boundary to demarcate itself from these larger families. It is a dynamic push and pull to say that, "We are a part of you, but we are separate." While being an adult and perhaps not living at home makes it seem as if the person is distinct from their family, the influence of the family on the person—and the couple—is still present. Bertoni and Bodenmann (2010) found that satisfied couples had better relationships with their families-of-origin than did dissatisfied couples or couples who were in therapy. These authors highlighted that one aspect of marital quality was this intergenerational dimension.

Young and Long (1998) identified several characteristics of couples. These include the relationship being voluntary, having both stability and growth/change, having a past, present, and future, merging two perspectives, giving and receiving support, and having a separate identity while also being respectful of the other person's identity. So while we may use the word "couple" in this book to refer to the unit, we understand that within that unit are two separate individuals. These distinct entities, however, are intimately connected in a process of mutuality—they create the other person in the relationship. For instance, a partner who frequently says negative things to her partner is helping to create a partner who may be quite defensive. Or a partner who does not engage the other emotionally helps to create a partner who more actively seeks out this emotionality.

As we've explored, all couples have problems; some more than others. Even couples who are very satisfied with their relationship have areas of their relationship they find as negative. Yet, those who are dissatisfied in their relationship will tend to have higher levels of negative behaviors (Bertoni & Bodenmann, 2010). These authors found that there were distinctions between satisfied and dissatisfied couples as well as those that seek therapy. Satisfied couples had more positive than negative behaviors, dissatisfied couples had more negative behaviors than positive, and couples in therapy had about equal amounts of positive and negative behaviors.

The couples that come to see you will come in all shapes and sizes and with a wide variety of presenting complaints. It is important for you to recognize that regardless of the configuration between the two members (i.e. their gender, sexual orientation, age, religion, culture, race, etc.) as well as the length of time they have been a couple, they are seeking something very important: change. The various specific issues that couples come to counseling for are beyond the scope of this book, which is more focused on operating from a specific model rather than focusing on the presenting complaint. However, having an understanding of some of the main reasons couples come to counseling can be quite important. For instance, problematic communication and lack of emotional affection are the most common reasons couples say they seek therapy (Boisvert, Writght, Tremblay, & McDuff, 2011; Doss, Simpson, & Christensen, 2004). Other prominent reasons for couples to go to therapy include making the couple relationship better for the children, lack of physical affection and sex, as well as trying to increase positive feelings between the partners. Therapists may also need to know how long a couple has been together and where they are in their developmental stage of couplehood (Henry & Miller, 2004; Miller, Yorgason, Sandberg, & White, 2003). While the problems that couples report tend to be the same whether they are newly together, are at the having children stage, or have been together for a long time, how these problems play themselves out in the relationship may be different.

However, the two members of the couple are often not in agreement as to what the agenda is for therapy—sometimes having two very different goals for the process (Goldberg, 1992). For example, one partner may come to couples therapy in hopes of salvaging the relationship while the other partner wants to use it as justification for the relationship not working and thus needing to end. Or one partner may come to therapy hoping for increased sexual intimacy while the other partner desires emotional connection rather than physical connection. This difference in agenda may be, for heterosexual couples, based on gender, as women tend to report more problems about their relationship than do men (Miller et al., 2003). Given that there are two separate individuals coming to therapy, it is important for the therapist to distinguish where the members' goals and intents for therapy overlap, as this will be the foundation for moving toward a mutually satisfying outcome.

Couples Counseling

As for what we might call what is happening when the couple comes to see you, this might be referred to as psychotherapy, therapy, marital counseling, relational counseling, couples therapy, etc. We are not going to distinguish between these sorts of terms (i.e. what might be the differences between "therapy" and "counseling"). However, in this book, we use the phrase "**couples counseling**" as a broad overview of what occurs when at least one person who is in a romantic relationship comes to a professional for some type of change in their relationship.

Couples counseling can be done with one person as it is not the amount of people in the therapy room that distinguishes it as couples counseling but the focus of the therapy—a focus on what is occurring between two people. As such, there are several types or forms of couples therapy (Sholevar, 2003); individual therapy, concurrent couples therapy, conjoint couples therapy, combined couples therapy, and couple group therapy. Individual therapy for couples occurs when just one member of the couple comes to sessions, but the focus is on improving the relationship. The other partner may not come for a variety of reasons including they are seeking a divorce, have a mental health issue, or do not believe in therapy. Concurrent couples therapy is when both partners are attending therapy, but doing so individually with the same therapist. Conjoint couples therapy, which is the most frequently used type, occurs when both partners attend the same sessions. Combined couples therapy is an integration of concurrent and conjoint when some sessions are held individually with each partner and some sessions both partners participate. Lastly, couple group therapy occurs when multiple couples are seen together in a group format. In this book we will be focusing on conjoint couples therapy.

We believe the term couples counseling encompasses the vast array of couples who come to therapy: people who are married, divorced, dating, engaged, as well as other configurations and allows room for one or more people to be in the therapy room. The important idea here is that regardless of how many people are present and regardless of the stage of relational development, the focus of the sessions is on the relationship. However, this focus may not always be the maintenance of the relationship as some couples come to therapy to seek ways of having a more amiable separation.

This decision to utilize the term couples counseling instead of marriage counseling is significant as it is inclusive rather than exclusive. The use of the term "marriage" may imply a more heterosexual dyad rather than nonheterosexual or nonmarried (Del Rio & Mieling, 2010). For some couples, laws and societal demands have not allowed them to formally marry. Other couples may not believe in the purpose of marriage or may see it as an institution. Thus, marriage is just one option for couples. Given the negative climate surrounding homosexual couples and recently transgendered couples, where a formal and legal marriage was mainly unattainable and even unsafe (by people outside of the couple threatening those within it), we believe the word "couple" is much more respectful than "marriage."

For many years the fields of couples counseling and family therapy have overlapped and were perhaps viewed as one and the same. This can be seen in associations such as the American Association of Marriage and Family Therapy. While many of the ideas between couples and family therapy are similar (i.e. that problems that people have are relational), we can distinguish between these fields. However, within this joint presentation, couple therapy was presented as of secondary importance to family therapy—which could be seen in the scarcity of presentation in family therapy textbooks (Gurman & Fraenkel, 2002). This secondary status can be placed in historical perspective.

What was considered as marital therapy (now couple therapy) is approximately 80 years old (Sperry, Carlson, & Peluso, 2006). Couple therapy may be viewed to have developed in four phases—some of which overlap (Gurman & Fraenkel, 2002; Gurman, 2015). These include "Atheoretical Marriage Counseling Formation" (1930–1963), "Psychoanalytic Experimentation (and Reemergence)" (1931–1966 and 1985–current), "Family Therapy Incorporation" (1963–1985), and "Refinement, Extension, Diversification, and Integration (1986–)."

The "**Atheoretical Marriage Counseling Formation**" phase was a time in which "marriage counseling" developed but was practiced by people who were not counselors as we know today, but rather doctors, family life educators, and clergy. Much of the counseling was about teaching the individuals in the couple about family life/roles rather than addressing "problems" as is current. It was during this time that marital therapy became a profession, which was seen in the establishment of the American Association of Marriage Counselors in 1942. This organization later changed its name to the American Association of Marriage and Family Counselors and is currently called the American Association for Marriage and Family Therapy.

The "**Psychoanalytic Experimentation**" was a time in which the marriage counseling of the previous stage, which did not really have a theoretical base, found a home in the psychoanalytic paradigm. In this phase the practice of conjoint therapy—working with more than one person in the room at the same time—emerged as a common practice. This was a major shift in the practice of therapy as traditional psychoanalysis was predicated on a one-on-one analyst and patient relationship.

The third phase, "**Family Therapy Incorporation**," contrasted the psychoanalytic influence on marriage counseling. Since many of the early family therapy founders had their roots in psychoanalysis, but had rejected that model and began to adopt a more systems-focused lens, they brought a brand new epistemology to work with couples. It was in this stage that family therapy, in many ways, devoured marriage counseling, leading the two fields to be virtually one and the same.

In the last stage, "**Refinement, Extension, Diversification, and Integration**," a greater focus on research into couples counseling emerged, such as emotionally focused couples counseling, the Gottman method, as well as behavioral couples counseling. This stage utilized "diversification" by bringing in ideas from feminism, multiculturalism, and postmodernism. Also, clinical models and techniques became more formalized and researched in terms of efficacy as well as couple therapy being utilized for presenting problems outside the scope of normal couple therapy—issues such as individual psychiatric disorders.

During the last part of the twentieth century, couple therapy went through several major changes (Johnson & Lebow, 2000). This included couple therapy becoming legitimized as a treatment choice for couples, the focus on the science of relationships, evidence-based efficacy for couple therapy, a greater focus on various aspects of diversity, as well as a movement toward integration. Burbach and Reibstein (2012) hold that there is a "coming of age" of couple therapy. This leads to the importance for therapists to have a strong grasp on the various couples counseling models that are present in the field.

Training programs for therapists have not traditionally emphasized couples counseling as they have other methods, such as group or family therapy (Long & Burnett, 2005). One of these reasons is that many graduate programs have degrees in family therapy and assume that covers couple therapy as well. However, some couple therapists view what they do as very different than family therapy (Lebow, 2013). This is a difficult distinction sometimes as couple and family therapies both rest on the assumptions of relationships, regardless of the number of individuals in the therapy room.

Not only is couples counseling not formalized in many therapy graduate programs, but is not recognized in some agency and practice settings. Couples counseling is at-risk in the managed care field, as it may not fit in some ways with the timbre of health insurance policies (Hoyt & Gurman, 2012). Many insurance companies insist on the insured person receiving a Diagnostic and Statistical Manual diagnosis. This may go against some couples therapists' sensibilities.

Yet, the importance of couples counseling as a distinct mode of working is paramount. Therapists should have a thorough understanding of couples' issues as well as various theories of counseling couples as approximately 50 percent of people who come to counseling do so because of some type of couple problem (Sholevar, 2003). For those whose primary presentation is something else, approximately 25 percent of cases involve some type of couples' difficulties. Thus, almost all therapists, regardless of specialty, or training background (i.e. marriage and family therapist, mental health counselor, clinical psychologist, clinical social worker, etc.) will work with individuals and dyads that are having problems in their romantic relationship.

Book Organization

This book is organized to allow you to compare and contrast five of the most popular post-positivist couples counseling theories by developing a case conceptualization of the same couple through each of these approaches. Chapter 2 presents a couple that was used by each of the chapter authors to conceptualize based on their specific approach. This fictionalized couple is a conglomeration of many couples that we (MR & RC) have worked with throughout our careers. We believe that people learn best when they can compare and contrast ideas. As such, we have organized this book so that you can understand five different models of couples counseling via this recurrent case.

Each of the theory chapters is organized similarly, with four main sections. The first is a brief history of the model. This is followed by a section on the theory of problem formation. In this section, the chapter authors explain how the model views why couples have difficulties. This is done through exploring the case of David and Natalie presented in Chapter 2. The third section explores the theory of problem resolution—how that model understands change. The last section provides a mock first session with explanation for why the therapist made certain interventions. We provide the same case and format for five constructivist, critical, and integrative approaches in a separate book (Reiter & Chenail, 2017).

References

Bertoni, A., & Bodenmann, G. (2010). Satisfied and dissatisfied couples: Positive and negative dimensions, conflict styles, and relationships with family of origin. *European Psychologist*, *15*(3), 175–184.

Boisvert, M.-M., Wright, J., Tremblay, N., & McDuff, P. (2011). Couples' reports of relationship problems in a naturalistic therapy setting. *The Family Journal: Counseling and Therapy for Couples and Families*, *19*(4), 362–368.

Burbach, F., & Reibstein, J. (2012). Focusing on couple therapy: Going forward. *Journal of Family Therapy*, *34*(3), 225–228.

Copen, C. E., Daniels, K., & Mosher, W. D. (2013). First premarital cohabitation in the United States: 2006–2010 national survey of family growth. *National Health Statistics Report*, *64*, 1–15.

Copen, C. E., Daniels, K., Vespa, J., & Mosher, W. D. (2012). First marriages in the United States: Data from the 2006–2010 national survey of family growth. *National Health Statistics Reports*, *49*, 1–21.

Del Rio, C. M., & Mieling, G. G. (2010). "Marriage" misnames "couples" and familial therapies. *The Family Journal: Counseling and Therapy for Couples and Families*, *18*(2), 169–177.

Doss, B. D., Simpson, L. E., & Christensen, A. (2004). Why do couples seek marital therapy? *Professional Psychology: Research and Practice, 35*(6), 608–614.

Goldberg, M. (1992). The impasse in couples therapy. *Psychiatric Annals, 22*(10), 520–525.

Gurman, A. S. (2015). The theory and practice of couple therapy. In A. S. Gurman, J. L. Lebow, & D. K. Snyder (Eds.), *Clinical handbook of couple therapy* (5th ed., pp. 1–18). New York, NY: The Guilford Press.

Gurman, A. S., & Fraenkel, P. (2002). The history of couple therapy: A millennial review. *Family Process, 41*(2), 199–260.

Henry, R. G., & Miller, R. B. (2004). Marital problems occurring in midlife: Implications for couples therapists. *The American Journal of Family Therapy, 32*(5), 405–417.

Hoyt, M. F., & Gurman, A. S. (2012). Wither couple/family therapy? *Family Journal, 20*(1), 13–17.

Johnson, S., & Lebow, J. (2000). The "coming of age" of couple therapy: A decade review. *Journal of Marital and Family Therapy, 26*(1), 23–38.

Lebow, J. (2013). Editorial: Couple therapy and family therapy. *Family Process, 52*(1), 1–4.

Long, L. L., & Burnett, J. A. (2005). Teaching couples counseling: An integrative model. *The Family Journal, 13*(3), 321–327.

Miller, R. B., Yorgason, J. B., Sandberg, J. G., & White, M. B. (2003). Problems that couples bring to therapy: A view across the family life cycle. *The American Journal of Family Therapy, 31*(5), 395–407.

Moore, K. A., McCabe, M. P., & Brink, R. B. (2001). Are married couples happier in their relationships than cohabiting couples? Intimacy and relationship factors. *Sexual and Relationship Therapy, 16*(1), 35–46.

Noack, T., Bernhardt, E., & Wiik, K. A. (2014). Cohabitation or marriage? Contemporary living arrangements in the West. In A. Abela & J. Walker (Eds.), *Contemporary issues in family studies: Global perspectives on partnerships, parenting and support in a changing world* (pp. 16–30). Chichester, UK: John Wiley & Sons.

Pinsof, W. M. (2002). The death of "till death us do part": The transformation of pair-bonding in the 20th century. *Family Process, 41*(2), 135–157.

Reiter, M. D., & Chenail, R. J. (2017). *Constructivist, critical, and integrative approaches to couples counseling*. New York, NY: Routledge.

Sholevar, G. P. (2003). Couples therapy: An overview. In G. P. Sholevar & L. D. Schwoeri (Eds.), *Textbook of family and couples therapy: Clinical applications* (pp. 417–437). Washington, DC: American Psychiatric Publishing.

Sperry, L., Carlson, J., & Peluso, P. R. (2006). *Couples therapy: Integrating theory and technique* (2nd ed.). Denver, CO: Love Publishing Company.

Young, M., & Long, L. (1998). *Counseling and therapy for couples*. Pacific Grove, CA: Brooks/Cole.

2

THE CASE

David and Natalie Johnson

Michael D. Reiter

Presenting Problem

David and Natalie Johnson (28 and 30 years old, respectively) made an appointment for couples therapy after Natalie discovered that David had been having an internet affair for the past six months. She happened to look in the history section of David's laptop and found a lot of personal messages between David and a woman named Devyn. In reading the messages, Natalie was heartbroken to read David saying that he wanted to divorce Natalie and move across the country to live with Devyn.

When she first confronted him with the affair, David denied it. She then made him open up his email folder and bring up the emails. He then explained that, yes, he had been conversing with the woman, but that it wasn't anything serious and he was just saying those things to her to get Devyn to continue talking with him. The following is the conversation they had during this argument:

Natalie: What is going on between you and this Devyn woman?
David: Nothing.
Natalie: Then why all the emails saying that you love her?
David: What are you talking about?
Natalie: David, I've seen the emails. Don't play stupid.
David: Okay, I am talking to someone, but it's not what you think.
Natalie: It's not that you love her, don't love me, and are going to divorce me and move in with her?
David: I might have said something like that, but I didn't mean it. I just said it to keep talking with her. It was just something fun to do. You know, kind of like catfishing.

Natalie: David, I'm not an idiot. If you want to be with her, then admit it and leave. But if you want any chance with me, then you better start telling me the truth.

David: Okay, okay. Look, you know things between you and me haven't been great recently. When's the last time we had sex, huh?

Natalie: And you think that's my fault?

David: You think it's mine?

Natalie: I'm not the one that's an alcoholic!

David: I forgot; you're perfect.

Natalie: I'm not perfect, but I'm not having an affair with someone on the internet. Have you ever met her?

David: No. It's only been via email.

Natalie: You never Skyped her? And don't bullshit me.

David: Fine, we video chatted.

Natalie: And did you talk naked and have sex online.

David: What does it matter? Do you think you've done everything to make this marriage work?

Natalie: I haven't led anyone else on.

David: But you've thought about divorce, right?

Natalie: I have, but I wanted to try to make things work out first. Do you?

David: Of course, otherwise I would have left already.

This conversation led the couple to agree to go for couples counseling to give the relationship one last chance before they contacted lawyers for a divorce. They had never gone for any type of individual or couples counseling before.

In terms of prior relationships, David is much more experienced than Natalie. David has had several long-term serious relationships, the longest of which was a two-year relationship he had during college. Natalie's longest relationship was for five months. She had several boyfriends in college, all of which cheated on her.

History of the Couple

David and Natalie Johnson have been married for three years. They met two years previously via an online dating website. David was 25 at the time while Natalie was 27. They talked to each other via online text chats for approximately three months before they agreed to talk on the telephone. While they were getting to know each other, David also was in conversations with several other women from the dating site. Only once did he meet up with one of these women, who lived in New York City, but the meeting did not go well.

After their first telephone conversation, Natalie and David started talking to each other several times per week. Natalie lived in Texas while David came from Maine. At the time of meeting, David was fully employed as a high school teacher. Natalie had established herself as a realtor in Texas.

After finding that their conversations were very fulfilling, the couple arranged for their first meeting five months after first contacting each other on the internet. David flew down to Texas and spent four days with Natalie. The two got along very well and sexually consummated their romantic relationship. For the next year David and Natalie visited each other at least once a month, flying back and forth from Texas to Maine or Maine to Texas. David did more of the traveling during this time.

The couple talked about being together and where they would live. Natalie thought it was much easier for her to stay in Texas as the real estate market was a lot larger than in the smaller town where David came from in Maine. During this time David applied for teaching jobs in Texas and eventually got one in the neighboring school district to where Natalie lived, however, he had to wait until the following school year to begin. In July of 2012 he packed up all of his belongings and drove across the country to move in with Natalie.

For the first year of their relationship David and Natalie both felt very much in love with one another. They shared an enjoyment of going out to restaurants, both having similar palates for food. They also enjoyed going to the movies, sitting at cafes drinking coffee and talking, as well as watching Dallas Cowboys games together. They had made Friday night "date-night" and had gone to new restaurants, theater shows, and other interesting activities. At the time, they each believed they had an active and enjoyable sex life.

During their second year together, they both noticed differences starting to emerge in the relationship. They began to argue more about small (i.e. where to go for dinner, which movie to see) and big things (i.e. whether, and if so when, to have a child). Natalie wanted to begin having a family right away while David wanted to wait until he found a better job. Natalie's argument was that she did not want to be an older mother and that she was already approaching 30. David stated that he wanted for them to have more time as a couple, although he began spending more nights out with friends at sports bars and sporting events.

In this past third year of their marriage, they have been finding themselves drifting apart from each other. David has gained weight over the three years of their marriage to where he is now 5 foot 8 and weighs 215 pounds. He also has increased his smoking of cigarettes from one every few days to now one pack a day. Natalie, while overweight herself, has become quite concerned about David's health and attempts to get him to be healthier. Earlier in the year, she attempted to get him to stop smoking. The conversation is below:

Natalie: David, are you going to have another cigarette now?

David: Perhaps. Why?

Natalie: Because I don't want you smoking in the house anymore. It makes everything stink.

David: You know, it's my house too.

Natalie: I know. But we both need to keep the house clean. And cigarette smoke not only makes the house smell, but I have to breathe it if it's in the air.
David: Fine, then I'll go out on the patio.
Natalie: That's better. But I still don't want you to smoke.
David: Why not? It's my body not yours.
Natalie: But I want you to be healthy.
David: I am healthy.
Natalie: You've been gaining weight, and now you're smoking even more.
David: What about you? You're overweight.
Natalie: I know. We both need to get in better shape.
David: Yeah, it would be nice if you lost weight.
Natalie: David, don't be mean.
David: I'm not being mean. Just truthful. I'm going outside to smoke.

Currently, the couple has not engaged in any sexual activity for seven months. At times, after they have argued, David has slept in the guest bedroom.

David's Family-of-Origin

David is the third child of three from Dana and Sheila. His siblings are his sisters Susan and Regina. Dana and Sheila met while they were both working together at a bank in Portland, Maine. Dana was a bank manager and Sheila a teller. They married two years after first meeting, when Dana was 27 and Sheila 24. After one year of marriage they had their first daughter, Susan. One year later, their second daughter, Regina, was born.

Sheila had only wanted two children, but Dana very much wanted a son. After many conversations, Sheila agreed to have another child, but warned Dana that this was the last, whether it was male or female. Three years after Regina was born, Sheila conceived and gave birth to David. When he was nine, Dana and Sheila divorced. Sheila has dated occasionally, but not seriously. Dana married Barbara in 2000.

David and his older sister, Regina, have not talked for the past six years. This was after many years of Regina's drinking and David telling her how irresponsible she was; especially as a mother. David is also somewhat distant from his father, Dana. Since the divorce of his parents, David has only talked with his father occasionally, mainly on holidays and birthdays. One of the reasons for this is that David tends not to initiate interaction, expecting his father to make the connection.

While he was growing up, David was on the shorter side. He was also not the most athletic kid in his class and was a little pudgy. Dana had been an athlete in high school, primarily playing varsity baseball. Dana had tried to force David into playing baseball, but David was usually one of the worst players on the field. This was a disappointment for Dana.

David's oldest sister, Susan, is close with their mother, Sheila. She is married to Alfredo, the only marriage for both of them. Ten years ago Susan had gotten pregnant but then had a miscarriage. This impacted her emotionally and physically. It was a tough situation for her, which brought Susan and her mother, Sheila, closer together. The doctors also told her that she would not be able to conceive another child. Susan and Alfredo then decided to adopt and eventually adopted a newborn from China, who they named Jordyn. Susan is very close to her daughter, Jordyn.

David's sister Regina is 31 and has been in recovery for the last three years. When she was 19 she gave birth to her daughter, Anna. Her boyfriend at the time, Don, left when he found out she was pregnant and would not get an abortion. When Anna was born, Regina was drinking and drugging and Sheila took over primary caretaking duties. Instead of getting help and cleaning up her life, Regina took this time to party even harder than she had been. She was arrested once for DUI and would ask Susan and David for money. Six years ago, at a family function, Regina had gotten drunk and began to berate David. He was also drunk at the time and their argument actually came to physical blows. David was arrested, but released on bond and put on probation. After that incident he refused to speak to Regina again. That event, though, led Regina to begin a program of active recovery and she went into a treatment center and joined Alcoholics Anonymous. She has been clean and sober and in recovery for over five years. She currently has full custody of Anna.

Natalie's Family-of-Origin

Natalie is the oldest of two children to Fred and Laura. Her brother, Scott, is three years younger. When Scott was two years old her parents divorced. Two years later her mother, Laura, married Nicholas. Together, they gave birth to Natalie's sister, Robyn, 10 years younger.

Scott is currently 27 years old and is married to Michele, which is his second marriage. He was married to Norma for one year, during which they had their daughter, Emma. Scott and Norma had met in college and married once Norma had become pregnant. However, during her pregnancy the couple had become contemptuous of one another and six months after Emma was born they divorced. Norma has full custody of Emma, with Scott spending time with Emma approximately once a week. Scott and Norma have frequent conflict, especially around the area of money. Two years ago Scott married Michele.

Natalie's younger sister, Robyn, is 20 years old and is going to college at a university in Oregon. When Fred and Laura divorced, Natalie and Scott lived with their mother. When Natalie was 10, her sister Robyn was born. Natalie played a parental role in taking care of her.

Natalie does not have a close relationship with her father, Fred. She was five years old when her parents divorced and seven when her mother remarried to Nicholas. However, she has not had a close relationship with either Fred or Nicholas. Natalie felt that Nicholas attempted too hard to be her "father" and throughout her childhood, and especially during adolescence, she had a love/hate relationship with him. Once the divorce occurred, Fred backed out of the children's lives, and spent sporadic time with Natalie and Scott. During early adulthood, Natalie made an attempt to reconnect with Fred, but found that while he cared for her, he didn't initiate much interaction. This infuriated Natalie as she believed that it is the parent's responsibility to initiate and maintain connections.

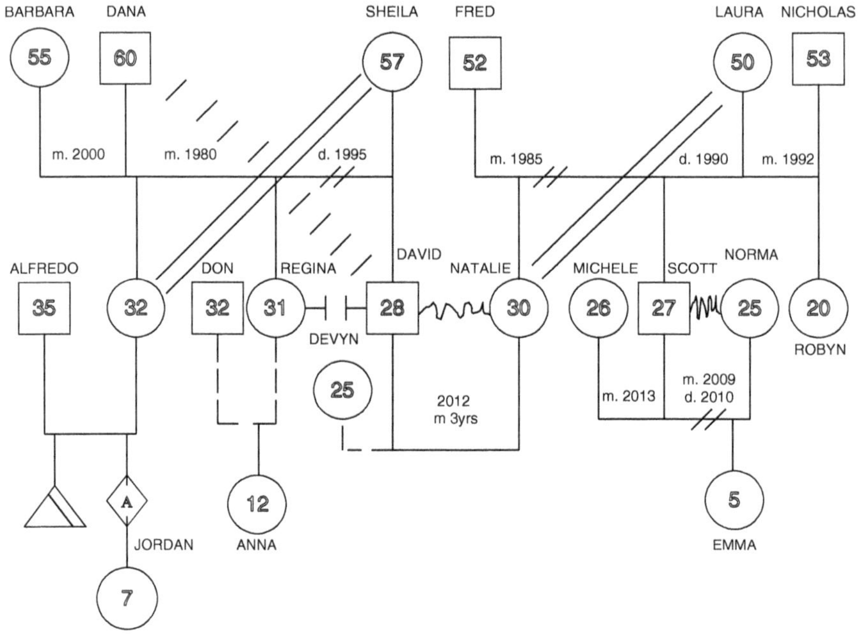

FIGURE 2.1 Genogram of the Couple.

3

PSYCHODYNAMIC COUPLES COUNSELING

Albert J. Brok

A Brief History of Psychodynamic Couple Therapy: Thinking up to the Present

Psychodynamic couple therapy is not only a theoretical model but an important clinical method necessary for understanding the self as well as an "Other" from the perspective of uncovering unconscious conflicts. It is the offspring of parental figures ranging from Classical Analysis, Object Relations theory, Self Psychology, Inter-subjective theory, and many other approaches developed by acutely observant and thoughtful clinicians, who took a keen interest in the profundity and complexity that makes up the mixture of individual psychodynamics, couple relationships, and the human desire to link with an other. Psychodynamic models are not static; they evolve and integrate concepts derived from systems, attachment, cognitive, and other theoretical perspectives (Brok, 1998, 2007).

Psychodynamic thinking has a long history and heritage that goes back as far as human beings took an interest in metaphor, symbolic thinking, and unconscious processes that may cloud one's reflective capacity and perceptions. We can go as far back as the "Allegory of the Cave" from Plato's *Republic*: "And if they could talk to one another, don't you think they'd suppose that the names they used applied to the things they see passing before them."

In other words, we may not be aware that what we initially name or assume is actually a belief, shadow, or distortion, rather than a fact. This is a problem that emerges in many couple relations. It involves the tendency to see another not only by objective experience, but also through the lens of unconscious assumptions termed transferences. By **transference** we mean the phenomena of relating to another unconsciously, in a way deeply colored by experiences from one's past (Freud, 1914).

The capacity to make assumptions is a useful human ability, but when we rigidly live by our assumptions, they can be misinforming and lead to deadly self-fulfilling prophecies. Assumptions curtail the efficacious use of our inquiry and imagination and the building of a more complex varied sense of one's partner. A maxim of use here is "where assumptions are, there inquiry should be" (Brok, 2014a). Psychodynamic couple therapists routinely help the couple and its members work through transferences by which they organize each other.

In a lovely exposition of the history of psychodynamic thinking, Ellenberger's (1970) *Discovery of the unconscious* ranges widely in providing excellent albeit brief coverage of the work of Pierre Janet, Freud, Adler, Jung, and others. These early "depth psychology" clinicians developed useful foci concerning "what lies beneath" and furthered the awareness that humans are not superficial creatures who are primarily rational, but rather complex beings whose emotional depths and beliefs need to be understood from many dimensions: internal, cultural, interpersonal, and historical, all of which are consciously and unconsciously organized. When setting therapeutic goals, these many dimensions need to be taken into account.

In short, psychodynamic couple therapy involves the education and elucidation of what goes on for both the couple and each member outside of awareness and its impact on the couple organizational climate. A major principle of all psychodynamic approaches is that only when someone has a sense of what goes on internally can he or she truly have a grip on choices in work, friendship, and love relationships (Brok, 1976, 2013). We shall see later in this chapter that choices that rest too much on illusion, phantasy assumptions, or unconscious needs can have powerful impacts on how a relationship emotionally functions. We may also stress that a crucial aspect of the model is experiential as well as cognitive. Couples often have difficulty sharing their felt experiences and need to be helped.

The early psychodynamic clinicians clarified and introduced clinically relevant theoretical concepts, such as transference, projective identification and collusions.[1] Such processes distort and prevent a sense of discovering who an "Other" actually is. A corollary to this is that an "Other" may not find it easy to allow him or herself to be discovered. Part of the therapy in couple work involves helping both partners recognize these dynamics and to become mindful of how they provoke, use, or react towards each other via transference, projective identification, or an unwitting unconscious collusive process. Bringing awareness of how they collude in co-creating problems in their relationship is crucial. In addition to each member's individual issues, there needs to be a realization that the couple is trapped in a system of their own making. Unconsciously, each member of a couple can evoke responses in their partner which repeat couple defeating behaviors. We shall see this dynamic when we later discuss the case example of Natalie and David. Interpreting such collusion and the role each member plays can enable partners to come together to solve their conflicts (Aznar-Martinez, Perez-Testor, Davins, & Aramburu, 2016). This is not always a simple or easy task.

One new elaboration of psychodynamic couple theory, originated by the present author, involves noting the difference between **finding** (in the sense of looking for someone who will validate your assumptions, as being quite different from the curiosity based interest in "**Discovering**"; Brok, 1998, 2007, 2011). A good example of the tragedy of finding what you are looking for via the dynamic of transference and projective identification in an **unconsciously collusive relationship** is illustrated in the award-winning film, *An Affair of Love* (1999).[2] It narrates a story of a man and woman who meet for an anonymous liaison. They meet, go to a hotel, and seem to get along well as long as they do not share anything about their personal lives. Slowly, the male protagonist attempts to know the woman better. He offers to drive her home; she replies "better not." Eventually, however, the couple begins to break down their barrier of anonymity. They both privately and independently admit to themselves that they love the other; they each imagine saying this to the other, and are ready to fight for their beliefs—even if the other doesn't admit to it. At one crucial juncture, they arrive at their meeting place, both prepared to declare and fight for their love. It is precisely at that point that assumptions creep in. The male protagonist looks at her face and thinks (needs to think) he sees her as serious (actually, she is thinking of how much she wants him) and he says: "I've decided it's impossible, this will never work." She replies, going by his statement and disavowing her true feeling, "Yes, I was thinking that too, it will never work." It is poignant that neither inquires about what happened nor brings out their true feelings. They misread each other terribly. They just stay with their assumptions and are left with not discovering each other's true feelings. Each individual had no idea what the other individual had been privately thinking but dared not share. So they "named" each other, erroneously. One gets the sense that history is repeated, through transference, projective identification, or fear of sharing a hope. They each erroneously validated each other's disavowal.[3] What each momentarily thought and desired, but never articulated, was thereby slowly strangled by internal conflicts (Brok, 2007).

An additional contribution to the evolving history of psychodynamic couple therapy include the notions of Cognitive Maps, theories of involvement, and the role of wisdom (Brok, 2007, 2011, 2014b). A **Cognitive Map** is a term-meant to articulate how people organize themselves and others in terms of unconscious beliefs strongly influenced by impingements to their curiosity motive. It is an elaboration of object relations notions, perception, and human ecology (Brok, 2007). It is also related to inquiry and curiosity. The more we are interested in discovering, the more we can learn about something, and someone.

Below is a humorous/serious illustration of what I mean. It is represented by a famous *New Yorker* magazine cover meant to depict the limited mental geography of certain denizens of Manhattan. Its title, *View of the World from Ninth Ave*, is a way of poking fun at those who think that everything is centered narcissistically on themselves and little else is worth being curious about.

FIGURE 3.1 Steinberg 1200.
View of the World from 9th Ave © The Saul Steinberg Foundation / Artists Rights Society (ARS), New York. © Condé Nast. Ink, pencil, colored pencil, and watercolor on paper, 71 cm × 48 cm. First published in *The New Yorker*, March 29, 1976. Published with permission.

We see a map of the United States with very little detail. New Jersey, Chicago, Las Vegas, the Pacific Ocean and then some slivers of Russia, etc. are depicted. I have used this as a metaphor to illustrate how members of a couple might limit their interests in each other's internal geography. In a difficult, blocked couple, they only see a few details, have some general suppositions and no interest in exploring what else is there.

Couples "map each other" in terms of unconscious beliefs, categories, and conflicted fears which a skilled therapist, through careful observation, intervention and interpretation, can help them notice, rework, and move towards previously uncharted interesting emotional territory. A corollary to this is how well each member of a couple allows oneself to be mapped. How much of his or her internal territory will they allow to be seen? We shall see this applied later in the case of Natalie and David.

Couples in therapy can suffer with a dynamic similar to the protagonists in *An Affair of Love*; thankfully, couples in treatment are working with a therapist, a valuable "third" who can help them gain perspective and shift things. One of the methods within a psychodynamic perspective I have developed and used is to heighten more detailed awareness of an "Other" by helping each member of the couple to be an **involved witness**. In this process a member of a couple narrates previously unknown aspects of their personal history while their partner is listening[4] as an interested (involved) witness. This technique amplifies their "maps of each other" so they understand each other in new ways (see Brok, 2007 for a case example). Another process is **dream sharing** (Brok, 2007), an exercise to be applied in later rather than initial sessions. Dreams in couple work often reflect how the couple is symbolically/metaphorically experiencing their relationship.

In sum, how each member of the couple organizes the terrain of the other in his or her imagination, and how the couple self-organizes, can have powerful implications for experiencing satisfaction in the couple relationship. Each of us carries an implicit map of our partners and ourselves. The map provides boundaries and familiar terrain through which we can keep located and comfortable. Our own emotions and assumptions about others are part of that map. The map is filled in with points through which we orient ourselves. In a well-functioning person, there is space in the map to discover new points that were previously not on the map. It seems clear that discovering novel aspects about a partner enables each individual member to grow (Aron, Norman, Aron, & Lewandowski, 2002).

Another very important consideration in the history of psychodynamic models of couple relations involves the evolving shift in the theory of love. Psychodynamic theorists classically thought of romantic attachment as based on a process of symbolically re-finding one's earliest love object (Freud, 1905/2001) and/or as narcissistically experiencing one's ego ideal as an aspect of the other (Chasseguet-Smirgel, 1985; Freud, 1914/2001). Most theorists have essentially followed Freud's original conceptualization of romantic dynamics, though amending it by adding the notion that love relationships are unconsciously organized around the hope that one's partner can play a role in "healing the wound inflicted by the less than good-enough early object" (Bergmann, 1987, p. 503). In other words, we hopefully find a "better edition" of our early love objects.[5]

In such formulations, the other becomes a container for positive expectations, but to repair, not necessarily to transform and evolve the self. Clinical experience certainly bears this out. However, the story does not stop there. For example, Brok (1998, 2007) coined the term **Involvement theory** as important in both understanding intimacy and love but also in formulating approaches to clinical work with couples.

In light of the above, the concepts of Attachment and Separation Individuation have also been reworked by psychodynamic theorists (Benjamin, 1995; Brok, 1998). **Attachment theory** is based essentially on a homeostatic model of human behavior, wherein self and other are intertwined in an interaction pattern that serves to sustain a secure base for *one* of them. Mother serves as a secure base for the infant by keeping tension at optimal levels out of her interest in her infant's developing autonomy. In his seminal work on attachment, Bowlby (1969) focuses on the development of spatial separation but says little about the infant's capacity to take *an interest* in the mother beyond her function as a secure base. As Brok (1998) has noted, becoming separate *from* an Other does not guarantee interest *in* an Other.

My own point of view, enlightened by Benjamin's (1995) critique is that attachment is indeed important and a life-long quest, but needs amplification. Mother needs to be viewed as not only serving as a base for autonomy, but also for the infant's discovery and *interest in* the mother. This is typified by there being enough focus by the child on Mother, so the child's interest in Mother is available to the child without it becoming a parentified relationship. Mother has to be allowed her separation too, and also curry an interest in the child about her thoughts (obviously appropriately relevant ones) and life. This is one of the early developmental building blocks for mutuality.[6] This recent psychodynamic oriented inter-subjective critique of separation individuation theory and aspects of attachment theory leaves room for the significance of discovery of, and interest in, the "Other" in a relationship that can become intimate.

Witnessing

The importance of **witnessing** is a modern psychodynamic concept that is also important in working with issues of intimacy in couple relations. Initially discussed by Poland (2000) and elaborated upon by Brok (2007, 2008a), witnessing alludes to the shock of otherness as defining what it is to be a person. For Poland, one's very sense of being alive is always shaped by the surprise of otherness and a function of the ability to be a witness to the "Other" rather than an interpreter, empathizer or sympathizer. Witnessing involves the capacity to be involved without impinging, thereby setting the stage for surprise about, interest in, and discovery of, an Other. In this sense, the feeling of being in love is partly a function of loving and feeling loved via another's interest in one's subjective self, based on that other's ability to be a witness.[7] In particular, an involved witness is not just an observer, but communicates a sense of interest in what he or she is witnessing. Healthy partners do this with each other and those that cannot need to be helped to develop such an interest (i.e. they may defend against the anxiety of knowing details of someone's historical map).

The Role of Play and Intimacy in Couple Relationships

The idea of ludic experience and the concept of play goes far back into history of human experience. In psychodynamic thinking, it has been elaborated upon by Winnicott (1953) and discussed in detail as a major ingredient in healthy couple relationships by Brok (1998, 2008b). By play, I am referring to a state of being, and not to the idea of sports or other pastimes.

Intimacy involves the experience of a non-judgmental climate as existing within the couple context. The potential for judgment exists and is in the background, rather than the foreground of the couple experience. One aspect of intimate experience is analogous to the existence of a state of play between the couple. **Play** is being used in the sense of there being space for spontaneity, freedom of expression, and no concern about being shamed. In other words, no serious impingements. Of course, this implies a consideration of the role of the superego in adult play states.[8] The Healthy couple can play. Here is an example of this concept:

> When I was a professor at Columbia University, I would sometimes be walking in the halls of Teachers College. Once I came across a bunch of students with their professor leading them by playing "*choo choo train*" right there in the hallway. They were not crazy. Rather they were a training class for kindergarten teachers and they were practicing an activity for 4 and 5 year olds.
>
> What caught my interest was in this lineup of about 20 budding teachers going *"chug chug, toot toot"* and having a great time (which hopefully they would do with their future kindergartners). There were three or four folks way in the back of the line, looking meek and ashamed and not doing the exercise. Even though they knew it was just that, an exercise, and it was ok to do it, and it wasn't silly. The point is they could not leave their shame to loosen up sufficiently to be contextually appropriate. It looked like they couldn't "make believe" lest they would be seen as silly (or crazy). They held on to some objective demeanor of behavior, coming from some internal source when in fact it was not necessary to do so. They just could not play. We might imagine it would be difficult for a kindergarten class to be able to enjoy such a teacher.

In adults, the capacity of play ameliorates the tendency to objectify subjectivity—that is, to be non-romantic and solely pragmatic. Play that is internalized during development of a secure base is an important epigenetic factor in relating spontaneously and not rigidly. Suppose you are in Miami, with your girlfriend (or boyfriend) and by the ocean, on a balmy summer evening looking at a lovely "Moon over Miami." You are enjoying a warm moment, holding each other and looking out to the sea and enjoying the stars and moon. You turn to her and look into her eyes, she looks lovingly back at you and you say, "Isn't it amazing how light reflected by the moon from the sun travels so fast, 186 thousand miles a second!" I daresay that it would not be considered very romantic by your girlfriend, even if she was a physicist.[9]

Or, let's say you are watching a magician, and you're busy focusing on how he does the trick, rather than enjoying the wonder of the illusion for the moment. Sometimes over-focusing on "reality," pragmatics, and seriousness can stifle the enjoyment of the magic of a moment—literally, in the example of watching a magician or magical moments between lovers.

Attachment versus Involvement

Attachment and Involvement are two different modes of romantic coupling. These two concepts, when unpacked dynamically, describe significantly different modes of loving. **Attachment** tends to focus on the subject re-finding what is missing, for example, a lost love, or a wished for fantasied mother or father. **Involvement** represents a comfort with the uncertainty in a possible relationship and is organized around the concept of being open to discovering previously unknown qualities in the other, or at least appreciating in a deep way "slightly" known qualities (Brok, 1998). The alternative is looking for what was lost, and trying to find it, or mold it through projective identification.

Hopefully, once you are with the other, you desire to move from finding to discovering and exploring. **Discovering** requires the work of involvement, which includes mutual capacity for empathy, mutual interest in each other's thoughts and ways. Specifically, it is marked by a transformational as opposed to a transitional relation. In an enduring love relationship, each Other is experienced as a transformational object in addition to a transitional object. In essence, the couple can tolerate sufficient benign tension to provide a degree of uncertainty and stimulate interest, curiosity, and enjoyment of change in one's self and the other.

Transitional versus Transformational Relationships

Following Winnicott (1971), a **transitional object** is something to be used but not developed.[10] (Think of the cartoon character from *Peanuts*, Linus with his security blanket.) It enables one to make a developmental change while simultaneously avoiding the anxiety of being alone. Transitional objects are by definition temporary. Linus's transitional object is a security blanket. In interpersonal relations this is marked by the use of another to develop one's self rather than develop the couple. The other becomes like Linus's blanket: an inanimate object as opposed to an interesting and interested subject. As a result, the partner being used as such an object tends not to develop his or her self.

It is not uncommon to see how some relationships endure because they evolve while others de-energized themselves and slowly end. In this sense, **transitional relationships** are concerned with attachment rather than involvement and have a narcissistic tinge. Transitional relationships exist so that a person can make a transition in one's life, and sometimes couples use each other for transitional purposes but not to mutually evolve as a couple. In such cases, the two individuals might slowly become apart. Such couples may be doomed to stagnation, disruption, or a fragile and stagnant narcissistic equilibrium.

Towards a Theory of Mutual Transformation and the Role of Play Discovery States

Transformational relationships are marked by a mature form of **play-discovery states**, which encompass old wishes and experiences with new developmental interests. Each partner is not only secured by the other, but also has an ongoing curiosity and interest in discovering what the other is continuously about. As long as both partners keep changing, so does the interest in discovering. The mutually transforming couple loves each other for all the old reasons, but in addition plays with each other and discovers qualities in each other for new reasons as well. Couples who approach this mode of relating live in a paradox of security, idealization, and the flux of the unknown and risk (Brok, 1998; Mitchell, 2002).

Viewing Coupling Through Time

Coupling can be conceptualized in terms of three distinctive qualities, plus their *before-couple* qualities. These are:

The Historical Couple: The original dynamic basis for the relationship.
The Current Couple: The actual dynamic quality of the relationship at present.
The Potential Couple: The potential inherent in their relationship. Where are they going, what is their "project"?[11]

Thus, we now end the brief historical review through current times of varied yet linked aspects of psychodynamic thinking as applied to couple therapy.

Theory of Problem Formation

In general, couple problems are attributable to both individual idiosyncratic styles of each member, combined with the collusive reality they may have unconsciously created by their styles. The basic approach then is to work with the individual as well as the couple aspects of the relationship (Brok, 2007),[12] the goal being to help the couple understand and reframe their personal *as well as* their couple dynamic. In formulating their difficulties, one caveat is important. The case of Natalie and David given to the authors of each chapter in this book contains valuable but limited details. This is quite different than a consultation in vivo with a couple, where the therapist can sense the way they come in to the consulting room. For example, do they sit close or far from each other? Their state of posture, dress and the many nonverbal communications and verbal intonations that can reveal much and help the therapist organize the wisest way to create a positive therapeutic climate. Thus, the case will be discussed in terms of various hypotheticals which may be relevant as an exercise but might be different in vivo.

The couple, Natalie and David, are certainly in the midst of significant difficulties. Let's look at them from the timeline perspectives outlined above: The Historical Couple, The Current Couple, and the Potential Couple. In addition, the individual members' histories (the genetic history) prior to their meeting is important to factor into the conceptualization.

The Historical Couple

The original dynamic basis for the relationship: we know that David was 25 and Natalie 27 when they met online, and that after at least one year of communication, they married. We know that David dated at least one other woman during his conversations with Natalie. His date did not go well, we don't know why or what "well" means in this context. We also know that David was apparently eager enough to meet Natalie in person, to fly down to see her in Texas and did "more of the traveling." He even accommodated her by moving from Maine to Texas. We know they got along very well and had a sexual relationship.

We do not know what they liked about each other at first, and what initially attracted them to each other. To get to some of these unanswered questions in initial sessions, the therapist may ask some of the following questions:

- *"What got you interested in David?"*
- *(with humor) "What did you see in this character?"*
- *"What made her different from others you dated?"*

Their responses can reveal initial aspects of the dynamic such as panic, dependency, sexual vitality, fun-loving, etc. Here are some of many possible examples:

Dependency: *"I know he would take care of me."*
Sexuality as primary: *"She/he was so hot."*
Idealization: *"He was like a God."* Or *"She was a dream come true."*
Self-esteem issues: *"I couldn't believe someone like that would be interested in me."*
Intimacy: *"We both understood each other and were on the same page. I thought we could easily be friends and lovers."* Or *"She was so warm"* or *"She was so rational and secure."*

From the case history we have an idea that they enjoyed many specific things together, such as shows, restaurants, and sports. They also had a satisfying sex life. We also know that in their second year, they bickered about small things, and had a difference about when (or hypothetically whether) to have a family. David wanted to wait, while Natalie did not want to be an "older mother." By their third year of marriage, they had both gained weight sufficiently to argue about it, and seemed to be devolving as a couple. Counter-arguments ensued with David claiming he wanted more time for them alone as a couple, while paradoxically, he was going out by himself with friends to sports bars. We have little information about Natalie, beyond her interest in having a baby and her concern about David's health. David seems to have interpreted this concern as an attack on his individual freedom, rather than as her love for him and her interest in his health.

The Current Couple

The actual dynamic quality of the relationship at present: the current couple is in conflict, yet healthy enough to not seize on differences to abruptly break up. There is some thread of hope within and between both of them to not break up precipitantly. Rather than break up or continue fighting, they seek out a "third" (therapist) to help them in some way. This already is a positive position for them to take. But there could be many other reasons. For example, it is also possible that one partner goes into couple work to "get rid" of the other, by leaving that other in a safe place. This does not seem to be the situation with David and Natalie. They are coming for hopeful reasons, but are at a loss about what to do. Reaching out to a third party may be an indication that the couple has an inkling that they do not have to be in a collusive process of hopelessness. Both come from divorced families, and we might hypothesize that they might sense a desire to not re-enact aspects of their parents' lives, but feel caught in a strong pull to do exactly that. Theoretically, instead of re-finding a lost object (mother or father) or re-finding a better edition of a lost object, they may be on the brink of discovering each other in a new way and having a relationship based on evolving together—a transformational relationship as opposed to a transitional one. This is all supposition, but given their history, such a thought would be likely from a psychodynamic perspective.

The Potential Couple

Where are they going, what is their "project"—do they have one? The current couple has put the potential couple on hold. The one clear future-oriented goal discussed by the current couple is to have a baby. However, this discussion seems to have been a precipitating factor for the revival of an old symptom for David. What is his anxiety? What does "not ready yet" mean? We would need to explore that from at least two points of view. First, is he experiencing Natalie's wish as a transference-based demand of some sort, which he resists out of fear of losing his autonomy or some other anxiety? He has every right to have his own opinion about when to start a family, but a hint that his resistance is symptomatic of something deeper is the apparent correlation with his cyber-affair. Does he run to a safer place geographically (the internet affair) out of anxiety of having something extracted from him by Natalie, out of a paranoid mistrust or sense of inadequacy on his part? Is there an underlying difficulty in full commitment and intimacy? Is there anxiety about becoming a father? One gets the sense of a serious conflict on the part of David, not with sex, but with taking the position of a father.

The second viewpoint rests on Natalie. Can Natalie wait for a mutual decision? Has she organized yet another person in her life that will hold out on her and eventually leave? Does she push too much or has she made a bad emotional decision in expecting her husband to want to have a baby? Is Natalie perhaps misreading David's need to escape his work and familiar location in life (where his family-of-origin lives) as a loving dedication to her? Just why has he gone to great lengths to be with her? Is this for a sense of connectedness or possibly an escape? Might this be some type of intricate combination? Did he think she would never expect to have a baby?

All this implies the couple is on the verge of devolving rather than evolving. This creates an existential crisis for both individuals as well as the couple. In fact, as the case history indicates, there is a sexual crisis between David and Natalie in that they have not been having sex for a long period, this in a couple that previously claimed no problems during their courting and their first year of marriage. Now, David is having a cyber-affair with a woman via the internet. Natalie has found out by looking into his laptop and was devastated. We might also note that David did not carefully hide his communications. This sometimes implies unconscious desire to be "discovered" and is meant as some sort of message, whether it be guilt, or attempt to show without personally saying it in vivo to his wife, that he is moving towards someone else. Of interest dynamically is that someone else (Devyn) is also geographically removed from David; just like Natalie was at the beginning of their relationship. This could suggest two things. The first is **repetition compulsion**; that is, reliving a past experience. The second is that there may be some unconscious fear of staying too close to "home" under certain emotional conditions.

Often enough we see a partner remove oneself in some way from an Oedipally exciting figure by running away. David and Natalie did have good sex. However, we could speculate he has run into an unconscious block when it came to enjoying his potency to have a baby. One thing is to be a husband; another is to proclaim that he wants to, and can be, a father. There are many other possibilities underlying such behavior, including the notion that a far removed idealized object is safer for David than a fully live person in close proximity. The film *Her* (2014), where the protagonist falls in love with an "operating system," is one such extreme example. In this groundbreaking film about relationships in the digital age, the protagonist literally falls in love with a digital woman; she is nothing more than an electronic creation. On the one hand, it demonstrates the power of idealization. On the other hand, it shows how idealization is a way of diminishing and protecting oneself against the neurotic fear of a real living person. In a similar way, for David, fear of involvement with a real person with whom he can father a baby seems to be an important dynamic.

We also need to understand that Natalie, who appears to be submissive and dependent at times, might have unwittingly colluded in repeatedly being rejected by a man. Natalie's relationship history is marked by bad experiences: Natalie's longest relationship was for five months. She had several boyfriends in college, all of which cheated on her. So these experiences with other men would be a dynamic worth exploring. Was it bad luck? Or is it something she unwittingly communicates about being too dependent that is enough to drive someone away? Or could it be she gets *used* as an object and has trouble representing herself as a subject? And what was the impression that David had about this? Is he at all interested in her subjectivity? And she with his?

It would seem that past experiences from their history have infiltrated their present and corrupted their future. However, they have come into therapy, apparently to accept there may be a different solution than to simply break up.

The Current Couple and Genetic History

Before David and Natalia met they had personal histories, which impact in various ways how the current couple functions. Natalie is the product of divorced parents, both of whom remarried and as a result Natalie has one stepsister, Robyn. This is a stepsister towards whom she played a parental role. She has no close relationship with either her biological father or her stepfather, Nicholas, who is described as "trying too hard to be a father to her." She is also described as having a very difficult relationship with Fred, her biological father. To quote, "Natalie made an attempt to reconnect with Fred, but found that while he cared for her, he didn't initiate much interaction. This *infuriated* Natalie as she believed that it is the parents' responsibility to initiate and maintain connections." Was her attempt to connect with David, to have a baby, that precipitated his fleeing the scene emotionally and involve himself with an other, a repetition of her experience with her father? She wanted something from both, and received nothing.

David has two female siblings. His father always wanted a male child and it is implied that his mother reluctantly accepted to get pregnant again (and for a final time). During his younger years, David was a disappointment to his father, who apparently pushed and pressured him to be athletic, and in particular to play baseball. David was not a good athlete and his father is described as disappointed in his son. It is implied that this was expressed very clearly to his son, and David likely felt put down. At the age of nine, David's parents divorced. So, David is a product of a mother, who out of love for, duty toward, or fear of her husband, accepted getting impregnated so that her husband can have a prized object for whom he had pre-conceived plans, plans severely disappointed because his son was not the idealized version of a boy he wanted. We can hypothesize that David's father was quite immature, and was intolerant, perhaps threatened by vulnerability. Given this, how significant in the eyes of authority could David feel?

Further, there is the dynamic of falling short of an internalized ideal, an ideal his father had for him and for whom David felt inadequate and disappointment in that he could not fulfill it. This can lead to a deep sense of shame. We must also consider that David's sister lost a child to miscarriage and eventually adopted one with her husband. His other sister, Regina, was an alcoholic and drug user. David once physically attacked her, when drunk. He was arrested, but was released and put on probation.

These are some background issues in David's life, and we do not know how they were unconsciously processed and reworked internally. Did they organize a conflict about fathering and success with children of one's own? In sum, here are some formulations about the couple that would need to be verified and, if appropriate, worked on in therapy.

1. Degree of transference-based phantasy versus reality observations of each other.
2. Projective identification of each toward the other.
3. Capacity and interest of each member of the couple to be witnesses for each other's life experience.
4. Determination of capacity to work with metaphor and symbolic meaning in an experiential way.
5. Helping this couple understand how they co-create their relationship.
6. Helping develop mutuality, awareness, and developing a benign emotional climate.
7. Determine capacity for play and imagination in the relationship, determining their strengths as a couple. Perhaps work out some of their conflicts via the transference experience with the therapist.
8. Attachment versus involvement issues in the couple organization.

9. Ability for the couple to have the capacity to commute between individual interests and the couple interests.
10. Anxiety versus free choice about fathering a child. Fathering seems to be a very conflicted issue for David. For Natalie, perhaps, there is an issue of pressuring out of desperate need, in addition to a normal desire to get pregnant. These may be focused on if they emerge during the first session. In subsequent sessions we would move more deeply into dream sharing, and what deflates capacity for passion as well as other dynamic issues that emerge, enabling them to work toward better understanding themselves and the relationship.

All the above approaches are relatively generic, in that with some exception they apply to most couples. In addition, and most importantly, it has been my experience, and noted by others, that a psychodynamic diagnostic understanding of each member of the couple as well as the couple itself by the therapist can be of great help in organizing intervention strategies (Mendelsohn, 2014).

Theory of Problem Resolution

In an initial session various things are of great importance. First, therapist and clients must all get to know each other and establish a comfortable enough climate for the couple and therapist to proceed productively. Step 1 in this process is to get the message across that the therapist is not a judge, but rather a significant intermediary they have chosen to help the couple discover what is possible and define what has been blocking the evolution of the relationship. The therapist can orient the couple to the idea that it would be a shame if they could never find out how to flourish together. So one of our goals is to discover what is in the way of a positive evolution of their relationship.

While not a requirement, the therapist could explain that the therapeutic focus needs to be twofold. The first avenue is how the couple functions. The second is how they, as two separate individuals, can mutually appreciate their own autonomy. In essence, they need to be good commuters between what is best for the couple and what is best for each individual in the couple.

The therapist can also introduce the importance of being involved witnesses with each other and try to understand each other's subjective experiences. So, when one partner seems to deny the other's subjective experience the therapist should intervene (unless the couple realizes this on their own) to help the criticized partner from feeling invalidated. Helping each member to be an involved witness is an important technique, in that it opens up hitherto unknown or little known aspects of each other's internal geography (i.e. feelings, interests, and capacities, including previously unknown experiences of each other's pasts). Such an exercise of listening and witnessing is itself a process that involves the couple in sharing. Not only is the content shared, but also the process of linking with each other in an exercise guided by an interested therapist who can clarify and interpret the way they listen to and organize each other's narrative (see Brok, 2007, 2011 for clinical case examples).

Another technical factor is the therapist's capacity to maintain what I term "**evenly hovering involvement**." Each partner's subjective position should be treated as valid (this is different from being correct), but neither should be elevated to being the whole story. Only through the establishment of such a therapeutic climate can a multi-subjective perspective become the way things are looked at, thereby allowing sessions to become safe enough for deeper dynamics such as transferences, projections, and narcissistic desires to emerge and be open for discussion.

A general goal for couple counseling involves helping the two individuals understand, reflect, and discuss in session what inhibits the quality of their relationship. The therapist also needs to leave space by not intervening too quickly, thereby cutting off the couple process. This of course depends upon the couple, their level of tension, the therapist's diagnostic acuity and other factors. For example, a couple where both members quickly regress in the face of tension and thereby reactivate desperate needs from each other to be taken care of emotionally, may need the therapist to be a parenting/guiding figure who initially structures things in order for them to feel safe. Their transference needs may be for an interested parent, a parent they never had. This happens under the guidance of the reflective observation of an empathic rather than challenging therapist. Such a couple might do well in initial sessions, until it is no longer necessary as they mature and individuate through the therapeutic work. Simply put, the developmental level that each member of the couple and the couple as a unit is at, must be taken into account. Some couples need soothing, some need confrontation, some need space, etc. One paradigm for understanding different levels of interventions related to developmental states, can be found in the work of Gedo (1979).

It is important to note that the couple therapist not only helps the couple resolve problems, but also to evolve as a couple. In other words, to grow by developing new ways to view each other in addition to old ways, and to reflect and think about the trajectory of their future lives. How a psychodynamic couple therapist approaches this will be clarified in the following section, but for now, we can list some general techniques:

1. Helping the couple be involved witnesses for each other.
2. Encourage the couple to share aspects of their past as well as recent history with each other and the therapist.
3. Enable discussion about how they envision their future and any disjunctions between couple members that appear as a result. Often present conflicts are not only about issues from the past, but anticipation of the future.
4. Helping each member understand their transferences and projections with the therapist and toward each other.
5. Sharing of their internal worlds with each other through dream sharing.

6. Helping the couple learn to make an inquiry rather than go by assumptions.
7. Helping the couple understand that their negative actions are symptoms of something more fundamental.
8. Helping through inquiry and interpretation by the therapist for the couple to take an interest in what underlies symptoms.
9. Encouraging the couple to work with metaphor. This is an important diagnostic issue. It concerns how well the couple can move from concrete facts to metaphoric meanings of their actions toward each other.
10. Helping the couple share their experiences of the therapist as part of the process.
11. The role of the therapist is also important. In particular, the therapist needs to be able to commute between styles of being with the couple as soother, challenger, perspective setter, transference interpreter, communication facilitator, and be capable of what I term **field relevant behavior** and self-disclosure.[13] In short, the role of the therapist includes use of his self in many varied ways during the session, dependent upon the couple's emotional state being presented. One technique does not apply to all. Interventions by the therapist should be made taking into account the diagnostic and developmental level of each member of the couple and of the couple itself (Gedo, 1979; Mendelsohn, 2014).
12. Finally, the therapist is hopefully not wedded to only one theory or way of relating, as this brings to the therapy a rigid one-style-limited approach that supposedly fits all. People are all individuals, and couples are quite idiosyncratic, though they may reflect some common themes. Put another way, nomothetic theories miss out on the ideographic nature of individuals as well as couples (Cone, 1986).

A Note on Termination

Psychodynamic couple therapy is not only focused on resolving specific problems, but also aims at unblocking the couple so they can evolve. By evolve, I mean a sense of ongoing growth marked by an incrementally increasing diversified sense each member has of the other, as well as a more diversified quality of couple life. For example, one aspect of readiness for termination is the successful negotiation by the couple of life stage issues and crises (see Brok, 1992 for a clinical case example). A further example is the capacity for the couple to develop wisdom.[14]

Ending the treatment often emerges through the awareness of all parties that the couple has created and reached a new developmental stage in their relationship. This new stage would be evidenced by experiences both in the session and in their out of session daily lives. Such awareness as "we don't argue with each other anymore, we actually listen and discuss" is one type of example. Another, among many, is realizing initial goals such as achieving newfound space for and with each other. This is space that seemed previously unachievable, such as taking personal time (i.e. leisure time or vacation time with each other; Brok, 1976), and not mixing it with or allowing it to trump functional time, such as paying bills or caring for children. According to Brody (1988), what is critical is that sufficient useful/working insight be attained to modify behaviors so that mutually reinforcing destructive behaviors are replaced by mutually reinforcing constructive ones, to the degree that gratification replaces conflict as the primary product of the couple's interaction. In practice, this will manifest as both partners subjectively experience and demonstrate therapeutic success by reporting increased satisfaction and diminution of disturbing friction to a level insufficient to be brought up in therapy. In essence, the couple lets the therapist know when they are ready for termination.

In another vein, Mendelsohn (2014) points to the importance of accurate diagnosis for successful termination. He cites the example of a couple misdiagnosed as sadomasochistic rather than paranoid-masochistic as having influenced a negative termination in couple work. Diagnosis, in general, seems to be overlooked in deference to generic "one technique fits all approach," which is a basic issue in American therapeutics founded upon primarily pragmatic ideals (Brok, 2009).

Below is a sample of some general criteria for termination:

1. Couple awareness of but not enacting their transferences to each other.
2. Couple realizing what climate their transferences were activating for each other.
3. Couple learning to become involved witnesses with each other.
4. Couple understanding their behaviors as symptoms of unresolved underlying issues.
5. Couple relating in less defensive and more empathic ways with each other.
6. Couple not getting provoked by the other, nor provoking each other.
7. Couple discussing rather than arguing with each other's differences of opinions; and not using differences to provoke a fight.

Hypothetical Initial Session

I received a call from Natalie, who identifies herself as being referred by her internist to see me and her husband. She advises they are having "trouble" and want to see someone before making any rash decisions. She cries on the phone and I assure her that I will do my best to understand what's going on once we meet and see how I can help. I ask if she discussed coming with her husband and she advises that she informed him this morning and after a brief argument he agreed to come with her. We discuss the fee, set up a time and then I take both of their names, address, and phone number. I advise that I look forward to meeting them and will do the best I can to help them both work on what's getting in the way of their relationship. I will usually also ask for their email, which is to be used with their permission only for appointment messages. Note: Depending upon what is presented and how the call goes, I try to stay an adequate time (not too short and not too long on the phone) to see if we can establish some connection. I don't want to stay too long or get into details or speak to both of them on the phone as that can create and generate a crisis. I try to stay not too short, to see if we can establish a rapport and also to get some basic information such as does the spouse know about the call and are they both willing to come, etc. There also may be some insurance issues to briefly discuss.

First Session

Unless there is a pressing "need" for one or both to start the session, I will start for the purpose of orienting them further and to set the stage for listening. I start because I believe, in general, it is a good idea to set some preliminary organizing experiences as to how the session might go (please note the subjunctive, *might go*, not *will go*). Also, I will be careful not to dominate the session but to serve as a helping facilitator and later on interpreter of what is going on between them. Also, I don't distract the focus by asking about their work or other aspects of their lives at these initial moments. This will most certainly come later, but it is important to see if they can communicate why they decided to come and what they hope. I will also carefully note where they choose to sit (i.e. together, separate chairs, far away, close, etc).

Therapist: Hi. Good afternoon. Glad to be here with both of you.
(Natalie and David walk in, she sits on the couch. David tries to sit next to her, and she moves away from him, not to a separate chair, but further away on the couch.)
David: What the hell?
Therapist: I see things have not been easy.

This comment acknowledges Natalie's nonverbal behaviors and David's perturbed complaint. My comment is clearly addressing both members of the couple. Note that I do not then ask David what he felt when Natalie distanced herself, nor do I ask Natalie what she felt or why she moved away. That's important, but will come later. For example, is Natalie showing me nonverbally how she feels rather than saying anything, and is David attempting to sit next to her out of fear of losing her? Is he putting on a show for me to see how he is rejected? Is he contrite?

I also don't want them to each have a solely dyadic relationship with me, but rather I make comments that encourage thinking about each other's reasons for their actions. This is different than asking to tell the other what they felt. I do this so their assumptions can be expressed and validated or invalidated by the other.

This process yields information of how "in tune" they are with each other and how much their assumptions are based on transference displacements and/or split off projections in to the other.[15] It is very important to note that when relationships are overly organized by erroneous assumptions, the members of the couple never get to really know each other as they are busy enacting their respective "namings" of each other. We all, in milder forms, are influenced by our transferences and projections without knowing it. In a healthy couple, these transferences and projections are minimally influential, can be reflected upon, and are trumped by the maturity of each member.

It is important in the first session to set the primary goal of therapy to encourage the couple's level of awareness of each other's feeling states and rationales. As suggested earlier, from a psychodynamic perspective it also elucidates projections and transference distortions. This is crucial if the couple is to understand themselves and resolve issues.

During this opening, the therapist also has assumptions and hypotheses about what is going on but keeps those in the background as they need to be validated by in-session experience. What is in the foreground is an inquiring interest to discover what's getting in the way of the two people having a satisfactory relationship.

At the beginning of therapy, the therapist really doesn't know what is going on or why.[16] The therapist does not take sides and is interested in both their actions. The reason for that is that couples have difficulties, based on their own individual dynamics, but also because they unwittingly co-create their manner of relating via unconscious needs. Once we can get an inkling of their out of awareness conflicts, needs, and desires, the therapist can help them understand alternative ways to organize themselves as a couple. Further, the therapist is more than a mere observing witness but rather is an involved witness. This occurs while keeping in mind that they may both be pulling for the therapist's sympathies by their actions.

In hypothesizing about what is going on for the couple, the therapist may wonder if their actions towards each other are re-creations of past experiences. It is important to help each member of the couple discover unknown things about oneself and the other as opposed to finding what they are looking for and reacting in keeping with a self-fulfilling prophecy. What the therapist is experiencing are early manifestations of transference in the session. Assumptions based on earlier developmental experiences are mixed up with their historical experiences as a couple. Such assumptions inform how they've come to view each other in the present and also how they anticipate their future (i.e. hopelessness sets a different tone than a sense of manifest hopeful feelings about "coming to therapy"). The very act of showing up is usually a sign of hopefulness. It can mean a wish to genuinely repair, reorganize, and possibly enliven a dying relationship. However, it can also communicate finding a way to leave a blocked relationship. These matters are often determined by how the initial session proceeds.

So letting the couple know the therapist sees what is happening is important. It signals the therapist is not ignoring either one of them and is interested in both their experiences. This also means the therapist is in control of his or her countertransference (Goldklank, 2009). It is often the case that one can have sympathy for one member of the couple and antipathy toward the other. Recognizing this can help the therapist not act upon those feelings. One way to handle this is for the therapist to remind him or herself, "Remember, they are both your patients!"

The Session Continues

David: Did you see that? (*Referring to his wife moving away.*)
Therapist: Yes.

It is important for the therapist to validate the client.

Therapist: Can you tell Natalie what you imagine why she didn't want you to sit next to her?

This is an attempt to do an early "empathic bridge" to see if David is interested in reflecting about his wife's behavior as opposed to merely reacting. I will also ask each partner to indicate if each of their spouse's assumptions are accurate.

David: I don't know, she just wants me out, I did nothing bad (*attributes a rejecting intention to his wife*).
Natalie: Nothing? You were carrying on with another woman on the internet! You want me to greet you with open arms?
She negates his self-attribution of doing nothing wrong
Therapist: I see you have separate takes on what just happened.
I stick with the action for the moment and not the content of what was said; then immediately address Natalie in a linked intervention.
Therapist: Can you imagine what David was thinking when he tried to sit next to you?
Natalie: He was trying to make believe he loves me, but I'm sure he wants to leave me. He's just putting on an act for you!
Therapist: (thinking to self) Is she right? Is she negating his intention and trying to draw me into taking sides to protect her? I am feeling sorry for her. Who am I in her transference? She is making an appeal to me! She feels like a victim. Is she reliving and re-creating a self-fulfilling prophecy on her part? And what is he doing? Why is he feeling victimized? Is he a liar? Or is he not able to communicate what drove him to look for others on the internet, etc.?
David: No, Natalie, I'm not fucking acting. I love you.
Natalie: (*addressing the therapist*) I am so hurt and now he wants to sit with me. He has betrayed me and I am lost.
David: (*with some anguish*) Not true! I love you.
Natalie: I am so hurt, I thought you were truly different, but you're just like the others!
Therapist: (thinking to self) Ok, here is a possible first clue of something.
Therapist: David, do you know what your wife means by "just like the others"?
David: No, what others? What are you talking about?

Natalie: (*cries*) You know!
Therapist: (*to Natalie*) That seems important. Can you share what you mean? What do you imagine David knows?

> *I am asking Natalie to share more about her background. A background David does not claim to know. By doing so, I am asking David to be a witness to her experience.*

Natalie: I've been left a lot. I thought you were different, David. You know that! (*Natalie cries and goes on to reveal in detail how all her previous boyfriends in college and after—five to be exact—cheated on her. She could never count on any boyfriend! She continues sobbing and narrates how she thought David would "never do such a thing" repeating herself, "I don't want this to happen again. I feel like such a loser."*)
David: (*unempathically*) Don't be a drama queen, Natalie! You caused me a lot of grief.
(*Turns to therapist*) She's always got to bitch about something!
Therapist: I can see how you argue. You both feel so misunderstood. (*To David*): Did you know about Natalie's experience with loss in her life?
David: (*more calmly, which is a good sign*) Not all the details. I know you feel bad "Natie" (*calls her by an endearing nickname*), but you worry too much. I am here now, right?
Therapist: (*since David responded calmly, I decide to approach one of the hot issues and take an inquiring risk; first with a slight preamble*) Sometimes couples resort to actions because they don't know how to articulate or communicate their thoughts to each other. Sometimes it's a repetition of what their parents have done or what they've learned to do in anxiety creating situations.
Here I educate a bit of how couples might recreate what significant others in their lives, such as parents, have done. This also touches upon earlier nonverbal actions about sitting together.
Therapist: (*to David*) Is it true what Natalie says about your involvement with someone else? It's certainly not pleasant to be discovered by your wife doing that? If it's true, it would be good to understand why you need to do it.
David: Well, yes, I went to my computer, but just to have some peace.
Natalie: See, Doctor. He's on the internet with her. I saw it with my own eyes on his laptop. (*Natalie sobs.*) See, he admits it. Why, David, why?
David: She means nothing to me! I'm playing around because we don't have sex anymore and you're bugging me about smoking and my health. Meanwhile you're gaining weight like crazy! Jesus, leave me alone! (*David is no longer calm.*)
Natalie: You're not interested in making love with me, David!

I hesitate but conclude better to bring this dynamic up in future sessions. I think to myself I will need to come back to David's statement of "She means nothing to me." If true, it is a statement of how he can use others to meet his temporary needs without thinking of his impact on them (a transitional as opposed to a transformational relationship). If he was lying to protect himself, it revealed an insecurity with his wife. So, at this juncture we have the couple devolving with its members scurrying towards their respective narcissistic corners. This is potentially useful as they demonstrated how they can remove themselves from a reflective capacity and an empathic stance with each other—which they are somewhat capable of. I think I will have to help them a lot in developing a reflective capacity rather than a reactive response. If they've never been reflective or empathic, that's a more difficult situation for the therapy. I will see how far we can go.

Natalie's revelation in the first session that she always feels left and David's anger with her about being a "drama queen" may be important data points. David apparently has not considered how provocative his behavior was to his wife. A thought about David occurs to me: even if she had not found out, he apparently did not wonder why he was avoiding dealing with issues between them by taking an escape route via the internet. I begin to think that distancing from tension, rather than moving into it, was an important dynamic for David.

I also wonder if Natalie's experience was bad luck or if she misread people or if she had unwittingly done anything that sabotages an ongoing interest in her. How much did David know about her being left by so many boyfriends, and what it meant to him internally? Was he a savior? Did he look down and devalue her? Was he afraid of her vulnerability? Did he feel pulled and also rejected by her apparent neediness? Why did David resort to the symptom of going behind his wife's back on the internet instead of confronting what he was angry or worried about? Was the sneakiness a way of buttressing a fragile sense of masculinity?

Later we would discover that he was identified with and acting toward her like his father did with him (berating and devaluing him). We would also determine that his own weakness and vulnerability was assuaged by splitting it off and projecting it onto his wife and devaluing her for it (a projective identification). There was also a sense that he treated his troubled and drug-addicted sister in the same way. The saddest thing is he did not trust in his sense of maturity and self-confidence as a full adult and a man. Although Natalie certainly gave the impression of being a victim, David too impressed me as one. Yet they both had a strength and belief to do what neither of their parents had done, which was to seek therapy to give themselves a chance to see what was going wrong. Underneath it all, they both seemed to have a desire to deal with their own internal dynamics and how they colluded unwittingly in creating a difficult rather than evolving and maturing relationship. Coming to couple therapy was part of a hopeful process. If I could engage them sufficiently to be patient enough with each other to begin a shift in their ways, we could get somewhere.

Therapist: I can see that you are both hurting big time. (*Again, bridging with both of them.*) Do you know what Natalie means that "she's been left a lot." Sounds like she's been counting on you to be there for her.

David: Well, yes, but then it became hard. Things began moving too fast! She just wants too much at times. (*Is David implying that he began to retreat from the relationship when she wanted a baby?*)

Therapist: Do you know what David means by "too fast"?

Natalie: He's bothered that I want to have a family.

Therapist: (*I think to myself, "Bingo."*)

David: No, not true, just not now, I told you I'm not ready yet. Yet… Natalie, "Yet." Get it?

Natalie: Yes, David, I want to get pregnant with you, have a baby, someone I can care for and have a family!! I want that, and you go on the internet!

David: I told you I need time. Must you rush everything? I've done so much for you. I moved all the way across the country to be with you!

Therapist: There is much here, folks. It will help me if we can get a bit of history. Get some perspective. Can you work with me on this? Can you share how each of you met?

By this intervention, I temper the incipient volatility and move them to considering what might influence their points of view. We move away from the present, not as a distraction, but to gain perspective and context. If they come along with me it's a good sign. History, when used properly, can be an asset for understanding and help develop a reflective capacity with themselves and each other. This is an important aspect of Psychodynamic Therapy.

Therapist: I need you both to help me help you untangle some knots you find yourself creating.

The hope with this intervention is to help both members of the couple understand that both their points of view are important. This will educate them about the impact of historical experience on current life and its potentially corrupting effect on future hopes. This therapist directive is also aimed at gaining a perspective on how to develop what seems to be a missing mutuality at certain times. This couple devolves into a hierarchical relationship marked by control issues and avoidance. Do they abort a transformational evolving relationship in deference to a transitional one? Is that what they are unconsciously co-creating as a function of their having been used by parental figures for their own purposes?

David: I was so attracted to her. She was considerate, and better yet, she would not bug me and lived far enough away to not be involved with my crazy family. She lived good and far away!! Though we visited each other when dating. We could talk and she seemed interested in me. We like a lot of the same things. I even got to like her Cowboys, over my Patriots!

Therapist: (thinking to self) What dynamic underlies his shift in sports team loyalty? Could it represent his eagerness to get away from his "crazy family" to "run away" from his home of origin? A rapid new identity? The cost being unconsciously resentful?

Therapist: (*to Natalie*) What got you interested in David?

Natalie: I didn't think he would cheat on me. He seemed so stable, together. Boy, was I wrong. I thought he would never leave me. I liked that he took an interest in me even though he lived so far away. We managed to hold our relationship together by traveling to each other's houses every few months. This took effort. And we could talk and he liked sports and the same movies I did. And ok, he was sexy… (*smiles a little*).

Therapist: (*I note to myself that the first thing Natalie refers to is security*) Of course security is important in every relationship. You both certainly need it in different ways. You had a lot of things in common. I see many strengths, including managing a relationship at long distance. That is not so easy. You both are troopers!

I am here reminding them of a truth and applying a self-psychology concept of ***mirroring***,[17] *in effect acting (genuinely) the tuned in and affirming parents that neither of the couple members fully had.*

Therapist: (*thinking to self*) *Did Natalie via her neediness and enthusiasm not sense the level of David's need to get away from his family? Or was she unconsciously rescuing him? And did David unconsciously think she was a pushover and that he could over-rely on her? Perhaps to save and stabilize him, without thinking much about his role or desire to create a family with her? These were open questions about the unconscious dimensions of their attraction. And there is the issue of "cheating." Was David diminishing it, thereby thinking how could it be important? Was his defense "I did not have sex with that woman" problematic because he was trying to fool himself by a technicality? Many reasons are possible for such a defense, including not trusting his own masculine intentions, trying to get his wife to identify with his denial, to protect him from guilt and shame, or of course a sociopathic streak where he doesn't care much about the impact of his actions on another.*

Therapist: (*to both*) Can you also share some of your individual history? What was it like growing up in your homes before you met? In my experience, sharing some of your history can help me get a sense of what you may be organizing about each other based on past experiences as well as the present. Sometimes history can blind us to what is going on in the present. And we miss out big time.

Here I am implying that they may be finding negative qualities in each other, rather than discovering potentials they don't know about nor know how to enjoy. We move into a more psychodynamic understanding by encouraging both members of the couple to share their beginnings together as well as their life histories as they emerge through inquiry in the session. This exercise is done together, with each partner being a witness to the other's experience (rather than via a genogram). What and how they spontaneously share can be helpful for discerning couple strengths as well as couple mutual distortions.

Therapist: So, tell me a bit of your life experience as children, your histories, etc. It might be important in terms of what blocks you from being more content with each other.

This is to help them formulate their transferences and define our future work around ameliorating blocks and liberating couple evolution. They also further learn to be involved witnesses for and with each other.

Natalie: Well… Uh… ok, I grew up in a broken family of sorts.

Therapist: Can you share what you mean "of sorts"?

Natalie: Well, my parents divorced when I was five. I hardly remember it. My mom remarried and I have a stepsister, Robyn. I was really a mother to Robyn. My mom was too busy and not really into it.

Therapist: Wow, so you were put into the role of a caretaker early on. Who took care of you?

Natalie: (*cries*) My stepfather, Nicholas, was ok. He tried to win me over but I couldn't really be comfortable with him. And my real dad, Fred is his name, disappeared on me. He was and is a lousy father. I tried to connect with him after college but no way was he really interested in me. I had to chase after him and eventually just got disgusted. He would not call me or see how I was unless I called him. Story of my life… I guess he left me too. (*sarcastically*) Why not? Get in line, men! (*This is another clue to her vulnerabilities*)

Therapist: (*to Natalie*) How difficult for you! (*To David*) Did you know much about her experiences at home with her father, and everyone?

David: I knew her parents divorced… but no, not that she was that angry with her dad. Well, maybe… only time I met him was at our wedding.

Natalie: Yea, 'cause I begged him. Made my stepfather uncomfortable but I didn't care. I wanted my real father to give me away to you!

Therapist: (*to David*) Have some thoughts about it?

David: Not really. He was alright. I didn't know all that was going on. I feel bad for you, Natalie. I know about "fathers" (*David's response is a good sign, shows some empathy and some reflective capacity*).

Therapist: David, can you share about your father?

David: (*angrily*) My father was a sadist. He pushed me to play ball. He wanted me to be a great ballplayer. He embarrassed me in front of my friends; made fun of me. I couldn't do anything right (*continues with some agitation and raised voice*). He was the big shot who played ball in high school. His varsity pictures are all over the house. He was a minor league player for a while. He would brag about his baseball exploits and say I would never live up to his achievements. He would throw a tantrum if we played catch and I missed the ball.

Therapist: It must have made you pretty angry?

David: I just sulked…

Therapist: You kept it in but showed it anyway by sulking. You must have felt very hurt. I wonder if you became allergic to anyone you experience as pushing you. Not an easy time.

David: Are you fucking kidding! I couldn't wait to get out of there. I felt better when he left. Fuck him! Pardon my language, Doc!

Therapist: I bet you missed him a bit, even if you don't remember now. Do you remember any close moments with him?

> *Here I am seeing if he is in touch with mixed feelings rather than purely hateful ones. If he has some degree of mixed feelings, it bodes well for his ability to be in touch with his needs for a relationship in addition to his distancing in anger as a way of feeling safe.*

David: Well, maybe I wished he could be a different kind of father, but not really. Besides, he left the house when I was a kid. Why are you even asking these things?

Therapist: I'm asking because I am interested in your experiences at home. It can help all of us understand you better. (*To Natalie*) Did you know about his dad's treatment of him?

Natalie: Not all the details. Just that he was angry at his dad. He didn't come to our wedding. I urged David to call him but he wouldn't do it. David's uncle took his place.

Therapist: (*mirroring*) What terrible struggles for both of you at a time of celebration! (*To David*) Is it ok that Natalie witnesses listening to your experiences when you were a kid at home?

David: It's ok. I'm not so great with the psychology stuff. Though when I was 15, I wanted to talk to someone about my crazy family.

Therapist: Did you see a counselor?

David: No, my mother said I didn't need it. She told me, "Just keep yourself out of trouble."

Therapist: What was going on?

David: Dunno. I was confused, depressed I guess. Also, I would lose my temper at home with my sisters when they would cheat at board games. I stole some magazines from our local drug store and got caught. I also took some kid's snow shoes from his locker at school, got caught for that too. I grew out of it I guess. I did ok in high school, especially in math.

Therapist: (*going beyond mirroring, to inquiring*) You certainly went through a low period. Any inkling why?

David: Hey, Doc, you gonna blame it all on my parents? (*Laughs*) Well, I guess my mother being a wreck after my father left.

Therapist: I know you think it's funny, and people do make fun about stereotyped thinking by therapists, but for us, let's keep things open, because our early life experiences can influence how we organize ways of being as adults for good and for bad. You yourself knew something was not right, 'cause you were then and I think now a bright insightful guy maybe still looking for a guiding experience with someone you trust.

This is a supportive statement from within his early positive transference to me. He had been quite collaborative with me, and in effect was being the opposite of what I imagined his father to be like. The disjunction between what might have been an expected transferential parental response with that of the therapist's actual (and genuine) response is a road to feeling more confident for the patient.

David: You got me, Doc!

Therapist: (*thinking to self*) *I am not sure what he thinks I got, except maybe he resonated to my being what I thought was the opposite of his father's way of relating to him. We are hopefully in a positive transference state for the moment. However, it may not be wise to dwell on it, as much as demonstrate it. So I should proceed with the genetic historical experience.*

Therapist: Can you share how old were you when your dad left?

David: Nine.

Natalie: (*who had been listening attentively empathically*) David, I'm sorry you had such a hard time. I feel so bad for you, but don't know what to do with you.

This empathic statement from Natalie as an involved witness is a hopeful reflective sign.

Therapist: (*to Natalie*) I understand your mixed feelings. Can I ask David some more about his early life? Are you interested?

Natalie: Ok. David didn't tell me about all this. Some I know, but not all of what went on. I feel so bad for you. David, you never told me about your depression and that you wanted to see a counselor when you were 15 years old!

Therapist: (*thinking to self*) *This may be a beginning shift in how she "maps" David. How does her witnessing of the additional details of his historical geography affect her?*

Therapist: (*to David*): Your mom, what can you tell me about her?

David: (*now very collaborative and in a calm mood*) She was helpless. A good person, but helpless (*sighs noticeably*). She couldn't set limits with Regina, my crazy sister, who was a total drug addict. I stepped in to help but it was useless. My mother was a bundle of nerves, and needed help from me (*lamenting*). It didn't work. Just didn't work. Got into a bad fight with Regina once. I hated her helpless needy way. I hate drugs. I teach high school now and see it all around. Parents are blind to it, and sometimes helpless.

Therapist: Boy, we have a lot of disappointment in both your lives. You really are troopers to try to make a life. I am wondering how you see yourselves different, not the same, as your parents?

Here the therapist is inquiring about what they do not identify with, and also what identifications they might fear. It's a question calculated to help them think of what they are not repeating or recreating, at least consciously. It paves the way to differentiating themselves more fully from bad internal objects (introjects—identifications) and focus on what they might be doing better than their parents.

David: I'm a lot unlike my dad. I don't want to be like him. I don't want to be divorced and I am easy-going. I am more sensitive, but don't like to be pushed.

Therapist: Makes sense wanting to make a commitment and not wanting to be divorced unless there is good reason. Guess you never gave up on the hope of having a better relationship than your parents.

David: Guess so… ok, yes…

Therapist: And you, Natalie?

Natalie: My mom was a good person. I too don't want to be divorced! Not for me, but I need to be wanted. (*Cries*) I need to be wanted, and needed. (*To David*) Wanted, you get it? I'm so sorry for your troubles as a kid, but I need you to be with me now!

Therapist: Looks like both of you are on the same page with some things. You have both experienced trauma in your lives, broken families, difficulty with parents, and yet you remained optimistic and wanted to make a relationship. Even over long distance at the beginning.

Therapist: (*thinking to self*) *I wonder about the distance. Could it unconsciously be a metaphor for fear of "short distance," a sense of intimacy? Not the time to bring it up. Would be a premature interpretation based on flimsy evidence. And it would be jarring, given their rapport at the moment. Better to continue as we are.*

Therapist: (*to both*) In some ways you never had the chance to be full children with normal concerns at school and with friends. (*To David*) I take it that your interest in sports is part of not letting your father's attitude block you. Could that be true?

David: You got it, Doc. Of course, I liked sports. I was a Patriot and Red Sox fan and followed them a lot. I even created my own scorecard, with ruled paper, to score baseball games I saw on TV. My dad made fun of me 'cause I did that. One time I remember he laughed at me and said, "I guess that's where you belong, pushing a pencil instead of holding a bat in your hands."

Therapist: I understand how you don't want to be pushed or bullied and am thinking that you might have experienced Natalie's enthusiasm for wanting a baby as bullying you. Using my imagination here. You're allergic to being pushed. Anything that reminds you of those experiences with your father can really bug you; to put it mildly. Further, I'm thinking that having children in your family meant having trouble, responsibilities like with your sister; and also, some anxiety well out of your awareness that you are not allowed to be a "full man" though indeed you have all the qualities of being one. Creating a scorecard and using it is a very creative way of putting yourself "in the game."

Therapist: (*thinking to self*) *Doing a scorecard is not like actually playing, but could also be thought of as a rehearsal for eventually being in the game. David is a bit of a voyeur, preferring the distance of an internet relationship to the real intimacy of a full relationship. I think of the recent film* Her *where the protagonist eschews a real relationship and falls in love with a computer operating system. His marriage may be a rehearsal for eventually becoming a father, but he is needing more time to get used to the idea. Can he compete with his father, procreate and be a better father? One can imagine his father making fun of his small pencil (a little impotent penis?) compared to his father's big bat. I am hypothesizing that David is suffering from a major Oedipal trauma and feels inadequate. Not about sex, as he and Natalie had satisfying sex at the beginning. His conflict is about sex for the purpose of procreation. Being a father. If so, can I help him shore up his masculine potency sufficiently? Will he need individual treatment? We shall see.*

Therapist: And for you, Natalie, perhaps your push to have a baby seems couched in terms of desperation rather than enthusiasm and frightens David a bit. He might not understand your communication or readiness. It is of course important to want things from someone you love, especially a baby, but let's explore the meanings it has for both of you. I'm wondering if it is a matter of both of you understanding and perhaps shifting what assumptions you project on each other.

Here I am opening further the exploration of transferences and styles of projective identification as well as what dynamics underlay the baby issue.

Therapist: The fact that David went on the internet and looked for another is indeed provocative, perhaps also a symptom. (*To David*) You might want closeness but you also seem to need distance when you feel pushed.

Geographical distance is how he started. I leave out the Oedipal dynamic at this point, though I risked using the word "frightens" earlier, it is in my opinion too early in the treatment to go there. We need to have a more profound working relationship for that.

Therapist: So maybe both of you need to edge slowly into comfort with intimacy and family. In your experiences they do not seem to go together. Can we work more on this next session? I greatly appreciate your collaboration in here today as well as your interests in each other's stories. It makes me think you can develop a sense of mutual understanding and be clearer about how you see each other, and differentiate that from things you took in from past experiences.

David: Doc, you're making some sense to me. I thought you were gonna come down hard on me!

Here we see his transference based expectation of a rigiditiy similar to his father, on my part, rather than understanding the symptom—without condoning his behavior.

Therapist: We need to explore your symptoms further. For you, it may sometimes be easier to look elsewhere instead of speaking up for yourself. I am glad you might want to work on it with your wife. (*To Natalie*) Are you ok with this?

Natalie: I don't know, but I'll give it shot. He is my only hope.

Therapist: I think it might be important to not see David as your "only hope" but to put it in perspective that he represents a legitimate hope for your happiness, but not *your only hope.* We need to attend to your tendency to feel a sense of desperation which can corrupt hopefulness and even chase away someone who is wary of the intensity of your neediness. It seems like you almost expect to be left and need to be proven wrong. Perhaps you can gain more confidence in the person you are and not feel you can only be happy by not being left? You actually get along so well together when there isn't major conflict. It seems to me, Natalie, that you might unconsciously hold on to your experiences and old memories about being left, in such a way that they are not only memories, but current likelihood. This can sabotage things as David might interpret it as you being pushy like his father was with him—rather than your enthusiasm to have a good and full life with him. I think you both want similar things, a good relationship, a sense of security and a feeling of being recognized. Looks like some experiences from your family have colored the way you look at those things. I'd like you to think about what we discussed today and pick up next time. You both have been helpful in sharing your experiences and in responding to my interests in your lives. I'd also like you to think about alternate ways of understanding each other based on what we discuss in here. Ok?

In this initial session we have dealt with a number of things: primarily, establishing a relatively calm and benign working environment. No one argued with me and the couple was able to reflect and take time to share about their lives in a collaborative way, allowing me to ask questions. There was rancor between them, but they both hung in, seemingly to temporarily, at least, get through what could have been big bumps in the session. Through the experience of witnessing each other's life narrative, along with my involved interest, they seemed to calm down, and hopefully understood themselves and each other better.

Much work needs to be done with this traumatized couple. But it seems hopeful. This was a good beginning for our initial session. I would estimate that this is a process that would take a good length of time, but the outcome of developing a relationship marked by the present and future being enjoyed, rather than the past re-lived, is a worthy endeavor.

They each might also need individual therapy to further clarify their individual issues. However, at this point, I think they might be able to work in couple therapy, on both their individual issues and how these collude to create a distorted inter-subjective space, framed by mutual interactive transferences and projections. I believe they can incrementally move towards a mature, more realistic relationship based on discovering each other, as opposed to finding what they were defensively looking for in each other.

Notes

1 **Transference** is a dynamic whereby one unconsciously displaces experiences, feelings and attitudes one had with and toward someone, in the past (parents, teachers, etc.) on to someone in the present. This process frames one's relationship with some current person on that basis. There is also always some degree of truth in transference feelings. **Projective identification** is a dynamic whereby one discharges unwanted feelings about the Self, and "puts them in the other" thereby relieving themselves from anxiety, etc. This is called splitting. Through this process you attempt unconsciously to get the person to identify *and* to act in accordance with your projection. Like a director with an actor, you get the other to play out what you want. In the process you never discover who that other actually is, as the projection blurs that. You find an unwanted aspect of yourself in another. Couples do this regularly. **Collusions** is a dynamic the couple co-creates to relive experiences from the past or to avoid experiencing alternate ways of relating. It is an unconscious dance that is a negative collaboration. For example, some couples will collude to fight to avoid anxiety about intimacy. Please note this is a highly simplified set of concepts just to have some basic clarity of these dynamics. These are very complex processes that are necessary to unpack in a therapeutic process.

2 Venice film festival, Best Actress award to Nathalie Baye (1999).

3 Disavowal is different from denial; in **disavowal** you realize something momentarily but then wipe it away, in **denial** you do not even realize you know something.

4 See Brok (2007) to understand the differences between witnessing and one of Gottman's exercises, such as love maps, as well as from Bowlby's (1985) internal working models.

5 When the original relationship to the parent left a residue of unhappiness and trauma, the wish will emerge that the lover cure the wounds the infantile objects have inflicted. In the unconscious, where contradiction does not exist, the two manifest themselves side by side, but once the attempt is made to translate these two contradictory wishes into a real relationship, difficulties will ensue. The turbulence in many love relationships is explained by this contradiction. In the analytic situation, both wishes—the wish to re-find and the yearning for the healer—become powerful. There is still another set of contradictory wishes associated with falling in love. In falling in love, symbiotic wishes to merge become strong, but as Mahler (1971) has pointed out, the reawakened symbiotic wishes for oneness also reawaken the fear of the engulfing mother, creating conflict.

6 In this light, Benjamin (1995) explains the Separation-Individuation theory and Attachment notions:

> Focus on… the child's interaction with the mother as object, It leaves in the unexamined background the aspects of engagement, connection, and active assertion that occur with the mother as other. This perspective is infantocentric, unconcerned with the source of the mother's responses which reflect not only on her pathology or health ("Narcissitic vs good enough") but also her necessarily independent subjectivity. It also misses the pleasure of the evolving relationship with a partner from whom one knows how to elicit a response but whose responses are not entirely predictable and assimilable to internal fantasy.
>
> *(Benjamin, 1995, pp. 31–32)*

7 Obviously, other factors such as idealization in moderate forms, sexual passion, interest, and many other factors go into the process of initial and enduring love.

8 For example, a rigid, rule-oriented person may make it very difficult for a partner to feel spontaneous, lest they be judged or sense they are making the rule-oriented partner anxious or angry.

9 This vignette comes from an actual clinical experience.

10 Winnicott and others have noted that a transitional object may be internalized and sublimated into culture.

11 By this, I mean a sense of the future with some specific or general goal whether it be a baby or spending more time together, etc.; a sense consideration of their future life together beyond the present. This is based on Brok's (1976) notion that life is a construction process, not a random process (see also Aron et al., 2002).

12 See Aznar-Martinez, Perez-Testor, Davins, and Aramburu (2016) for a slightly different approach.

13 By field relevant, I mean self-disclosure that is related to the current session field, rather than disclosing out of field thoughts and feelings about one's personal life. For example, a therapist can under certain circumstances share his experience of tension in the session, or a sense of relief and joy with the current couple's empathy towards each other or share his experience of the climate the couple is setting. He may comment on the couple's comfort with his presence and inquiring if he is accurate in this perception. Or, in a different example, that he is experiencing the couple as comfortably dependent rather than overdependent upon him, and might inquire if they have noticed this change—or is it solely his subjective experience? For some couples it becomes a surprise to understand that the therapist welcomes feedback about his activity and thoughts, perhaps unlike their parents, etc.

14 The present author is currently developing the value of wisdom as one of the important capacities of couple relating. There is little written about this capacity in the psychodynamic literature, and would be added to the concepts of passion, tenderness, and mutual recognition marked by interest in an "Other" and self-awareness as important components in relationships.

15 Simply put for purposes of this chapter, **transference** is a process of displacing feelings onto another person that are not fully accurate, and are based on historical experiences. Projections into the other are derived from Melanie Klein's (1957) object relations theory of **projective identification.** This is a process that puts into the other what we don't want to see about ourselves and thereby getting the other to play an unwanted role. Couple relations are very much influenced by these processes (Brok, 1998).

16 An overly anxious therapist or one who has difficulty with uncertainty might too quickly begin giving suggestions to assuage his or her anxiety, or resort to too much structure or structured techniques. We must remember that technique derives from the Greek word *technae* and can relate to two concepts: one art, the other mechanical technique. Much of American therapeutics tends to focus on the pragmatic usage of technique. Pragmatics are crucial, but when too much in the forefront, diminish the uniqueness of the couple and the individuals that comprise it. One approach for all is

not a very good idea if one values human uniqueness (see Brok, 2010). Getting from here to there is important—but how? Psychodynamic couple therapy relies on both the art of understanding what is relevant in the moment and the various known techniques that can be applied.

17 **Mirroring** is a concept develop by Heinz Kohut, the originator of Self Psychology theory. A short definition of mirroring is when the parent confirms and responds to the child's inner sense of vigor, greatness, and perfection (Kohut, 1978). It is a self object function I chose to act upon with this couple, as I surmised they had been failed by their parents around this dynamic. I recognized they had done much to attempt to develop a positive relationship that was not corrupted by pathology. This, I hoped, would help cement a constructive working relationship based on an empathic understanding of what they were about.

References

Aron, A., Norman, C., Aron, E. N., & Lewandowski, G. (2002). Shared participation in self-expanding activities: Positive effects on experienced marital quality. In P. Noller & J. Feeney (Eds.), *Understanding marriage: Developments in the study of couple interaction* (pp. 177–196). Cambridge, UK: Cambridge University Press.

Aznar-Martinez, B., Perez-Testor, C., Davins, M., & Aramburu, I. (2016). Couple psychoanalytic psychotherapy as the treatment of choice. *Psychoanalytic Psychology, 33*(1), 1–20.

Benjamin, J. (1995). *Like subjects, love objects: Essays on recognition and sexual differences.* New Haven, CT: Yale University Press.

Bergmann, M. S. (1994). The challenge of erotized transference to psychoanalytic technique. *Psychoanalytic Inquiry, 14*, 499–518.

Bergmann, M. V. (1987). *The anatomy of loving: The story of man's quest to know what love is.* New York, NY: Columbia University Press.

Bowlby, J. (1969). *Attachment.* New York, NY: Basic Books.

Bowlby, J. (1985). *A secure base: Parent child attachment and healthy human development.* New York, NY: Basic Books.

Brody, P. R. (1988). Couples psychotherapy: A psychodynamic model. *Psychoanalytic Psychology, 5*(1), 47–70.

Brok, A. J. (1976). Existential, instrumental, and developmental issues relevant in counseling and applied human development. *Society and Leisure, 7*, 61–72.

Brok, A. J. (1992). Crises and transitions: Gender and life stage issues in individual, group and couples treatment. *Psychoanalysis and Psychotherapy, 10*(1) (The Journal of the Postgraduate Center for Mental Health, New York, Brunner Mazel).

Brok, A. J. (1998). *Attachment and involvement as modes of romantic coupling.* Invited presentation, American Psychological Association, Division of Psychoanalysis, Eighteenth Annual Spring Meeting, Boston, MA.

Brok, A. J. (2007). Expanding couple cognitvie maps. *Group, 31*(3), 183–199.

Brok, A. J. (2008a). Presentation. Section 1 Invited Panel on "Discovering vs. Finding in Analytic Work for Both Analyst and Patient," Annual Spring Meeting, Division 39 (Psychoanalysis), APA, New York, NY, April 4.

Brok, A. J. (2008b). *Disavowal of knowing: A factor in a good relationship or malady of an ideal?* Invited presentation, Symposium on "Limits and Limitations to Intimacy: Quasi Affairs,

Convenient Assumptions and Induced Responses," Division 39 (Psychoanalysis) Annual Convention, American Psychological Association, Boston, MA, August.

Brok, A. J. (2009). Time to kill? What we are up against. *Round Robin, Newsletter of Section I, Division of Psychoanalysis, APA, XXII*(1), 1–22.

Brok, A. J. (2010). *Getting from here to there: Important – but how? Round Robin, Newsletter of Section I, Division of Psychoanalysis, APA, XXIV*(1), 2–13.

Brok, A. J. (2011). Working with couples from a psychodynamic perspective using cognitive maps. In D. K. Carson & M. Casado-Kehoe (Eds.), *Case studies in couple therapy: Theory based appraches* (pp. 53–64). New York, NY: Routledge.

Brok, A. J. (2013). Individualismo, benigno y maligno en la cultura Americana [Benign and malignant individualism in American culture]. In A. Brok, M. Cruppi, N. Goldstein, A. Mariona, R Meygide-Sharagorodsky, J. Scvartzman, C. Tewel, & S. Zusmande Arbiser (Eds.), *Una Travesia por la fabrica de sueños* (pp. 177–184). Buenos Aires: Letra Viva.

Brok, A. J. (2014a). Attachment, perversion, play and involvement: Film screening and discussion of "An Affair of Love." Invited presentation, The Southeast Florida Association for Psychoanalytic Psychology, Fort Lauderdale, Imperial Point Medical Center, FL, December 7.

Brok. A. J. (2014b). "Un enfoque psicodinamico-creativo sobre Terapia de Pareja" [A creative psychodynamic focus on Couple Therapy], Asociacion Psicoanalitica de Madrid, Seccion de Familia, Grupos e Instituciones, Madrid, Spain, November 25.

Chasseguet-Smirgel, J. (1985). *The ego ideal: A psychoanalytic essay on the malady of the ideal.* New York, NY: W.W. Norton.

Cone, J. D. (1986). Idiograpohic, nomothetic, and related perspectives in behavioral assessment. In R. O. Nelson & S. C. Hayes (Eds.), *Conceptual foundations of behavioral assessment* (pp. 111–128). New York, NY: Guilford.

Ellenberger, H. F. (1970). *The discovery of the unconscious.* New York, NY: Basic Books.

Freud, S. (1905/2001). Three essays on the theory of sexuality. In *The standard edition of the complete psychological works of Sigmund Freud, volume VII (1901–1905): A case of hysteria, three essays on sexuality and other works* (pp. 123–246). London: Vintage Books.

Freud, S. (1914/2001). On narcissism: An introduction. In *The standard edition of the complete psychological works of Sigmund Freud, volume XIV (1914–1916): On the history of the psycho-analytic movement, papers on metapsychology and other works* (pp. 67–102). London: Vintage Books.

Gedo, J. (1979). *Beyond interpretation: Toward a revised theory for psychoanalysis.* New York, NY: International Universities Press.

Goldklank, S. (2009). "The Shoop Shoop Song": A guide to psychoanalytic-systemic couple therapy. *Contemporary Psychoanalysis, 45*, 3–25.

Klein, M. (1957). *Envy and gratitude and other works.* New York, NY: Delacorte.

Kohut, H. (1978). Disorders of the self and their treatment: An outline. In H. Kohut, *The search for the self: Selected writings of Heinz Kohut* (pp. 359–385). Madison, WI: International Universities Press.

Mahler, M. S. (1971). A study of the separation-individuation process: And its possible application to borderline phenomena in the psychoanalytic situation. *The Psychoanalytic Study of the Child, 26*, 403–424.

Mendelsohn, R. (2014). Revisiting the sadomasochistic marriage: The paranoid-masochistic relationship. *Psychoanalytic Review, 101*, 647–673.

Mitchell, S. (2002). *Can love last?* New York, NY: W.W. Norton.

Poland, W. (2000). Witnessing and otherness. *Journal of American Psychoanalytic Association, 43*(1), 17–43.
Winnicott, D. W. (1953). Transitional objects and transitional phenomena: A study of the first not-me possession. *The International Journal of Psychoanalysis, 34*, 89–97.
Winnicott, D.W. (1971). *Playing and reality*. London: Tavistock.

4

ADLERIAN COUPLES THERAPY

Jon Carlson, Leigh Johnson-Migalski, and Ebony Spriggs

Unhappiness in marriage is merely a mistake, a defect in one's life pattern.
Alfred Adler, *Reading Times*, p. 24, November 29, 1929

Alfred Adler was the first therapist of the modern era to do family therapy and is also believed to have been the first to systematically provide help to couples (Bitter, 2009). As one of the three originators of psychotherapy (with Sigmund Freud and Carl Jung), his approach stressed the importance of relationships and the social context. It is probably fair to state that Adler's operational definition of mental health is when an individual has good relationships with all of the significant people in their life. This chapter presents Adlerian couples therapy applied to the case of Natalie and David. The theory applied to couples, the key concepts, the treatment formulation, and the four-step process will be presented.

Brief History of Adlerian Couples Counseling

Alfred Adler may have believed in good relationships and the importance of marriage but according to his biographers (Bottome, 1939; Hoffman, 1994) he was not very good at it (i.e. marriage). Actually, Adler's best solution for his own marriage to his wife, Raissa Epstein, was to live on two different continents. Alfred and Raissa, however, remained married for their lifetimes and produced four children of whom they were fond—three girls and one boy. The boy, Kurt, and one of the daughters, Alexandra, became psychiatrists and carried on the work of their father.

Adler believed in marriage and was able to help others to translate his ideas into creating happy satisfying relationships. We use the word *satisfying* and not *love*.

The goal in couples counseling is to increase satisfaction. Love is present in most relationships. Even when people divorce, they often love their partner, but they just aren't satisfied in their marriage.

The Adlerian approach involves helping couples to create or restore both social and emotional equality. Adler noted that a quality marriage was one in which each person was more concerned about the wellbeing of the other than they were about themselves. In essence, "Love is the wish to make another happy" (Carlson, Peluso, Figenbaum, & Oles, 2012, p. 244). It is this attitude that helps couples to feel and act like a unit and to place value on the relationship while still respecting the individuality of each partner. In couples work it is important to realize, as well as clarify to the couple, that there are three entities in a marriage or partnership. For example, Natalie and David need to understand that in their marriage there is "him," "her," and "us." The Adlerian therapist is concerned with what is best for "us" or the relationship and does not get caught up in refereeing between David and Natalie's individual needs.

The Adlerian therapist realizes the importance of education or **psychoeducation** in working with couples (Carlson, Watts, & Maniacci, 2005). Couples learn about marriage from their families-of-origin and can only do what they have been taught. Many partners say that they will not be like their father or mother but despite their best intentions what else do they know? The Adlerian therapist attempts to remove blaming and to normalize relationship problems by helping the couple realize that their behaviors towards one another are not as much intentional as they are learned. The task of therapy is to unlearn behaviors that create distance between one another and to create those that create connection and togetherness. Unfortunately, we have created a throwaway society with a sort of planned obsolescence where things are not designed to be permanent or last. We have a means of externalizing problems and believe that everything should go our way. When our marriage is not going well we don't look at ourselves but rather at how our partner is not meeting our needs. The solution is often to get a divorce. Recent research seems to highlight the fallacy of this thinking and to provide the basis as to why Adlerian therapists are marriage-friendly therapists who believe choosing your original partner again is often the best choice. A pioneering research study by Waite, Browning, Doherty, Gallagher, Luo, and Stanley (2002) showed:

1. Unhappily married adults who divorced or separated were no happier on average, than unhappily married adults who stayed together.
2. Divorce did not reduce symptoms of depression for unhappily married adults, or raise their self-esteem, or increase their sense of mastery, on average, compared to unhappy spouses who stayed married.
3. The vast majority of divorces (74%) happened to adults who had been happily married five years previously.
4. Unhappy marriages were less common than unhappy spouses.

5. Two out of three unhappily married adults who avoided divorce or separation ended up happily married five years later.
6. Many currently happy married spouses have had extended periods of marital unhappiness, often for quite serious reasons, including alcoholism, infidelity, verbal abuse, emotional neglect, depression, illness, and work reversals.

Unfortunately, according to psychologist John Welwood (2005), this is the first time in history that couples lack clear guidelines, supportive family networks, a religious context, and a compelling social meaning to be married. Training and support, therefore, need to be an important component of couples therapy. Alfred Adler and his followers provided the theory and strategies necessary to help therapists guide couples to learn how to create satisfying partnerships.

Some of the most prominent Adlerians who influenced Adlerian couples counseling include Rudolf Dreikurs, Jon Carlson, and Don Dinkmeyer. In 1946, Rudolf Dreikurs wrote *The challenge of marriage* to provide guidance to couples to help them learn how to have a more satisfying marriage. In 1984, Don Dinkmeyer and Jon Carlson developed a comprehensive marriage enrichment training program, *Training in Marriage Enrichment* (TIME; Dinkmeyer & Carlson, 1984), for couples to learn the skills needed to create satisfying marriages. The couples guide, *Time for a better marriage* (Carlson & Dinkmeyer, 2003), provides the important information, homework, and experiential activities that guides couples towards healthier and fulfilling ways of cooperating and connecting in their relationship. The ten-week program was shown to be effective (Bowling, Hill, & Jencius, 2005; Hawley & Olson, 1995; Matteson, Christensen, & England, 1988). Some of Adler's key concepts that are incorporated in *The challenge of marriage* and the *TIME* program, and are important when working with couples, are as follows.

Equality and Mutual Respect

Adlerian couples counseling emphasizes equality and mutual respect for the relationship (Carlson & Englar-Carlson 2016; Carlson et al., 2005). Spouses are equal. Both partners need to have a voice with regards to their life together. The couple needs to co-develop common goals in order to have a mutually compelling future.

There may be an agreed upon division of labor or roles that may be culturally specific but the Adlerian therapist hopes that each couple can find ways to respect each other. Relationships have been moving toward equality and respect as larger systems have been transitioning to more democratic processes. Partners have found ways to share power as opposed to one having all of the power. Not having a set structure of knowing who has the power or how to share leaves couples mystified on how to operate.

Dreikurs (1971) articulated that the changing systemic ideas of power and superiority have left men and women confused on gender roles. Established, unspoken dynamics for men and women (i.e. men are in charge and women follow, men work and women stay home) used to guide behavior in North America but now positions or powers are not resolute. Men and women do not follow the old models and are unsure of how to act in the present. There is a lot of confusion in the couple's dynamics (Carlson et al., 2005). *Who has power in the relationship? How is it negotiated?* David and Natalie lacked effective role models of cooperation and equality for them to learn healthy respect as intimate partners. As a result, their learning curve, as it relates to the ability to deal with differences, is extremely steep.

Being Responsible for Yourself

Each partner contributes to the partnership in ways that will either promote the desired goals for the relationship or create dissonance and conflict. The problem behaviors that couples experience are understood by the Adlerian couples therapist as creative, yet perhaps ineffective ways that the individuals have been attempting to reach their goals whether conscious or unconscious. Alfred Adler emphasized the importance of personal responsibility for marital success. Unfortunately, partners often believe that the only thing wrong with the marriage is their partner. Each partner often feels this way and blame one another. Because of this they have trouble seeing their role in why the marriage doesn't thrive. We see this in the case of David and Natalie, as they both blame the other for the relationship problems and seem clueless as to their own role. The Adlerian therapist believes the answer for them (as for most couples) is not to find or choose a new partner via divorce or affair but to actually learn to be a different partner through counseling and psychoeducation (Carlson & Lorelle, 2016).

Life Tasks

It is important to make sure that each partner is mentally healthy and living a balanced life. In Adlerian terms, this means to address what are called **the Life Tasks**. Adler (1956) originally defined three universal tasks that represent the main challenges people experience in life—work, love, and community. He felt that all three must be addressed in order to function effectively. In addition to focusing on the challenges of the marriage, the Adlerian couples therapist assists each partner to meet each of these. Both Natalie and David need to improve their relationships with themselves. They report that they have not taken very good care of themselves. Both David and Natalie could be helped in terms of designing programs around fitness, diet, job satisfaction, and helping others. People who feel good about these core areas are likely to be better companions and open to developing novel ways to have fun together.

Movement

The Adlerian couples therapist understands the importance of monitoring the couple's **psychological movement**. What is their behavior? What are they doing as opposed to what they say? How are they interacting with each other? Sometimes, Adlerians will use the language of vertical versus horizontal movement, which reflects the attitude and way of operating or the dynamics a person demonstrates. **Vertical movement** implies one person is taking a *better than stance*—the relationship is not seen equally but that there is a winner and a loser while horizontal connotes *equality*. **Horizontal movement** is similar to the term—an equal or even playing field—a person treats others as if they were of the same level of importance. The therapist stays aware of the progress or movement that the couple is making towards their stated goals. It is not as important where the couple is presently, but whether or not they are making progress that is important. The important question for the couple is: "Are we getting better even though we still have a long way to go?" Reminding couples of their accomplishments and what they have done together is motivating for them. The therapist also helps the couple to stay aware of what they have been through, and what is good about them. Often couples lose sight of the process and get discouraged because the goal has yet to be realized, even though they may be getting very close. This would be similar to the discouraged farmer plowing up the field just as the shoots begin to break the soil. Natalie and David demonstrate vertical communication and do not see themselves playing on the same team and both feel that the other is trying to put them down. An example of their conversation that demonstrates this might be:

Natalie: I'm not the one that's an alcoholic!
David: I forgot; you're perfect.

In this simple exchange of insults, neither are listening and both are trying to hurt and have the last word and not communicating. An example of horizontal communication would have been:

Natalie: I am really upset because I found emails between you and Devyn.
David: I understand and see how that would hurt…

Lifestyle

"The attitude of every individual toward marriage is one of the expressions of his style of life. We can understand it if we understand the whole individual not otherwise" (Adler, 1956, p. 434). Each individual partner has a lifestyle or a personality style. The **lifestyle** consists of the cognitive, emotional, and behavioral patterns that make up the individual's approach towards life, others, and their orientation to the world. It is shaped by their early experiences in their family-of-origin and biology. Adlerian theory is a biopsychosocial model that incorporates biology into understanding a person (Carlson et al., 2005). For example, a person with a difficult temperament may feel more disorganized in a chaotic family-of-origin than a child with an easy-going temperament; therefore, the easy-going child may perceive "life has its ups and downs but I can manage it," while the difficult temperament may conclude "life is chaotic and I can't handle it." In the case of David, we see the influence of genetics—he is a smaller perhaps not athletically inclined person; he grew up in a family with a father that greatly valued being athletic and a man. How can you succeed as an athlete when genetically it may be harder? People can do it but in David's case the pressure was too much and he consistently feels less than a man. Feeling less than a man will make it harder for him to feel fully loveable and accepted in a relationship. People with adaptive lifestyles feel the courage to engage in life's tasks and strive for both personal and couple goals. People with maladaptive and less effective lifestyles feel discouraged and may withdraw from life's tasks.

Adlerians gather specific information about each member of the couple to understand how they make sense of the world, themselves, their partner, and their identity as a partner. For example, a glimpse of Natalie's lifestyle may include the following: the world can be chaotic and exciting, I need to take care of people but don't have the skills to relate equally to my peers, therefore when I am in a relationship I need to control because I know people will leave me anyway which maintains the chaos that I expect. Adlerians would assess the following to understand and conceptualize each person in the dyad: biological influences, family/cultural values, modeling of problem-solving skills, birth order/sibling relationships, gender guiding lines, family/cultural atmosphere, and early recollections (Carlson et al., 2005; Bettner, 2007; Powers & Griffith, 2012; Mosak & Shulman, 1998; Yang, Milliren, & Blagen, 2009).

Each person approaches the relationship from this unique lifestyle and one's private logic or basic mistakes. **Private logic** is just a phrase that Adlerians used to communicate that each of us has figured a specific way of belonging in the world, our non-conscious beliefs or convictions. Adler also used the word **schemas**. Our perception of how we see the world and others is filtered by our current schemas. Individuals can develop mistakes as part of their lifestyle. These **basic mistakes** can be overgeneralizations (s/he must always love me; we must never argue; couples must agree on everything), impossible goals of security, misperceptions about life's demands, minimization of one's worth, or faulty values. Natalie's belief that men will leave her will influence how she may behave. She may be always misinterpreting more neutral behavior by David to indicate he is leaving. She may then become more controlling to try to avoid that but her reading his email probably makes things worse. These expectations create unspoken marital rules that are either helpful or destructive for the relationship. In many cases they are compatible. For example, some people want to be taken care of and others want to take care of people. Some enjoy leading and others following. Adlerians are looking for *complementarity* in lifestyles.

It is important to collect information on sibling relationships because through their sibships people learn how to interact with people in their adult life. This happens at an early age, but these lessons are carried out throughout the person's lifetime (Lew & Bettner, 2007). How a person interacted with their siblings will be reflected in their current relationship. Aspects of the same difficulties and patterns that occurred in the sibling relationship will occur in the romantic relationship. By understanding these sibling relationships, the therapist can gain a better understanding of the current difficulties that the couple is experiencing. In the case of David and Natalie, understanding their **birth order** helps to highlight their essential differences. She was the oldest or firstborn while he was the youngest. Oldest children tend to find their place by trying to do what is right while youngest children care less about right and wrong and seem to just want their way (Carlson et al., 2005). We will provide a comprehensive lifestyle summary and a summary of the couple later in the chapter.

Early Recollections

Early recollections (ERs) is a projective technique that can be used to help the Adlerian therapist understand each partner's lifestyle more deeply (Clark, 2002, 2013; Mosak & DiPietro, 2005). Each partner gives six to eight earliest memories recalled before the age of 10. The memories are not primed but by just requesting the earliest memories, they for some reason come to mind. Interpretations of ERs can help a couple see how they see themselves, the world and others. A well-trained Adlerian therapist can help the couple learn how their individual lifestyles either complement or irritate one another. Natalie's early recollections seem to show someone who believes that people cannot be trusted and it is necessary to control or over-function. David believes that it is important not to give in to others. When he stays on the couch after a fight because he does not know how to resolve differences this confirms Natalie's ideas that men leave her.

Holism

Adler (1957) emphasized understanding a person and the couple in a larger social context. The Adlerian therapist looks beyond the parts to the sum of the parts. Dreikurs (1971) underscored that the couples therapist must look at the systems that the person and the couple is embedded in. David and Natalie appear to be embedded in a North American culture that has evolving ideas on what it means to be a man and woman. David and Natalie's ideas of a husband and wife are also influenced by their experience of their families-of-origin. We live in a society that discriminates against women (Brown, 2015) who are not mothers and Natalie's desire for being a mother is impacting their relationship. David, like many men in North American society, wants to be a good provider but he wants to wait until he gets a better job. These outside social contexts influence and reinforce individual values but these individual values are clashing and creating friction.

Including culture, race, age, religion, sexual orientation, ethnicity, and social economic status are all contexts that Adlerians examine and fold into the conceptualization. For example, how is the couple managing the different religious values in the relationships and themselves (Duba Sauerheber & Bitter, 2013)? How is the level of acculturation of each partner impacting their feelings of belonging and social interest (Duffy, Carns, Carns, & Garcia, 1998)?

Adlerians would also consider the context for LGTBQ couples who are married and experience discrimination. Couples who are not in the majority of the culture experience heightened stress due to their minority status which will compound any problems they are facing. Not having any modeling of what minority couples do when dealing with stress or what is the norm for their relationship is also stressful. An example of this is when someone grows up gay in a society that only models how heterosexual couples behave. The stress of heterosexism and prejudice creates more difficulty for LGBTQ relationships (Yang, Milliren, & Blagen, 2009). Adlerians would make sure to address these larger systemic concepts to show how the couple is not alone and other couples struggle in the same way. This will help to shore up the relationship from "me versus you" to "us versus the society" and how the couple can manage this discrimination together.

Social Interest

Adler (1956) asserted every person has the innate capacity and tendency for social interest. He described **social interest** as caring for others, being considerate, and responsive to society's needs above the individual's own needs, and the ability to understand what another person is experiencing (empathy). The social interest extends beyond the individual relationships to the community and a sense of belonging to the community. The sense of responsibility to live cooperatively and improve the community is associated with social interest. While Adler believed social interest was innate, he suggested that it is nurtured by the social context. Marriage and forming intimate relationships are methods of exercising and developing this social interest. Adler captured this sentiment in this note he sent to his daughter Vali on her marriage:

> I ask you to fill yourselves with the brave resolve to think more about each other than about yourself, and always try to live in such a way that you make the other's life easier and more beautiful.
>
> *(Bottome, 1939, p. 131)*

David and Natalie appear to be self-focused and could benefit from increased social interest.

Theory of Problem Formulation

As has been alluded to earlier in the chapter, couples that struggle lack the knowledge and skills on how to cooperate and treat each other with equality and respect. Adlerian theory is a value-laden theory that argues for healthy functioning and that one needs to act in a socially interested or courageous, compassionate, creative, and common-sense way (Manaster & Corsini, 1982). Therefore, problems arise in people and couples when they cope with feelings of discouragement and feelings of inferiority in an unhealthy, unproductive, rigid, or unhelpful way. All people have feelings of inferiority. Healthy people strive to do better, to be better people, and improve themselves and these feelings can help motivate them as well as address the need to belong and be connected with others. When people have been trained from childhood to cope with these feelings effectively or learned this later then stressors are easier to manage, but if people lack this knowledge and training then problems surface. An individual's feelings of inferiority increase as well when they are in situations where it feels that others are not including them. This is why it is important for the Adlerian therapist to understand how each person's current perceptions of themselves, others, and the world influences their feelings.

The Adlerian therapist can apply Lew and Bettner's (2007) delineation of some key psychological needs to show how David is responding to high inferiority feelings and discouragement in the relationship. Lew and Bettner's "**Crucial Cs**" consists of connecting, capable, count, and courage. They defined connecting as wanting to belong or fit in, while capable is the need to grow and improve, to feel competent. People also desire to count and to feel significant, while courage influences how the other "Cs" are implemented. With courage, people will connect, be capable, and count in ways that are usually helpful for all.

Theory of Problem Resolution

Although Adlerian theory resides as one of the oldest approaches to counseling and therapy, it is very integrative and innovative. This section will review how an Adlerian couples therapist will formulate the change process; delineate the four phases/stages of Adlerian therapy/counseling that structure treatment; describe the first session with David and Natalie; and provide a list of some of the common and classic Adlerian interventions used with couples, including Natalie and David, that build skills, increase social interest, understanding and empathy, and decrease inferiority feelings and discouragement.

Basic Principles and Skills of How Adlerians Understand the Change Process

Adlerian couples therapists use the principles that Carlson and Dinkmeyer (2003) indicate are at the foundation of the change process:

1. *Developing and maintaining a good relationship requires a time commitment.* For the relationship to succeed, the couple must make it a priority now and in the future.
2. *Specific skills that are essential to a healthy partnership can be learned.* When the couple understands how a marriage works and the necessary skills for building a satisfying marriage, they can develop the skills that create a positive and rewarding relationship.
3. *Change often takes time and all change begins with you.* The first step in creating a satisfying marriage involves a commitment to change. Each partner begins by understanding what their role in the marriage has been and what they can do to make the relationship different. They must be patient in their growth and allow for different rates of change. As you proceed through the therapy process, some weeks will produce wonders and others will produce little apparent change.
4. *Feelings of love and caring that have diminished or disappeared often return when behavior changes.* Some days we are close to one another while others we are distant. Romantic feelings, intimacy and love often diminish over time in a relationship. When feelings change, many couples believe the relationship is over. This need not be the case. A change of feelings may mean that the partners are not being reinforced in the relationship and that the relationship deserves a higher priority. It is important at such times to act as if all were well. By acting as if the relationship is the intimate, satisfying relationship desired, new behaviors and feelings can be established.
5. *Small changes are very important in bringing about big change.* A happier relationship results from many small changes over a period of time. Even though both partners are committed to change, there may be times when unwanted patterns reappear. This does not mean that the new skills they are learning are not working in their marriage. When they continue to focus on the positive relationship they desire, these times of testing will pass. Lasting and satisfying marriages are created when marriage partners love and support each other. The question becomes, how can they learn to love and support each other more often? Like muscles, love and support become stronger with exercise.

There are many factors that can interfere with a relationship and many skills that can help create an ongoing atmosphere of love and support. The skills necessary for creating and sustaining an effective marriage are learned. Partners begin marriage with an assortment of skills, some effective and others ineffective in helping them achieve the desired sense of connection. The skills needed to enrich marriage are well known to the Adlerian couples therapist and can be expressed to their clients in simple terms. The Adlerian therapist is attempting to help the marriage partners learn to relate in the following positive ways (Carlson & Dinkmeyer, 2003):

- They individually accept responsibility for their behavior and their self-esteem.
- They identify and align their personal and marital goals.
- They choose to encourage each other.
- They communicate their feelings with honesty and openness.
- They listen empathically when feelings are being expressed.
- They seek to understand the factors that influence their relationship.
- They demonstrate that they accept and value each other.
- They make choices that are best for the relationship.
- They choose thoughts, words, and actions that support the positive goals of their marriage.
- They solve marital conflicts as they arise.
- They commit themselves to the ongoing process of maintaining a satisfying marriage.

Four Stages of Adlerian Therapy

There are four stages in Adlerian couples therapy: these stages are the relationship, assessment, insight, and reorientation (Carlson & Englar-Carlson, 2016; Carlson et al., 2005). Therapy proceeds along a series of progressive stages that seems quite logical. In practice the stages are not necessarily followed in a fixed sequential fashion but actually fluid and stop and start many times as therapy progresses (Carlson & Englar-Carlson, 2016).

An Adlerian therapist is very active within the counseling and change process, so it is very important that the couple feel that they have a strong and equal relationship with the therapist so that change can occur. It is also important that the therapist not favor one member of the couple over the other. Connection with both members of the couple occurs during the relationship phase, and also throughout the other phases. The therapist can go about doing this in several ways. One way that this can be done is making sure to treat each member of the couple with respect. There is also the added bonus that the couple can also learn how they should treat each other. The therapist can also offer encouragement and hope to the couple. When many couples enter therapy they are discouraged and cannot see a light at the end of the tunnel. Offering **encouragement** and hope, and also pointing out strengths, can help the therapist to create a stronger relationship with the couple. This stage is important as there needs to be a solid base on which the rest of sessions will be built.

The second stage is for formal assessment and is important as it allows the therapist to collect information that will be used to further the therapy. During this phase information about the couple system and how each person works within that structure is collected. Collecting this information allows the therapist, and the couple, to better understand the system. When this occurs each partner can become more aware of which problems they are contributing to and change their behavior accordingly (Carlson & Dinkmeyer, 1999). The **lifestyle assessment** is a the individual assessments and a couple assessment that will be explained at the first couple's session.

David's Conceptualization

David was the youngest child and the only boy following two sisters in his family. The family was led by a "manly" man who practiced vertical (up/down) rather than horizontal (equal) communication. His father and mother met while working at a bank where the father was the mother's boss. His father continued to be the boss and lead at home as he did at the bank. His mother went along with this arrangement until the children were grown and the marriage dissolved.

The family was child-focused or child-centered (i.e. Regina's pregnancy at 16 and decision not to terminate, a miscarriage that brought mother and sister closer, David fighting with Regina over her mothering skills, and the divorce of parents after the children had grown up). His father pressured the short and pudgy David to follow in his footsteps and to be a good athlete. David tried to be the "manly man" his father wanted but could never measure up to his dad and resented his father for pushing him so hard. David valued motherhood as seen with his alienation-inducing fight with Regina over her lack of mothering skills while battling alcohol—David embraced this value of the family. The family did not know how to resolve conflict and used quitting or "cut offs" as ineffective solutions to differences or disagreement. For example, David and his sister Regina have not talked in six years, his parents divorced, and the family called the police on David to handle the physical confrontation that erupted. David continues to lack the skills of problem resolution as in his marriage. He seeks fun from other women, sleeps on the couch after arguments, and blames Natalie for all of their marriage problems. David has found success in his career as a teacher, again embracing the family value of being child-centered. This job is perfect for him because he can show how children are important to him but he is not challenged as much in regards to authority since he is literally and metaphorically the "biggest man" in the classroom. He continues to struggle to be the "manly man" through exciting sexual conquests but then feels constantly disappointed by his high expectations for himself, which results in him not trying and instead focusing on short-term pleasures like eating and smoking. He is probably genetically predisposed to addiction given Regina's struggles, so when stressed he may self-soothe with eating and smoking. He pushes Natalie away by avoiding conflict, inappropriate contact with other women, gaining weight, drinking, and smoking. Through this action he shows Natalie that she can't make him be a certain way just like his father tried to make him into a certain type of man.

Natalie's Conceptualization

Natalie was the oldest child in her family followed by a brother who was two years younger. When she was 10, she became parentified as she was expected to care for her stepsister. Natalie did not see positive conflict resolution growing up and her parents divorced when she was five and they continued to struggle as her co-parents. She had an inconsistent relationship with her birth father and her stepfather. She did not learn how to communicate with a man. She grew up believing that she is not responsible for fixing the relationship with her father or for that matter anyone. She continues to try to caretake David but does not know how to interact with him as an equal. She practices vertical and not horizontal communication. Natalie mothers David but does not know how to trust him and does not expect him (or any man) to be faithful to her given that every boyfriend she has picked has cheated on her. Given her ambivalent experience with her father and stepfather and lack of experience in long-term romantic relationships, she does not know how to interact with a man nor does she (unconsciously) expect him to stay and treat her with respect. Natalie's brother married and divorced, indicating the lack of training or family pattern of poor relationship skills. Natalie has become a real estate agent, which seems to be a good job for her. She can caretake others during the exciting and chaotic time of moving, but does not need to have a long-term relationship with her clients. Natalie, as a 30-year-old female, is experiencing pressure to have a child as a typical female in the North American culture. She responds to this pressure by pushing David for a child.

The Couple's Conceptualization

Hawes (2004), Dreikurs (1971), and Carlson and Dinkmeyer (2003) have articulated that people are attracted to other people that match their unconscious expectations, which leads to problems later. David was attracted to Natalie's first-born caretaking skills which may also be viewed as a mothering style, matching his value of women being good mothers. Later, he resents her and sees her caretaking as controlling. Natalie was unconsciously attracted to David's youngest born qualities of fun and excitement but now resents his unwillingness to be responsible for his self-care and disloyalty to her.

Both Natalie and David grew up in families that did not know how to resolve conflict. Both families modeled excitement and chaos. Natalie and David unconsciously are accustomed to the chaos and it feels "normal" even if it is uncomfortable. The beginning of their relationship from online meeting to visiting each other engenders excitement, drama, and chaos. In their geographically distant relationship they were able to focus more on fun and romance and not get bogged down in everyday annoyances and cooperation. Both partners are participating in making chaos in a negative way—David with his pulling away toward infidelity and Natalie with her overcontrolling and snooping behavior. This is how each partner is managing their high inferiority feelings—they are doing the only type of coping behavior they know how to do because they never learned any different, even if they don't like what is happening. Their movement—their dynamics—would be called a distance–pursuer pattern. Both partners believe the one to blame should be the one to fix the situation. Both partners are struggling with how to find power and equality in the relationship. *How can a woman and man operate together and find hope that they can figure this out together in a way that a negative ending is not destiny?*

Adlerian couple therapists do not focus on just understanding the problems but look at the lifestyle to understand their clients' strengths. In fact, much of the Adlerian literature on understanding couples, or the love task, delineates on how successful couples and people act with social interest; a healthy functioning couple should be encouraging of one another and possess social interest (Adler, 1956, 1957; Dreikurs, 1971).

No wonder they fell in love. They both unconsciously felt comfortable with each other due to the similar ways of thinking about men, women, and life. In many ways, Natalie and David have a lot in common upon which to build success. They are both discouraged due to the larger societal pressures, lack of skills and absence of positive models, and personality dynamics of how to find significance in the world and in the relationship.

Treatment Plan/Problem List

The seemingly major or presenting concern of Natalie and David consists of David's infidelity. The Adlerian couples therapist focuses on the unsatisfying relationship and not the specific problems like affairs or lack of sexual frequency. Problems are just the arenas where couples do battle over their unsatisfying relationship. The infidelity needs to be looked at as a symptom of the *problematic relationship* and not *the problem.*

Dreikurs (1971) viewed infidelity as a form of superiority and power—a form of safeguarding against problems in the relationship. Yang, Milliren, and Blagen (2009) identify infidelity as a form of *eros* or erotic love, which is self-centered, versus *agape* love, which is other-centered. Both David and Natalie are struggling with their emotional and physical commitment to their relationship. Her emotional lack of connection safeguards her from the risk of being hurt like she has been hurt many times before from men and also reifies her ideas that she is right that all men let her down. She then can't tolerate this being alone and tries to further control David to fix the situation which makes it worse. David responds to the caretaking by backing further away and seeking out fun elsewhere. He does not have to face the stress of being a father if he does not commit to this relationship. Both Natalie and David are discouraged and not operating or behaving in a way that helps the relationship right now.

The couple will need to understand how their roles as oldest (Natalie) and youngest child (David) impact their current lifestyle. As an oldest child Natalie is over-functioning, trying to take responsibility for all that happens. David, on the other hand, is a youngest child who doesn't seem to want or know how to grow up.

Perhaps most important is that the couple needs to learn skills of conflict resolution and to learn how to resolve their differences without quitting or cutting off the other. Each partner has grown up with divorce helping them to believe that relationships do not last. The couple needs to learn that conflict and difference does not mean the relationship is over. Neither partner has experienced the safety of a close relationship.

The couple needs to understand that difference is acceptable and makes a relationship interesting. Olson, Russell, and Sprenkle (1989) have identified the importance of certain traits in the family-of-origin which will create harmony or struggle. Closeness versus distance and rigidity versus flexibility are some of the most important characteristics that couples learn from their families. Couples ebb and flow between distance and closeness, but individuals can be differentiated by their comfort level with distance and closeness. Both David and Natalie indicate they would like a close relationship but neither knows how to maintain this closeness.

This couple also needs to address problems of Natalie's rigid beliefs compared to David's more flexible outlook. Neither partner has very good self-care behaviors and needs to learn to take care of themselves as well as the relationship. "Love is the wish to make another happy" is a concept that seems to have evaded David and Natalie. They need to learn that a good partner needs to think of their partner's needs and not just their own.

Games of Probabilities/Readiness for Change Assessment

Mosak and Maniacci (1998) assess a client's perception on the likelihood of change occurring using a percentage system. We could ask David and Natalie, "If I were to meet you on the street one year from now, what is the percentage out of 100 that you two will be together?" Clearly, a low number indicates discouragement, a high number shows hopefulness, and if the answer is 50/50 that could be a sign of ambivalence. An Adlerian therapist could use this opportunity to teach the clients about perception and self-fulfilling prophecy, that the client could make the prediction true but not unless a new mindset is established. This also provides information as to each partner's level of readiness. Doherty (2011) estimates that 30 percent of the couples who come to therapy have at least one member who is ambivalent. When this occurs, the Adlerian therapist would follow Doherty's (2011) protocol for the mixed-agenda couple. The term "agenda" refers to the goal of the individual partner. A mixed-agenda couple have different goals regarding the future of the marriage. The therapist also needs to assess the stage of change the couple is at and to tailor the treatment accordingly (Prochaska, Norcross, & DiClemete, 1994). Knowing that a couple is committed to the relationship allows the therapist to begin interventions to help the couple reach their relationship goals. Hawes (2004) has found that couples often fear that their relationship is so dysfunctional that they will require years of therapy—this commitment feels overwhelming. With ambivalent clients, she encourages them to commit to one session at time. She asks the couple if they are ready to come again for the next week's session until the ambivalence subsides and a long-term commitment, if needed, can be agreed upon.

First Couples Session

The couples session begins with indicating to the couple that the therapist would like to begin the session by going over the information that was learned in the individual meetings. The results are presented in a hopeful and upbeat fashion that helps the couple to understand that the therapist sees them through a positive lens. The first two phases of Adlerian therapy (relationship and assessment) take place in this case with the separate individual sessions to collect the mini-lifestyle information. Adlerians could and do often meet with the couple together for the first session and collect some data with each person in the room. The therapy relationship is structured by articulating how Adlerian therapists operate and creating agreements for keeping the therapy safe. For example, Adlerians may inform clients that the therapist may make guesses about how the clients see themselves, the world and others but that the guesses may be wrong at times. Adlerians tend to be practical and pragmatic and if we have some ideas on how a person operates we would rather introduce that idea rather than spending months for the client to come to that insight. Also the Adlerian couples counselor would explain that the focus is on the couple and not on one person. Given the focus on responsibility the therapist would underscore that they can't make their partner change but that focus should be on each person being responsible for changing themselves. The therapist reminds them that they are "100% responsible for their role in the unsatisfying relationship."

With the focus on insight and helping each partner understanding themselves, it alters their viewpoint and allows for forgiveness and hope and trying new ways of operating. In this session the main focus will be on an intervention to address unfinished business, but encouragement will be used throughout the session.

Therapist: I appreciate the honesty that you both showed in our initial meetings. By your hard work in our individual sessions you have really helped me to get a good idea as to what is going on and how much you care. Before I go into the formulation I want you both to know that I understand that even though things may seem pretty hopeless lately that I am, however, encouraged from the patterns that I see.

Natalie: I don't know what patterns you are talking about.

Therapist: I wasn't very clear. (*Agrees with her in a non-defensive manner.*) The first is that you are talking with me and not lawyers. This tells me you want to stay married to one another. Second, you have described some patterns that were learned in your families and that we should be able to help you learn some new patterns since you are both committed to and wanting a more satisfying marriage.

This is an example of encouragement—reframing that it could be much worse if they were talking to lawyers but they are not at that point—and focusing on learning and not on the damage due to their family-of-origin.

David: You think the problem is that we haven't learned how to be married?

Therapist: That's a good way to look at it, David. You both learned everything that your parents taught you about being married even though you didn't want to be like them, that is all you know.

David: That makes a lot of sense. At times being with Natalie seems like *déjà vu* to when I was living at home.

Natalie: I feel that too.

Therapist: Let's go over what I learned.... (*The therapist goes over the couple's formulation as written above and the problem list.*)

Using a positive approach that educates the couple in what seems to be happening in their relationship provides a hopeful way of how to proceed. There is no blame. Both partners are responsible for their role in making the marriage miserable (or wonderful!). This is referred to as ***creating hope through encouragement****. The therapist then asks the couple:*

Therapist: Since you both seem to realize that you have a less than wonderful relationship with your same sex parent, what do you think you could do to make it better?

Natalie: I don't want to get along with my Mom, I want to get along with David.

Therapist: Believe it or not Natalie I think they are related just like I think David's impasse with his father is related to how he treats or mistreats you.

David: You want me to fix my relationship with Dad?

A discussion continued where the therapist was able to help each to design a way they that they could talk with their parent about wanting to have a better relationship with them. Each seemed to realize that they could be a good son or daughter even if their father or mother was not a good parent. They both indicated that they would make contact with their same sex parent indicating that they really needed their help in how to be a better partner. By asking for help or guidance from their parent they were changing the long-standing pattern of expressing anger and disappointment. It is less important how their parent responds to this new approach than it is that Natalie and David do their part as a good daughter and good son. Adler often prescribed activities for people to do to improve their awareness and feel better. By practicing new skills on an old relationship, as well as resolving feelings of discouragement, can possibly help them feel more courageous in fixing their current romantic relationship.

In addition to this suggestion, the therapist wants to get the couple working on some skill development that will help them to directly change the relationship dynamics and to start the process where small changes in loving behaviors often stimulate positive feelings.

Therapist: In addition to contacting your parents this week would you be willing to do another activity? (*Both nod.*) I would like you to talk with each other for ten minutes a day. (*Both look at the therapist with an OK but we already do this kind of expression.*) I want you to do this in a very special way. This activity is called a **daily dialogue** and on the even days of the calendar Natalie will begin and talk for five minutes and David can only listen and then you will switch places with Natalie listening and David talking … (*The therapist continues to clearly discuss what they are to talk about and helps the couple schedule a time to do this once each day until the next session.*)

The Adlerian therapist understands that much of the work that will change the couple relationship occurs outside of the actual therapy session (Carlson & Englar-Carlson, 2016). Each partner has homework to do which implies that both are responsible for changing. During the first session, the therapist assigns *encouragement days* and the *encouragement meeting* in addition to the *daily dialogue.*

Encouraging Days

To help Natalie and David the therapist asks the couple to do the **encouraging days exercise** (Carlson & Dinkmeyer, 2003). This activity asks each partner to make a list of seven to ten small pleasant behaviors the partner can do that will please the individual. Behaviors should be specific, positive, and unrelated to past conflicts between the partners. Behaviors are chosen that are possible for the partner to do on a daily basis. These lists are then exchanged. Each partner should try to do two encouraging behaviors each day. One item is added to the list each week. This is an important list as it is the key to the person's heart (Carlson & Dinkmeyer, 2003).

Encouragement Meeting

The **encouragement meeting** involves having each partner say one thing that happened to them during the day that they enjoyed and one thing their partner did that they appreciated. Hope for the relationship comes from encouragement and increasing the positive in their togetherness. To continue the increase in positive exchanges, David and Natalie are asked to have an *encouragement meeting* each day after their daily dialogue. In this activity each partner is asked to indicate one thing that happened that day that they appreciated and one thing their partner did in the past twenty-four hours that they appreciated. According to Gottman and Gottman (2015), satisfied partners have four positive exchanges for every one negative.

Future sessions

In future sessions, David and Natalie addressed the other aspects of their problem list. The remainder of this chapter shows some of the ways each of the problems are addressed as well as other strategies and techniques used by the Adlerian couples therapist. The therapist must make sure to tailor the treatment suggestions to David and Natalie (Carlson, Sperry, & Lewis, 2005). In order to accomplish this, there are many Adlerian techniques to choose from, but Adlerians are not limited to these techniques. If there is a technique from another theory that could benefit the couple then Adlerian therapists are free to integrate these into the treatment (see example below; Carlson & Dinkmeyer, 1999).

David and Natalie seem to both be expending energy to improve their marriage; unfortunately the energy is misplaced. Natalie believes she is helpful to David in a fashion that is psychologically similar to the way his Dad tried to help him. When this "constructive criticism" or suggestion occurs, David digs in his heels, refusing to do whatever is suggested.

Therapist: It seems like the two of you are doing the distance–pursuer dance. The more Natalie tries to get closer to David, the more he distances.

David: I guess that is the same thing that I did with my father.

Natalie: I did something similar when I was younger and it didn't work then either.

Therapist: It seems like you are both discouraged and not very connected. What do you think might happen if you responded differently?

Natalie: We might actually get closer together.

The therapist could introduce two interventions here to help: *catching oneself* as well as *reflecting as if* (Carlson & Englar-Carlson, 2016; Carlson et al., 2005). **Reflecting as if** could be very powerful here because it would help both of them stop behaviors that seem very automatic and help them discern the specific new skills needed. The therapist could have them both articulate a person that seems to have better conflict resolution skills. For example, has David seen a co-worker not dig his heels in during a conflict—can David reflect and then act as if he is the co-worker. The therapist would have David reflect on what does the co-worker tell himself, what does he think, what is he perceiving about the other person in the conversation, how does the co-worker feel, and what does the co-worker do? Oftentimes, clients can't think of new ways of operating but reflecting as if can help them move out of this stuck place.

Another intervention that could be used with David and Natalie is called **catching oneself** (Carlson & Dinkmeyer, 1999). In this intervention the therapist has each partner catch themselves when they fall back into negative patterns of communication. This will also work for any behavior, negative or positive, that the partner wishes to change. Catching oneself will be difficult at the beginning as the couple may find it difficult to notice the behavior, and once they are able to notice the behavior they may find it difficult to stop the behavior in its tracks. As each partner begins to get better at noticing triggers and patterns they can work to avoid situations that trigger undesirable behavior (Carlson & Dinkmeyer, 1999).

Addressing the Affair

There are times when couples enter counseling due to infidelity in the relationship. In this case, the infidelity will be a focus of treatment, as it could be difficult to repair the relationship with this large problem going unresolved. In the case of the Johnsons they decided to enter couples counseling after Natalie discovered that David had engaged in an online affair. Those who engage in online affairs can feel deeply connected to their online partners, even if the two have not met in person. The person who has been cheated on will also still experience the feelings of being betrayed and having their trust broken (Helms, 2010). As in other types of couples therapy it is important for the affair to be stopped before therapy can begin. It is also helpful to have both partners reaffirm their commitment to the primary relationship while engaged in therapy. In order for trust to be rebuilt between the couple, several things need to occur. First, the person who cheated needs to accept responsibility for the cheating. Due to the cheating taking place over the internet, especially if there was never any in-person contact, those who cheated may feel that having a cyber-relationship with someone is not really cheating. The partner must also be able to show their partner that they will not engage in cheating again and that they are willing to end the internet relationship. The person who has been betrayed also has responsibilities. They must be able to forgive the partner and find closure so that the relationship can continue to move forward. This is a beginning process of rebuilding trust in the relationship. Through other interventions, this process will continue (Helms, 2010).

As a general rule when these events occur it is necessary to talk about them as soon as possible and then agree to not talk about the affair again. Otherwise these situations have long-term impact and just like a chronic infection can lead to a gradual eroding of the relational bodies. It is important to not let the worst thing that happened in the partnership define them. The regrettable situations are not the person. They are exceptions. What Natalie and David need to do with the recent affair is to learn that it was a mistake that needs to be learned from.

Therapist: Talking about what happened between David and Devyn on a regular basis will probably ruin your chances of having a satisfying marriage.

Natalie: What do you mean? I need to find out about what happened.

Therapist: Are there things that you don't know?

David: I have told her everything because nothing happened.

Natalie: Each time I start to ask him about things he clams up and won't tell me anything.

Therapist: I have a suggestion that will take both of you to cooperate to make it work. When you are ready, Natalie, I want you to ask David any questions you need answers to. David, I want you to answer Natalie's questions with the best answer you can give and as honestly as possible. Once you have asked all of the questions and David has given you honest answers, you must both agree to never talk about this situation again.

Natalie: What if he doesn't tell me the truth.

Therapist: Then it won't work. It will be like putting a new building on a cracked foundation.

David: What if she won't let it go.

Therapist: Then it won't work. But if you don't do this, you will let it define your marriage and that won't be pretty. To the degree you both can keep this commitment, you can put this behind you. I understand that you will never forget that this happened. However, if you no longer talk about it, the impact will become less and less with time.

Improving Communication

Couples frequently have impaired communication patterns that need to be addressed. Healthy partnerships need relationships that are between equals and practice what has been called **horizontal communication**. When we practice horizontal communication we seek to understand, negotiate, encourage, and reveal feelings. Unsatisfying relationships use **vertical communication** where one partner speaks as though they are superior to the other. In this form we draw attention to ourselves, boss others around, and maintain or create distance or surrender (Carlson & Dinkmeyer, 2003).

Gottman and Gottman (2015) have observed that particular negative interactions are present when relationships are not satisfying (see Chapter 6). Criticism, contempt, defensiveness, and stonewalling will destroy a marriage. Criticism involves regular complaining, blaming, and character assassination. Contempt uses sarcasm and cynicism as well as other forms of hostility to communicate disgust of one's partner. Defensiveness involves defending our position but is really a way of blaming our partner. Stonewalling occurs when one partner mentally or physically tunes out or leaves. This usually happens when one experiences their partner as critical. We see this happening when David avoids Natalie. In their relationship all four of these variables are present and need to be removed.

Being Present

Being present involves being there for your partner. So many people in today's fast-paced world are seldom completely present for those we are talking with. It is important to practice meditation and empathy in effective relationships in order for each partner to know we value them. Couples are urged to start conversations with "I am here for you" to help them remember the importance of being present.

I Messages/Respectful Communication

Another intervention for increasing helpful and positive communication is **I messages**. The therapist teaches the couple to focus on communicating their experiences rather than commenting on their partner's behaviors. Couples will engage in criticism, which typically occurs when a sense of dissatisfaction is felt and the partner communicates this by talking negatively about a trait of their partner (Gottman & Gottman, 2015). When couples engage in criticism they often resort to blaming their partner and turning their opinions and feelings about their partner into fact. Talking in I messages or in "I feel" statements helps each partner to stop making assumptions about the other (Carlson & Dinkmeyer, 2003). These statements can be strengthened when each partner communicates what they need instead of what they do not need. This helps to make statements less challenging and negative to the receiving partner. When members of the dyad do not feel as challenged, then there is less chance that the conversation will be shut down. Learning to communicate in these ways helps each partner to maintain their dignity and promotes respect in the relationship (McCurdy, 2007). It is also important for each partner to communicate their feelings, but many people have difficulty telling the difference between what they are thinking and what they are feeling. In order to help couples with making this distinction, a therapist can provide couples with the instructions to replace the word "feel" with the word "think" when they are describing their inner experiences. If the sentence still makes sense once they have made the substitution, then the person is really describing their thoughts as opposed to their feelings (Carlson & Dinkmeyer, 2003).

Integrating a Non-Adlerian Intervention

David and Natalie need help with communication. This is not surprising as neither is very good at expressing themselves nor at listening. A helpful method that couples can use in communication is to teach couples the Imago process developed by Harville Hendrix and Helen Hunt (Hendrix & Hunt, 1988; Hendrix, Hunt, Luquet, & Carlson, 2015) (see Chapter 7). The following is the Imago dialogue process applied to David and Natalie.

It would be ideal for David and Natalie to always feel connected and present to the other, though it would be virtually impossible to do so. When one or both of them feels the need to establish connection, or when the connection is ruptured through an argument, fight, or frustration, the Imago dialogue process should be utilized. The process follows:

Begin by requesting an appointment for a dialogue.

The purpose of the request is to alert the receiver that there is a need for the sender to be heard and the receiver to begin the process of calming themselves to listen.

Natalie: Is now a good time to dialogue about your sleeping in the guest bedroom?

David: Yes, as long it does not require more than an hour.

Calm and center the body and mind, especially David, the receiver.

Both Natalie and David take three deep breaths and, if available, the receiver thinks about a safe place. The couple enters into a curious and meditative space with each other.

Make eye contact and look deeply into the other's eyes.

David and Natalie look deeply into each other's eyes compassionately. This relieves some fear and the pupils will expand to signal safety to the ever-alert brain.

Natalie says what she would like to say several sentences at a time using "I" statements as much as possible.

Natalie: I feel lonely when you sleep in the bedroom because I love you even if we don't agree about everything.

The receiver mirrors what they have heard and checks it out.

David: If I got it, you said that just because we fight and argue, you still love me and want me to sleep together in our bedroom. Did I get that?

Natalie: Yes. That's exactly what I said. I believe that if we can always go to bed together it sends an important message to me.

David: As long as we sleep together each night you feel connected even though we don't agree.

Natalie: I hadn't thought of it just like that but that is just how I feel.

After a few rounds of mirroring, the receiver checks out what they have heard in a global mirror.

David: Let me see if I got all of that. What I heard you say is that you want me to sleep in the bedroom each night because it helps you to believe that we are OK. Did I get that?

Natalie: You sure did. That would mean a lot to me.

If they have heard accurately, the receiver validates what they have heard.
Keep in mind that validation is not agreeing. It is saying that I can see that you see it that way.

David: That makes sense to me. Actually I sort of feel the same way.

Receiver checks out again if the sender feels validated.

David: Did I get that right?
Natalie: You got it.

Receiver offers empathy.
The receiver, paying attention to what they may be feeling in their own bodies that may be attributed to the sender, makes an attempt at empathy for their partner.

David: And given that I have been out of the bedroom for a long time, I can imagine you might be feeling pretty worried about "us." Is that the feeling?
Natalie: Yes, that is perfect!

A polite closing
It is always good to end on a polite note. This will encourage future dialogues as the brain interprets these encounters as safe.

Natalie: Thank you for listening.
David: Thank you for sharing.

If appropriate, Natalie and David can switch roles and repeat so both are heard.

Marriage Mission Statement

The **Marriage Mission Statement** is as an important activity that Carlson and Dinkmeyer (2003) created to help couples to develop and design the type of relationship they want. The therapist would ask Natalie and David to list what they believe, want, support, and value in their relationship. Some sample questions to be answered within the mission statement include: "How do we want to act as husband and wife? What are we all about, what is our identity as a couple? What is the purpose of our marriage? What do we want in our family? What are five or six of our values? How do we encourage one another? How will we divide up responsibilities?" (p. 10)

Encouragement

The Adlerian therapist realizes that we like someone who sees the best in us. We do not like someone who is critical or sees only what is wrong. Adlerians stress encouragement and help couples to realize and utilize their strengths (Dinkmeyer & Losoncy, 1980).

Platinum Rule

Both partners need to learn how to love one another in a manner that is received with the intention it is sent. Too many couples practice the "golden rule" and waste energy loving the way they want to be loved. Adlerians urge that couples practice the "**platinum rule**" where you love someone the way they want to be loved (Carlson & Dinkmeyer, 2003).

"Soft Start-Up" is Encouragement in Action

When it is necessary to be critical begin with what marital researchers John and Julie Gottman (2015) call a "**soft start-up**." For example, David might say to Natalie, "You do so many things well I am surprised that your weight has gotten beyond your personal level of happiness." Or Natalie might say to David, "Remember when we were dating and lived so far apart and were able to put out so much energy to see one another each month. I am sure we could do that now." We like someone who accepts us/listens to us/understands us. Most couples report that the thing they liked best about their partner was that they accepted them just as they were.

Finding Strengths

Another job of the therapist is to keep record of the strengths and weaknesses in the relationship and to encourage the couple to access their creativity. To do this, the therapist acts as an encourager, motivating the couple to take the resources that they do have and use them to strengthen the relationship instead of weaken it (Peluso & MacIntosh, 2007). The therapist also identifies and communicates the strengths of the couple, especially if the couple is not able to do so themselves. It is also important for the therapist to communicate to the couple how they find significance and to help the partners get their goals aligned.

Social Interest

A primary goal is to promote **social interest** in the relationship. Individuals in a healthy relationship are responsible for their own choices in the relationship. They do not expect their partner to give them a sense of self-esteem. They have communication skills that allow them to seek understanding and express empathy. They resolve conflicts respectfully, cooperatively, expressing feelings honestly and considering each other's needs. Partners in healthy relationships also balance togetherness and closeness by honoring the dyad, yet also maintaining a sense of separateness where both individuals are valued. Healthy couples are attracted to each other physically, but engage together collaboratively in all aspects of life including financial, intellectual, spiritual, and emotional. Couples also have equal power and do not dominate or manipulate.

Understanding Each Other's Perspective

As therapy begins it is important for the therapist to educate the couple about the fact that each person has their own perspective on the relationship; each person has a different meaning that they assign to the same experiences. Many breakdowns in communication occur when people in the relationship assume that they know what their partner is thinking. This can lead to the partners reacting to what they *think* their partner wants instead of what their partner *actually* wants. As people are acting from their own perspective their behaviors always make sense to them; they can understand why they have behaved in a certain way. Their partner though does not have this same perspective and so it is difficult for that person to understand why their partner is acting in such a way. When it comes to relationships there are always two versions of what has occurred. This is because each person has their own perspective, which is not typically communicated between partners. Understanding that there are differences between how partners perceive situations is an important step to repairing the relationship. There can be times when one partner views something as a problem while the other partner does not see that anything is wrong (Carlson & Dinkmeyer, 1999; Dinkmeyer, Jr., 2007).

Couple (Marriage) Weekly Meetings

The **Marriage Meeting** is another tool that couples can use to help to stay focused on their goals while dealing with the numerous challenges of daily life (Berger, 2014; Carlson & Dinkmeyer, 2003). When couples move in together, whoever sets up the kitchen or puts away the tools is in charge of those activities. Hopefully, they can negotiate a more equitable arrangement if this is talked about. Weekly meetings to deal with business of the partnership need to be scheduled. As problems occur during the week that cannot be resolved quickly, partners are instructed to write them down and save them for the next meeting. The suggested meeting agenda (Carlson & Dinkmeyer, 2003) is as follows:

Positive things I like
Discussion of work and chores
Plans for fun
Problems and challenges

Most items on the agenda can be discussed in a conversational manner following the guidelines provided in *Time for a better marriage* (Carlson & Dinkmeyer, 2003).

Couple's Conference/Daily Dialogue

Many couples have not really listened to each other for a long time. They are often stuck in wanting to be right/feeling superior/discouraged and not able to understand or "hear" what their partner is saying. Hawes (2004) established a **couple's conference**. A conference will be scheduled (usually in front of the therapist who will write the date and time down) ahead of time. The conference lasts sixty minutes with each partner having thirty minutes of uninterrupted time to say whatever they want to say. Due to the distraction of facial expressions that may trigger old perceptions, the couple should sit back to back—on the floor with their backbones touching so that they have to lean/support each other. This positioning also embeds a classic Adlerian technique of using a metaphor—that they have each other's back—in which they support one another. A timer is set and one person talks or not for thirty minutes, then the other person has a turn. The person who started first then starts second at the next couple's conference. The positioning, the structure, and the scheduling of the conference help productive listening to occur.

A version of this is called a **daily dialogue** (Carlson & Dinkmeyer, 2003). On the even days of the calendar, one partner talks for five minutes, then the other partner talks for five minutes. Then on the odd day the other partner starts first. Each gets a chance to talk and to listen to their partner and nothing more. Over time, deep insight and understanding will occur. This was suggested to David and Natalie at their first joint meeting.

Four-step Problem-solving Process

Adlerian couples therapists teach a four-step problem-solving process. The way a couple deals with conflict determines whether or not the conflict will be harmful to their marriage. Failure to deal with conflict constructively is the most powerful force in dampening marital satisfaction. Unresolved conflict may also be the most prominent cause of divorce as they tend to be repeated (Carlson & Dinkmeyer, 2003). The four-step problem-solving process is a helpful way for couples to resolve differences and conflict. These steps include: 1. Mutual respect, 2. Identify the real issues, 3. Look for areas of agreement, and 4. Both participate in the solution.

When David and Natalie were ready to learn to handle conflict appropriately the following steps were taught to them by the couples therapist.

Step 1. Show mutual respect. Rather than the issue itself, the attitude of one or both partners is often at the heart of the conflict. In a relationship with mutual respect each partner seeks to understand and respect the other's point of view.

Step 2. Pinpoint the real issue. Most couples have difficulty identifying the *real* issue. Who does what around the house, how money is spent, or whether or not to have sex usually are not the real issues. These disagreements do have to be resolved, of course. But the purpose or goal the partner is trying to achieve is the real issue. Once the real issue is identified it becomes easier to resolve surface disagreements. The concern usually centers around one of the following issues:

1. A person is feeling a threat to their *status* or *prestige.* "Why should I give in?" or "What will they think?"
2. A person feels their *superiority* is being challenged. "If I'm not on top, I feel inadequate."
3. A person needs to control or their right to decide is at stake. "If I don't boss them, they won't do it right" or "Why should I let him/her decide for me?"
4. A person feels that their *judgment* is not being considered and they are being treated unfairly. "Whose way is the best way?"
5. A person feels *hurt* and needs to *retaliate* or *get even.* "S/he won the last one" or "I'll get even this time."

Knowing each partner's lifestyle facilitates the therapist interpreting and the partner's guessing at the real issue. There is often overlap.

Step 3. Seek areas of agreement. In a conflict situation, the most comfortable solution that comes to mind is to suggest how our partner could change to alleviate the problem. A more effective approach is to ask, "What can I *do* to change our relationship?" By concentrating on what one is willing to do and by not requiring their partner to change, this creates an atmosphere in which agreement can be reached. Although the ultimate solution to conflict involves mutual change of behavior, the desire and decision to change is the responsibility of each individual.

By agreeing to cooperate rather than bicker, a couple sets the stage for discovering what they can each do to resolve the conflict.

Step 4. Mutually participate in decisions. As partners work on a problem and the issue becomes clear, either may propose a tentative solution. A partner may respond by accepting the proposed solution, modifying it, or making a counter suggestion. An atmosphere of give-and-take is most effective. For example, "I would be willing to go dancing twice a month if you would agree to leave at midnight." When an agreement is reached, the therapist can help clarify the role of each partner in carrying out the decision and decide what should be done if either partner doesn't follow through.

The Adlerian therapist decided to teach this model to Natalie and David by dealing with their conflict over David's smoking. Natalie is upset that David continues to smoke cigarettes.

Therapist: Natalie, what is your issue with David smoking?

Natalie: I do not want him to smoke at all in our house or around me because I am afraid of second-hand smoke. But my biggest concern is for David's health. I worry that he just doesn't take care of himself and this is just one example.

Therapist: David, can you verify that you understand Natalie's concern?

David: Natalie, I know you don't like cigarette smoking and you worry about my smoking because it is not good for my health and you love me.

Therapist: Your turn, David. Can you tell Natalie what your concern is?

David: I have a right to smoke or not smoke. I know it is not good for me but it is my choice not hers. This feels a lot like when my Dad would ride me all the time.

Natalie: So you don't want anyone to tell you what to do whether it is for your own good or not.

David: That's exactly right.

Therapist: OK, let's move on to the second step. What do you think the real issue is for each of you?

David: For me it is control. I want to control my own life and make my own decisions.

Natalie: I feel hurt and that my judgment doesn't matter to you, my husband.

Therapist: So the real issue doesn't seem to be smoking as much as it is David's control and Natalie not being valued. Let's move on to the third step and look for what you agree on.

Natalie: I don't want to control David. He is an adult and able to control himself.

David: I value you Natalie and I guess if I am being honest with myself I should stop smoking for so many reasons that we have been over many times in other discussions.

Therapist: It seems like you have shown mutual respect, identified some of the real issues, found some areas of agreement, and know what you think you can do.

David: It is probably time to stop smoking. We would have more money for sure. I will quit but I want to do it my way.

Natalie: I promise not to say anything else but I would like to know what your plan will be.

David: The EAP program at the school district has a smoking cessation program. I will call them tomorrow and get a referral.

The real issue seemed to be the way in which they were trying to solve this problem.

When both partners mutually participate in conflict resolution, they can develop creative agreements that are acceptable to both and that are in line with their common goals. Responsibility and power are shared equally, and cooperation replaces resistance.

Hidden Reason

Other interventions can be used to help each partner to better understand their partner's feelings and perspectives. One that could be used is the **Hidden Reason technique** (Carlson & Dinkmeyer, 1999). It is difficult for many people to identify the underlying purposes that drive their behaviors. This technique is used to help each partner identify these underlying purposes, or hidden reasons. This is a technique that involves both the therapist and the other partner. In this technique one partner's behaviors are examined in an attempt to find the hidden reason behind the behavior; both the therapist and the other partner make guesses as to what could be the underlying purpose and the first partner is asked whether any of these reasons resonate with them. This intervention has dual benefits. The first is that the first partner may not be able to identify hidden reasons for their own behaviors; and second, the other partner is be able to gain a new perspective on their partner's behaviors and understand what drives their partner.

Another way for partners to obtain a better perspective of each other's experiences is to have them switch roles (Carlson & Dinkmeyer, 1999). This is best done when there is a particular disagreement that the couple has had many times. In this intervention the couple is asked to recreate a fight that they have continually had, but instead of arguing their side they must take the side of their partner. Each partner will need to argue why their side is correct, which is actually the side of their partner. Partners initially may not take this intervention seriously and "argue" for their point of view under the guise of arguing for their partner's view. This will defeat the purpose of the intervention, so each partner must take this seriously and genuinely provide reasons for "their" point of view (Carlson & Dinkmeyer, 1999).

Paradoxical Interventions

Several paradoxical interventions can be helpful in showing Natalie and David how counterintuitive and unhelpful their behavior can be to their relationship. One type of paradoxical intervention involves prescribing the symptom. In this intervention the therapist prescribes the symptom to each partner, and each partner must consciously engage in the symptom so that they no longer fight the symptom. When this intervention is followed through the couple can see their behavior in a truer sense and better understand how it perpetuates difficulties and the consequences that result from the behavior (Carlson & Dinkmeyer, 1999). Another form of paradoxical intervention is called **spitting in the soup** (Carlson & Englar-Carlson, 2016). This intervention is used by the therapist to bring the purpose of behavior to the person's attention. This intervention works as some people will cease to engage in that behavior once the real purpose has been revealed to them. Effectively, their soup is ruined (McCurdy, 2007).

Reflecting as If

In **Reflecting as if** the couple is asked to reflect on how they would be different if they were acting like the kind of couple they wanted to be (Carlson et al., 2005). There are three parts to this intervention. In the first, the therapist encourages the creativity of the couple by asking reflective questions designed to help them think about how they would be different and what would be different. Alternative realities with alternative behaviors are created in which the couple engages in different activities than they do currently. In the second phase, the couple and therapist create an action plan—what the couple will engage in—based on these alternative realities. In the last phase, the couple engages in their action plan and they actually act *as if* according to their action plan. The couple then regroups and discusses the process with the therapist (Watts, 2003). The process of *reflecting as if* can be more helpful for couples as opposed to the *acting as if*, as it gives the therapist and the couple a chance to reflect on what they feel will work. By reflecting the couple can identify behaviors that are more likely to result in success (Watts, 2003).

Termination

Therapy is terminated when the couple and therapist come to a mutual agreement that the goals for the couple have been met. At this point, the couple will have developed the skills to be able to solve any future problems they encounter without needing the therapist. The couple will also continue to work on making sure they can meet the hallmarks of a healthy couple using the skills they have learned. The termination is not final as it is recommended that the couple make regular yearly follow-ups with the therapist. The purpose of these meetings would be similar to visiting a medical doctor for a yearly physical check-up. This would be a yearly relational check-up where the couple could assess their level of satisfaction as a couple and what they need to do to maintain positive movement toward their marital goals.

Summary

This chapter has presented a sample of Adlerian couples therapy applied to the case of Natalie and David. Throughout the course of treatment from an Adlerian perspective, Natalie and David would have learned not how to fall more in love, but how to gain more satisfaction out of their relationship. It is hopeful that by the end of therapy, Natalie and David would have made the decision to choose each other again instead of choosing new partners. Much like Natalie and David, many couples have difficulty communicating and cooperating with each other in the task of love. The Adlerian therapist works to teach the couple that they can regain satisfaction in their relationship if they are willing to take responsibility for the problems in the relationship, show mutual respect for each other, and identify the real issues. Sometimes, as in the case of Natalie and David, this means learning how to avoid criticism, defensiveness, contempt, and stonewalling; learning to value and respect the partner; and cooperating to find solutions to difficulties that leave both people satisfied. In order to do this though, the couple must understand what they are really fighting about. Many times couples will become stuck trying to fix the symptom of a problem instead of the problem itself. The Adlerian therapist is there to help cut through all the trappings and to help identify what it is each partner actually wants.

The Adlerian approach is an active educational model that utilizes a strong treatment alliance between the therapist and couple as well as a comprehensive assessment and treatment conceptualization to help tailor the skill-training necessary for each couple. Adlerian therapy is also a theory that focuses on health instead of sickness. As such, the Adlerian therapist does not forget to remind the couple about what they are doing right and the strengths that are evident in therapy and in their relationship. Encouragement between the therapist and the couple and between the members of the couple is frequently used to promote these strengths and to encourage the couple to find new ways to operate within the structure that they have built. Also, as this is a theory of use, the therapist makes sure to provide the couple with interventions that they can actually begin to use. Interventions and techniques are meant to be applied and practiced by the couple, mostly outside of therapy without the therapist present. Many of the interventions used are deceptively simple and can produce small changes, which lead to larger and larger changes in the couple, when done properly. Many of the tactics and strategies discussed in this chapter, even those that are not strictly Adlerian, are used by the Adlerian therapist because they are useful and can promote encouragement and respect between the members of the couple. As the therapist making sure to tailor treatment to the couple, operating in a respectful manner, and using techniques and interventions that focus on encouragement and respect, can lead to real changes within the couple and an increased sense of satisfaction.

References

Adler, A. (1956). *The individual psychology of Alfred Adler: A systematic presentation in selections from his writings* (H. L. Ansbacher & R. R. Ansbacher, Eds.). New York, NY: Basic Books.

Adler, A. (1957). *Understanding human nature.* (W. B. Wolfe, Trans.). New York, NY: Premier Books.

Berger, M. N. (2014). *Marriage meetings for lasting love: 30 minutes a week to the relationship you've wanted.* Novato, CA: New World Library.

Bettner, B. L. (2007). Recreating sibling relationships in marriage. *Journal of Individual Psychology, 63*(3), 339–344.

Bitter, J. R. (2009). *Theory and practice of family therapy and counseling* (2nd ed.). Belmont, CA: Brooks Cole.

Bottome, P. (1939). *Alfred Adler: Apostle of freedom.* London, UK: Faber & Faber.

Bowling, T. F., Hill, C. M., & Jencius, M. (2005). An overview of marriage enrichment. *The Family Journal, 13*(1), 87–94.

Brown, L. (2015). *Childfree women: Comparing narrative themes.* Unpublished doctoral dissertation, Adler University, Chicago, IL.

Carlson, J., & Dinkmeyer, D., Sr. (1999). Couple therapy. In R. E. Watts & J. Carlson (Eds.), *Interventions and strategies in counseling and psychotherapy* (pp. 87–100). Philadelphia, PA: Accelerated Development.

Carlson, J., & Dinkmeyer, D. (2003). *Time for a better marriage.* Atascadero, CA: Impact Publishers.
Carlson, J., & Englar-Carlson, M. (2016). *Adlerian psychotherapy.* Washington, DC: American Psychological Association.
Carlson, J., & Lorelle, S. (2016). Taking ownership. In G. R. Weeks, S. Fife, & C. Peterson, (Eds.), *Techniques for the couple therapist: Essential interventions.* New York, NY: Routledge.
Carlson, J., Peluso, P. R., Figenbaum, N., & Oles, K. (2012). An interview with Jon Carlson. In P. R. Peluso, R. E. Watts, & M. Parsons (Eds.), *Changing aging, changing family therapy: Practicing with 21st century realities* (pp. 229–246). New York, NY: Routledge.
Carlson, J., Sperry, L., & Lewis, J. (2005). *Family therapy techniques.* New York, NY: Routledge.
Carlson, J., Watts, R. E., & Maniacci, M. P. (2005). *Adlerian therapy: Theory and practice.* Washington, DC: American Psychological Association.
Clark, A. (2002). *Early recollections: Theory and practice in counseling and psychotherapy.* New York, NY: Routledge.
Clark, A. J. (2013). *Dawn of memories: The meaning of early recollections.* New York, NY: Rowman & Littlefield.
Conway, E. (2000). Using the crucial C's to explore gender roles with couples. *Journal of Individual Psychology, 56*(4), 495–501.
Dinkmeyer, D., Jr. (2007). A systematic approach to marriage education. *Journal of Individual Psychology, 63*(3), 315–321.
Dinkmeyer, D., & Carlson, J. (1984). *Training in marriage enrichment (TIME).* Circle Pines, MN: American Guidance Services.
Dinkmeyer, D. C., & Losoncy, L. E. (1980). *The encouragement book.* Englewood Cliffs, NJ: Prentice-Hall.
Doherty, W. J. (2011). In or out: Treating the mixed-agenda couple. *Psychotherapy Networker,* November-December, 45–50, 58, 60.
Dreikurs, R. (1946). *The challenge of marriage.* New York, NY: Hawthorn.
Dreikurs, R. (1971). *Social equality: The challenge of today.* Chicago, IL: Henry Regenry.
Duba Sauerheber, J., & Bitter, J. R. (2013). An Adlerian approach in premarital counseling with religious couples. *Journal of Individual Psychology, 69*(4), 305–327.
Duffy, T. H., Carns, M. R., Carns, A. W., & Garcia, J. L. (1998). The lifestyle of the middle-class Mexican-American female. *Journal of Individual Psychology, 54*(3), 399–406.
Gottman, J. S., & Gottman, J. M. (2015). *10 principles for doing effective couples therapy.* New York, NY: W. W. Norton.
Hawes, E. C. (2004). Marriage counseling and enrichment. In O. C. Christensen (Ed.), *Adlerian family counseling* (3rd ed., pp. 129–167). Minneapolis, MN: Education Media Corporation.
Hawley, D. W., & Olson, D. H. (1995). Enriching newlyweds: An evaluation of three enrichment programs. *The American Journal of Family Therapy, 23*(2), 129–147.
Helms, K. M. (2010). Internet infidelity: Guidelines for recovering intimacy. In J. Carlson & L. Sperry (Eds.), *Recovering intimacy in love relationships: A clinician's guide* (pp. 181–206). New York, NY: Routledge.
Hendrix, H., & Hunt, H. (1988). *Getting the love you want: A guide for couples.* New York, NY: Henry Holt.
Hendrix, H., Hunt, H., Luquet, W., & Carlson, J. (2015). Using the Imago dialogue to deepen couples therapy. *Journal of Individual Psychology, 71*(3), 253–272.
Hoffman, E. (1994). *The drive for self: Alfred Adler and the founding of Individual Psychology.* Reading, MA: Addison Wesley.

Johansen, T. M. (2005). Applying Individual Psychology to work with clients of the Islamic faith. *Journal of Individual Psychology, 61*(2), 174–184.

Leggett, D. G., Roberts-Pittman, B., Byczek, S., & Mores, D. T. (2012). Cooperation, conflict, marital satisfaction: Bridging theory, research, and practice. *Journal of Individual Psychology, 68*(2), 182–199.

Lew, A., & Bettner, B. L. (2007). Recreating sibling relationships in marriage. *Journal of Individual Psychology, 63*(3), 339–344.

Manaster, G. J., & Corsini, R. J. (1982). *Individual psychology: Theory and practice.* Chicago, IL: Adler School of Professional Psychology.

Matteson, D. L., Christensen, O. J., & England, J. T. (1990). The effectiveness of a specific marital enrichment program: TIME. *Individual Psychology: Journal of Adlerian Theory, Research, and Practice, 46*(1), 88–92.

McCurdy, K. G. (2007). Making love or making love work: Integrating the crucial c's in the games couples play. *Journal of Individual Psychology, 63*(3), 279–293.

Mosak, H. H., & DiPietro, R. (2005). *Early recollections: Interpretative method and application.* New York, NY: Routledge.

Mosak, H. H., & Maniacci, M. P. (1998). *Tactics in counseling and psychotherapy.* Itasca, IL: F. E. Peacock Publishers.

Mosak, H. H., & Shulman, B. (1998). *Manual for lifestyle assessment.* Levittown, PA: Accelerated Development.

Olson, D. H., Russell, C. S., & Sprenkle, D. H. (1989). *Circumplex model: Systemic assessment and treatment of families.* New York, NY: Haworth Press.

Peluso, P. R., & MacIntosh, H. (2007). Emotionally focused couples therapy and individual psychology: A dialogue across theories. *Journal of Individual Psychology, 63*(3), 247–269.

Powers, R. L., & Griffith, J. (2012). *The key to psychotherapy: Understanding the self-created individual* (2nd ed.). Port Townsend, WA: Adlerian Psychology Associates, Ltd.

Prochaska, J. O., Norcross, J. C., & DiClemente, C. C. (1994). *Changing for good: The revolutionary program that explains the six stages of change and teaches you how to free yourself from bad habits.* New York, NY: William Morrow.

Waite, L. J., Browning, D., Doherty, W. J., Gallagher, M., Luo, Y., & Stanley, S. M. (2002). *Does divorce make people happy? Finding from a study of unhappy marriages.* New York, NY: Institute for American Values.

Watts, R. E. (2003). Reflecting "as if": An integrative process in couples therapy. *The Family Journal, 11*(1), 73–75.

Welwood, J. (2005). *Perfect love, imperfect relationships: Healing the wound of the heart.* Boston, MA: Shambhala.

Yang, J., Milliren, A., & Blagen, M. (2009). *The psychology of courage: An Adlerian handbook for health and social living.* New York, NY: Routledge.

5

COGNITIVE BEHAVIORAL COUPLE THERAPY[1]

Terence Patterson

History of the Model

To understand the origins of cognitive behavioral couple therapy, we must go back to the early twentieth century when alternatives to Freudian psychotherapy began to emerge. First, however, let us differentiate between the aspects of behaviorism and cognitivism.

Behavioral Roots

Behavioral pioneers such as Ivan Pavlov and John B. Watson, and later, B. F. Skinner, Albert Bandura, and Joseph Wolpe, rejected "mentalism" as explanations for human behavior and emphasized observable behaviors and the forces that shaped and reinforced them. Previous methods based on childhood experiences, internal cognates, and symbolism that involved interpretation, transference, and insight were replaced by a functional analysis and the use of stimulus control and the management of the contingencies of reinforcement. For example, Pavlov's famous classical stimulus–response conditioning revealed the common ways that phobias develop, by associating an unconditioned stimulus (a black cat) with a conditioned one (an ominous experience). Skinner's pervasive influence in diverse fields was based on operant conditioning, which differed from Pavlov's classical stimulus–response conditioning by emphasizing reinforcement of desired behaviors following a response (for example, reinforcing a child's eating a new vegetable with praise and attention). Wolpe developed the concept of **reciprocal inhibition**, his reframe of an operant procedure (differential reinforcement of other behaviors—DRO) that indicates that an undesired response such as fear cannot exist at the same time as a desired one such as relaxation, a method he used in

systematic desensitization (Wolpe, 1958), which is used today as part of exposure treatment for traumatic experiences.

Bandura's contribution was **social learning theory**, which posited that our behaviors and ideas are modeled from significant persons in our lives. His famous Bobo doll experiment (Bandura, Ross, & Ross, 1961) demonstrated the powerful impact of reinforcement and punishment when learning from significant others. This type of modeling might be seen as a possible alternative explanation to Bowlby's attachment theory, indicating that attention and imitation of potential influential figures throughout our lives shape who we are. Although Bandura never felt his theory fully fit the behaviorist model, many view his work as a precursor to the integration of behavioral principles into psychotherapy practice that began in the 1960s.

It may be helpful to briefly describe some basic techniques that are commonly used in cognitive behavioral couple therapy (author's descriptions):

- **Reinforcement**—a comment or behavior that increases a desired behavior.
- **Clarification**—an inquiry to elucidate and specify a statement.
- **Validation**—reinforcement indicating understanding and affirmation of a client's comments or behavior.
- **Prompting**—cues that increase a desired understanding or behavior.
- **Noting cognitive distortions**—questioning or comments to point out faulty thinking that often results in maladaptive behavior.
- **Assertion**—direct expression that respects the position of others.
- **Reframing**—an accurate restatement of a negative perception as a positive event or intention.
- **Behavioral activation**—setting an action in motion to ameliorate a problem or to increase resilience.
- **Exposure** and **systematic desensitization**—systematically providing gradual experiences to a feared object or situation in order to decrease anxiety and avoidance.

Although certainly not exhaustive, these CBT methods are likely familiar to most clinicians, and the more specific aspects of models developed as part of empirically based couple therapy are described in the following sections of this chapter. These techniques highlight the focus of *changing behavior* as efficiently as possible, and posit that generalization and emotional and cognitive changes can often result from behavioral activation (see Spiegel & Guevremont, 2010).

Cognitive Origins

Rarely recognized in the field of therapy, the German-born Ulrich Neisser is seen as the father of cognitive psychology with the publication of his book *Cognitive psychology* (1967). According to Neisser, cognitive psychology focuses on the basic thought processes of perception, memory, and attention. The psychiatrist Aaron T. Beck is considered to be the pioneer in the field of cognitive psychotherapy, with the publication of his book *The diagnosis and management of depression* (Beck, 1967). Beck and his daughter Judith have promoted the role of cognitions as primary determinants of emotions and behavior, and a student of Beck's, the psychiatrist David Burns, is largely responsible for the popularization of cognitive behavioral methods with the publication of his book *Feeling good: The new mood therapy* (Burns, 1980).

Others such as Arnold Lazarus, Albert Ellis, Michael Mahoney, and Donald Meichenbaum developed major models integrating cognitive and behavioral elements, with some focusing on specific disorders such as depression or phobias.

Lazarus, in *Multimodal therapy* (1981), identified behavior, affect, sensation, imagery, cognition, relationships, and bodily function (**Basic I.D.**) and are all involved in problem formation, assessment, and treatment. Ellis (2004), in *Rational emotive behavior therapy*, emphasized cognitions, emotions, and behavior, and was known for direct, confrontive challenging of cognitive distortions. Mahoney was early known as a radical behaviorist and later was viewed as an integrationist, and was known for his emphasis on *self-control* (Mahoney & Thorsen, 1974). Meichenbaum is considered one of the founders of integrative CBT and is known for his work on stress innoculation (1996, 2008).

In essence, CBT generally views and treats problems on a cognitive and behavioral basis, and Ellis and Lazarus are perhaps the most integrationist of the theorists who are identified in the CBT orientation by including other facets of human existence. Although cognitive therapy and behavioral therapy came to be generally recognized in the therapy field as CBT, cognitive therapy begins with changes in thinking as the basic mechanism, and bases treatment on that premise.

Selected techniques developed in cognitive therapy include:

- Activity monitoring through charts and, increasingly, electronic devices.
- Pointing out and challenging automatic thoughts.
- Socratic questioning.
- Guided discovery.
- Self management.
- Providing information to correct misunderstandings.

Many of the above will be familiar to readers. A personal favorite is **guided discovery**, which may be considered a form of psycho-education. Rather than using a didactic or "information giving" mode, the therapist explores existing positive aspects of a couple's experience, cognitively and behaviorally, and assists them in using ideas and interactions to ameliorate the problem. **Self management** draws upon awareness of one's thoughts and emotions, and connects them to past and current behaviors (the current emphasis on *mindfulness* is similar). The therapist then works with clients on individual thoughts and behaviors that are adaptive, with the emphasis on each person taking responsibility to do his or her part to improve the relationship.

Although not all of these cognitive and behavioral methods are explicitly used in the case transcript in this chapter, they are derived from the works of Beck, Ellis, Meichenbaum, and others, and are entirely appropriate in individual, couple, family, and group therapy.

Sorting the Cognitive and the Behavioral

Perusing all of these variations within the CBT realm, the essence of Cognitive Behavior Therapy (CBT) presents some probing questions:

- Does it focus mainly on thoughts, feelings, or behavior?
- What is the origin of problems?
- What are the primary objectives?
- Which methods are critical?
- Does effective treatment require basic behavioral methods and/or cognitive techniques or a combination of the two?
- Is it basically a pragmatic, problem solving approach like many others?
- What about the role of early experiences?

In this author's experience, all of the above aspects have been incorporated into the practice of successful and effective clinicians. Based on the reality that many practicing therapists were trained in the 1960s and 1970s in a psychodynamic model and that Freudian concepts still pervade much of the field today, terms such as "countertransference," "defense mechanisms," "attachment," and "ego strength," along with their accompanying constructs, are frequently used by CBT practitioners. In everyday practice, the mantle of CBT encompasses a broad scope of methods for many practitioners who wish to use the term, rightly or wrongly.

Regarding the current use of the term *cognitive-behavioral*, Kelly and Halford (1993) have clarified the elements of **Cognitive Behavior Couple Therapy** (CBCT), with the premise that understanding the distinctive features of each allows for more effective implementation. The terms *cognitive* and *behavioral* will be used to identify the principles that are central to each model, and methods will be discussed in this chapter to properly apply them in an integrated, ethical, competent fashion with couples.

In many clinical settings today, CBCT is not applied as a singular model. Clinicians who identify with CBCT may often be widely eclectic, without truly adhering to behavioral or cognitive principles and techniques. When we recognize the haphazard approach taken by some CBCT clinicians, we do not endorse randomness and believe that a model's effectiveness is diminished if its principles are not followed with integrity.

In considering the integration of the various elements of CBT described earlier, excessive attention to cognitions, for example, may result in a low priority on activation of behavioral skills (Fincham & Bradbury, 1993). CBCT emphasizes behavioral adaptation as well as cognitive restructuring, and a thorough assessment (Epstein & Baucom, 2002) is essential in order to guide treatment planning and to blend the elements of CBT appropriately in meeting the needs of a particular couple. Rather than an argument for eclecticism, an empirical integration of the cognitive and behavioral elements provides a pathway to apply processes consistent with both domains in order to meet the needs of clients most effectively and efficiently.

Antecedents of Couple Therapy

Although prominent figures such as Rogers, Lazarus, and Ellis wrote and lectured on relationships and to some extent, couple therapy, their approaches are considered to apply more widely to various populations, problems, and groups. Carl Rogers, for example, in his later years applied humanistic principles to political and social movements (Barfield, 2004). Early family therapy pioneers such as Nathan Ackerman, Don Jackson, Paul Watzlawick, Ivan Boszormenyi-Nagy, Murray Bowen, Virginia Satir, Carl Whitaker, Jay Haley, Chloe Madanes, Salvador Minuchin, and others focused primarily on families, including the effect that marital relationships had on system dynamics. Ackerman, Jackson, Bowen, and Boszormenyi-Nagy's works were based on psychodynamic models; Satir and Whitaker promoted an essentially humanistic approach; and Watzlawick, Jackson, Haley, and Madanes were known for Strategic Therapy as part of the Palo Alto (MRI) group (Madanes, 1981; Watzlawick, Weakland, & Fisch, 1974; Weakland, Watzlawick, Fisch, & Bodin, 1974). Minuchin stressed the importance of structure in the family system, asserting that parents need to exert a degree of control in order for the family to function effectively and achieve homeostasis into the family system. Elements from all these early models can be incorporated into an integrative CBCT model, and Patterson's parent training (1971, 1982; Patterson & Chamberlin, 1994) and Minuchin's structural approach (1974) clearly integrate elements of social systems, social learning, and reinforcement principles.

It was not until pioneers such as Neil Jacobson and Gayla Margolin (1979), Robert Weiss (1980), Richard Stuart (Stuart, 1969, 1980, 1996; Stuart & Jacobson, 1987); John Gottman (1979), Robert Liberman (Liberman, 1970; Liberman et al., 1980), Ian Gotlib (Gotlib & Rusher, 1988; Gotlib & Beach, 1995); Nathan Azrin (Azrin, Naster, & Jone, 1973); Frank Datillio (1989); and Nathan Epstein and Don Baucom (Epstein & Baucom, 2002; Epstein, Baucom, & Daiuto, 1997) began to apply behavioral analysis and cognitive therapy principles and methods to the treatment of couples that CBCT began to emerge on its own and develop into an empirically based model. From these pioneers, many examples emerged that incorporate an integrative approach to cognitive behavioral couple therapy (e.g. Dobson, 2009; Lebow, 2014; Whisman & Weinstock, 2002).

Research and Integration

Experimental (including single subject) and meta-analytic research emerged initially in *efficacy* studies and along with them, treatment manuals and systematic protocols for use in clinical practice. More recently, research has expanded to include *effectiveness* studies in community settings with practicing clinicians, with a greater focus on diverse clientele and a variety of presenting disorders. This development emerged from the dual realizations that samples used in efficacy studies were often homogenous and that the rigid controls possible in the laboratory were not practical in community settings. Most significantly, increasing awareness of the need for *cultural competence* that emerged in the 1990s led to the development of more pragmatic, flexible methods (McGoldrick & Giordano, 1996; Sue, 1994). The majority of research in couple therapy has been in the behavioral realm due to its systematic, empirical, and quantifiable foundations.

CBCT is based on more empirical, experimental evidence than any other couple therapy model, due to the primacy of cognitive and behavioral dysfunction in relationships as the primary variable in research (i.e. Bradbury & Fincham, 1987; Bussod & Jacobson, 1983; Epstein & Baucom, 2002; Gotlib & Ruscher, 1988; Jacobson & Margolin, 1979; Jacobson et al., 1984; Waring, Stalker, Carver, & Gitta, 1991; Wills, Faitler, & Snyder, 1987). The field has generally moved away from research comparing CBCT with other models on constructs such as satisfaction, and is focusing more on process variables and integrative techniques and concepts (Butler, Chapman, Forman, & Beck, 2006).

This brief description of both cognitive and behavioral foundations has been summarized so that they may be clearly distinguished from each other. The following sections will attempt to elucidate a true CBCT integration based on cognitive and behavioral foundations. The main objective is for clinicians who employ CBCT principles and techniques to do so in a competent fashion, and especially for the non-behavioral clinician to grasp key concepts and determine when to use them effectively. Readers will see that CBCT is capable of addressing a wide range of clients and presenting problems, and the case discussion will illustrate methods to employ them in an appropriate fashion.

Problem Formation

Exploration of Foundational Issues

As we examine the formation of problems under a CBCT model, the first three sessions are considered to be the assessment phase. A thorough assessment establishes the foundation for treatment planning, and as we shall see under the problem resolution phase, assessment procedures can be therapeutic in themselves. Without a thorough picture of couple functioning, it is easy to focus on superficial or lower priority issues and to miss systemic patterns that can generalize to other aspects of the relationship. An added benefit is that higher functioning couples will often use the tools and awareness gained during assessment to modify dysfunctional patterns and develop greater intimacy with their partners. This brief period of assessment in itself may lead to problem resolution, which may be considered as *consultation* rather than psychotherapy, and is referred to as **brief self-change** in Halford's SRCT (2003) model, consisting of the following:

- Introduction, setting the affective and cognitive tone, contracting regarding ethical and legal issues, attending to each person's objectives and willingness to engage in therapy.
- Assessment by means of individual and couple history, interviews (individual and conjoint), observations of interaction and relational style, use of general and specific inventories.
- Feedback on assessment findings, including couple's presenting problems, individual issues to be addressed, and therapist's presentation of core issues.
- Prioritization of issues to be addressed and negotiation of the therapeutic contract, including logistics of frequency and length of sessions, and referrals for adjunctive services.

A CBT perspective on problem formation is based primarily on principles of reinforcement, cognitive reconstruction (Beck, 1967; Dattilio 1989; Epstein & Baucom, 2002) and social learning theory (Bandura, 1965; Jacobson & Margolin, 1979). The emphasis in drawing from each of these depends upon the orientation of the clinician. The essential dialectic between the cognitive and the behavioral depends on the orientation of the clinician and which aspect is dominant: faulty thinking, behavioral deficits, or dysfunctional behaviors. A workable synthesis in CBT allows for an interplay between the two. From this writer's perspective the formulation begins with **a functional assessment of behavior**: what are the strengths of the relationship, what exchanges are occurring in the current problem behaviors, and what occurs to reinforce problem behaviors? The critical aspect in developing a problem formulation (see Meichenbaum, 2008) is to identify patterns or sequences of behaviors that are reinforced through avoidance, improper or excessive attention, and behaviors that become familiar and routine. Examples are "giving in" to undesired behaviors and repeated prompts that elicit resistance ("nagging"). Nagging can be defined as doing the same thing over and over and reinforcing the opposite (undesired) results.

Problems also develop from skill deficits, such as lack of experience in social interaction in large groups or in sharing decision making in a new relationship. Faulty experiences in one's family-of-origin may be involved in maladaptive patterns of relating that may also include skill deficiencies. Attempting to determine whether a particular skill exists in a client's repertoire or whether habitual maladaptive patterns have become dominant can be complex. For example, did clients who do not utilize self-soothing and recognize trigger points to avoid escalation in an argument ever possess those critical skills, or did they habitually neglect to use them out of resentment toward their partner or because of a desire for control? It would be a waste of time to do psychoeducation to teach those skills for those who have them, as opposed to exploring a willingness to use them and identifying antecedents and consequences of escalation during arguments. A functional assessment will provide clarity in problem formation and enhance the efficiency and effectiveness of treatment planning. A clinician who emphasizes behavioral analysis may also explore cognitions during assessment, but the process begins with a focus on formation and maintenance of behaviors.

On the other hand, a more cognitively oriented clinician begins with the premise that cognitions are paramount and that thoughts elicit emotional reactions that result in problem behaviors. One of the most powerful constructs underlying conflicts in couples is **negative sentiment override** (**NSR**), identified by Robert Weiss (1980). Related to attribution theory, NSR involves generalization of negative affect, or viewing a partner's behavior as part of a negative fixed personality trait. From this perspective, if I believe my partner is inconsiderate of me, every mistake that occurs reinforces my perception. If he is often late because he doesn't think of my needs, his lateness because of an accident on the freeway is immediately attributed to his thoughtlessness. Negative constructs can be attributed to one's self as well, such as when a partner's warmth and affection are not reciprocated because "I'm not worthy of him or her." A corollary to this type of generalization is over-idealization of a partner, which often results in extreme disillusionment when she makes mistakes and evidence exists that she is actually human. The formation of negative or unrealistic thinking is based on the premise that cognitive distortion arises from processes such as faulty attribution, superstition (an inductive process that generates conclusions based on a single or a series of observations), arbitrary inference, self-recrimination, or a general tendency toward bias. The result is viewing fixed traits in a partner rather than behavior that is contingent upon specific situations.

Another major model which I shall refer to in this chapter is *Self Regulatory Couple Therapy* (SRCT), developed by W. Kim Halford (2003) with three key elements: self-guided change, psycheducation, and therapist-guided change. SRCT is integrationist in that it relies primarily on behavioral activation by each partner, while taking cognitive distortions and negative emotion into account. Psychodynamic clinicians may see a hint of self psychology in the essential goal of having each individual taking responsibility for his or her own actions in a relationship.

CBCT problem formation is grounded in a functional analysis of the couple's problems. While the ostensible issue that brought them to therapy must be addressed directly, the foundational issues of acceptance and commitment

(Hayes, Strosahl, & Wilson, 1999), their cognitive and emotional reactions, and their ability to communicate, problem-solve, and maintain role equity need attention and are essential to successful treatment (Jacobson & Margolin, 1979). Though some may view these as "deeper" or "core" issues that are focused upon more fully in approaches such as psychodynamic or existential models, CBCT views them as related or corollary to thinking, emotions, and behaviors, and in that light they may be considered as antecedents or consequences of problem behaviors.

In David and Natalie's case, questions such as the following regarding their expectations of each other at the time they made a commitment to be together are critical and should also be explored from the outset:

- Did they intend to be monogamous with each other, and was this an implicit or explicit understanding?
- Was each focused on a long-term relationship with marriage, children, and dual careers, or did they slip into it with some reluctance?
- Was there an agreement to support each other financially when one (David) was unemployed for an extended period?
- Did David consider the upheaval that would occur when he moved across the country to be with Natalie?

David and Natalie's level of awareness of their mutual understanding of these and other issues at the time of their decision to commit to a relationship may begin to elucidate the origins of the difficulties they are currently experiencing and their need to communicate more openly and effectively. Granted, many issues are assumed at the beginning of a relationship and most couples do not thoroughly discuss or negotiate expectations ahead of time, but major disparities can be seriously disruptive to the point where they become irreparable.

Next, once their differences and disillusionment with one another became apparent, was each able to prioritize issues so that they could come to accept each other without conflict, be appropriately assertive about the issues that they wanted changed in their partner, and understand that certain issues may be non-negotiable? This relates to the first element of expectations: could they accept the other's positions on having children, financial support, and be willing to negotiate or work through outside relationships and what and how to communicate with one another? Without these initial understandings and a willingness to accept the other person fundamentally, arguments around small and large issues, disruption, and alienation are bound to occur. With acceptance, the potential for *commitment* becomes greater, with accompanying *bids for intimacy* and *turning toward* each other (Gottman, 2002), rather than infidelity and divided allegiance. An agreement that is intended for a temporary period of exploration or entered into impulsively can result in behaviors that obviate the potential for a more lasting relationship.

Acceptance and Commitment

The foundational work on acceptance and commitment is based on Steven Hayes's work (Hayes, Strosahl, & Wilson, 2011), which focuses on acceptance of one's self and commitment to a change strategy. A strident inability to accept the essence of a partner or having non-negotiable critical items undermines the potential for CBCT (and probably most other approaches) to succeed. Acceptance and commitment to change have been included in CBCT as *Integrative Behavioral Couple Therapy* (IBCT) by Jacobsen and Christensen (1996; Jacobson et al., 2000) as behaviorally operationalized constructs and will also be referred to in this discussion. **Acceptance** first requires a prioritization of beliefs, emotions, and behaviors of one's partner, and an acceptance of basic aspects of the person. Partners can request that specific behaviors be changed, or if not, they can consider them "deal-breakers" or completely unacceptable, leading to separation and dissolution of the relationship. Lower priority behaviors need to be accepted and not become points of contention involving nagging and resulting in constant arguments and turmoil. **Commitment** is reflected in couple interactions that strengthen the trust and bond between partners, and precludes behaviors that indicate that the relationship is tenuous. Infidelity, greater allegiance to one's family-of-origin, friends, or other activities that interfere with emotional intimacy are signs of lack of commitment, along with threats of leaving, being unable to plan together for the future, and absenting oneself without declaring an intention to return.

Clarity around acceptance and commitment can provide both the couple and the therapist an initial view of the feasibility of couple therapy. "Letting go" of trying to change one's partner through acceptance (other than for major non-negotiable items such as violence) can lead to greater intimacy and respect. The commitment aspect of CBCT involves activating change and remaining consistent in one's own behavior and reactions in regard to trust and refraining from threats of leaving.

Major value differences, life stage incompatibility, personality or psychological disorders, and substance abuse may come into play and lead to a lack of acceptance and a wavering commitment to remaining in the relationship. When these become obvious, the therapist has a critical role in providing direct feedback to the couple on key concerns regarding acceptance and commitment, and while allowing them the choice of whether or not to proceed, the therapist should commit to a full therapeutic contract without a clear discussion of their differences in these areas. As stated previously, much actual therapy often occurs during this phase of assessment, which highlights the *brief self-change* aspect indicated above (Halford, 2003).

Synthesizing Problem Formation

Provided the couple can agree on basic levels of acceptance of and commitment, it is important to explore other areas of couple functioning through observation, structured exercises, and inventories. By observing spontaneous interactions, both verbal and nonverbal cues to their thoughts, styles, and sequences of behavior, we can begin to offer clinical impressions to clients for validation to determine whether they are artifacts of the therapy situation or typical of their relational style. This process is part of problem formulation as well as a technique at the beginning stage of therapy that is often therapeutic in itself. Many couples will have an "aha" experience that allows for self-change, while for others it may involve dissonance and confusion that can interrupt their typical problem cycles; in other words, articulation of the troubled aspects of their relationship can cause great distress and cause one or both partners to withdraw and discontinue therapy. Thus, it is important to proceed in a measured tone and emphasize both strengths and challenges to the couple. Structured exercises in session such as having them plan a vacation or a date night can provide real-time information and experiences. Marital inventories such as the Dyadic Adjustment Scale (DAS; Spanier, 1976), Marital Satisfaction Inventory (MSI-R; Snyder, 1979), the Couples Pre-counseling Inventory (CPCI; Stuart, 1996) and a host of others focused on overall interactions and specific problems are widely available to clinicians to assess problem formation. My personal favorite (although out of print) is the CPCI because of its comprehensiveness and dual-response items that indicate one's personal response as well as their perception of how they would respond to items such as household chores, child care, sexual relations, etc. Most recently, prominent psychologists such as Gottman (2015) and Pinsoff and Chambers (2010) have made theory and evidence-based assessment tools available online for wide dissemination. An added benefit of these and other assessment tools is that they can be highly therapeutic in themselves and promote self-change at early stages, both during the process of engaging in them and through feedback from the clinician.

Problem Formation with Natalie and David

In developing clinical hypotheses and the formation of the dysfunction between Natalie and David, the following appear to be salient:

- David and Natalie are experiencing a frequent pattern of allowing impaired communication, major life transitions, and annoying habits to accumulate and generate resentment and distance between them. Individual characteristics, such as David's impulsiveness, predisposed them to view each other in light of patterns experienced in their families of origin and to make them aversive to similar developments in their marriage.
- Natalie and David's distancing experiences in their families-of-origin allow us to view separation and alienation as themes in their experience. From a CBT perspective, they have had powerful social learning that makes separation a familiar and accessible solution to their problems.
- David, although younger, has had more relationships than Natalie. Cognitively and emotionally, David may not have transformed his self-image from that of a single man "playing the field" to being married and monogamous.

- Dating each other and others online for a significant amount of time has made this mechanism familiar to them both, making it easy for David to return to a previously successful practice.
- Differences between them did not emerge until the second year of their marriage, suggesting that the normal honeymoon phase was part of an over-idealization that reversed into negative sentiment override (NSR) and erupted into accusations during arguments ("Oh I forgot, you're perfect").
- David is sensitive to accusations of drinking due to his sister's alcoholism, and rejects Natalie's comments as nagging. Such reminders evoke a learned aversive response from him. He also resists Natalie's comments about his smoking and weight gain. This sensitivity may also relate to his father's pushing him unsuccessfully to be an athlete.
- David's resistance to having children with Natalie may be related to the difficult experiences both of his sisters had with their pregnancies, and his catastrophizing that a similar thing may happen with Natalie. She is aware of her "biological clock" and is looking to the future and wanting stability. She also has experience in a parental role with her siblings.
- David says he wants more time together as a couple, yet he is staying away from home more, indicating that his emotional and cognitive awareness is out of synch with his behavior.
- David is in a transition period, having relocated across the country and between jobs, giving him lots of free time to revert to old habits. As stated above, various aspects of his cognitions and emotions are incongruent and disorganized, and he fills his time with immediately gratifying activities. Questions arise about whether David fully considered the personal difficulties of uprooting across the country without a job to be with Natalie.

Although not viewed as causal, the above factors relate to social learning, in that the patterns that David and Natalie have become familiar with in their families-of-origin and subsequently are now easily reverted to in times of stress. Alcoholism, distancing, virtual internet connections, affairs, and even separation and divorce are being drawn upon from their intellectual and emotional memory banks. David and Natalie's flaws have become apparent to each other and the once idealized love partners have at times become objects of disdain. David's internet affair and history of multiple relationships has become a source of anxiety to Natalie and her picture of an ideal family life as she moves into her thirties. Typical after an affair, negative sentiment override (NSR) has taken over as Natalie now sees David as an untrustworthy, betraying person rather than a good husband who succumbed to a familiar pattern in times of stress.

Thus, although we do not know the precise causes of the problems that Natalie and David are facing, we can see some aspects in their histories that may have contributed to their intellectual, emotional, and behavioral responses to this crisis. There is no indication of early childhood experiences that necessarily underlie their conflict, nor would these be seen as causative, but perhaps as antecedents in a chain of events under a CBT model. We do not know if Natalie and David had conversations early in their relationship about expectations regarding differences in taste, alcohol and tobacco use, sexuality, open relationships, or having children, but large disparities in expectations about major issues can cause a relationship to come crashing down when they are unrealized. Cognitions about the other's behavior have generalized to global, negative attributions and shifted in the beginning of the relationship from idealized to negative traits in the current situation. David's behavior has become avoidant, involved an affair, and Natalie's thinking has also turned away from David in that she has considered divorce even prior to her discovery of the affair. It is difficult to determine whether their behaviors led to negative thoughts and emotions or vice-versa, and it really doesn't matter, as there seems to be a reciprocal pattern where each reinforces the other and leads to conflict.

Problem Resolution

The stages of therapy, as we move through a CBCT model from assessment to resolution, may be basically viewed as the processes described by Halford in *Brief therapy for couples* (2003) as brief self-change, psycho-education, and therapist-guided change. These are not viewed as one-dimensional or prescriptive stages, but as flexible core procedures that are drawn upon in a comprehensive model of treatment. As mentioned in the previous section on problem formation, feedback at the conclusion of the assessment phase may in itself be enough to resolve a couple's problems, so that the first stage of brief self-change, which is the major emphasis of the model described by Halford as Self-Regulatory Couple Therapy (SRCT), may be sufficient. This does not seem likely for Natalie and David.

Self-change involves the ability to reflect upon and identify one's thinking and behavior involved in an interaction, and the willingness to take action and modify it. Although self-change can require psycho-education and therapist training, it often occurs spontaneously. Whether this develops in the early stages of therapy or at a later point, it is essential to the change model. While couple therapy's essence fosters positive interactional sequences, the CBCT model presented in this chapter rests on the premise that each individual is responsible for his or her own actions and reactions to their partner, whether or not the other person is willing to change. In this regard, each partner has the responsibility to engage their respective cognitive, emotional, and behavioral skills in order to achieve problem resolution. These tools will be discussed further in the dialogue between David and Natalie.

Thus, while an integrative CBCT model will be reflected in the stages of therapy in the following transcript, clinicians with a more cognitive orientation would begin with faulty cognitions; clinicians with a more behavioral emphasis would explore the antecedents and consequences of dysfunctional behavior; and those following an Ellis or Lazarus approach would explore multiple dimensions of functioning during assessment and treatment. As in most other models, the more effective CBCT clinicians are generally not purists, and the methods described here are representative of the concepts, assessments, and stages of therapy generally followed in CBCT. Finally, in CBCT it is perfectly compatible to incorporate concepts and techniques from other models that are congruent with CBT principles (Patterson, 1997). One such principle is from Positive Psychology (Seligman & Csikszentmihalyi, 2000), in that offering *hope* to clients during each session can mobilize their efforts and provide momentum for therapy to continue. This is not to say that sadness and confusion are not appropriate at times, but reinforcing the couple for seeking therapy and attempting to reach a resolution can energize them and keep them engaged in working toward an appropriate resolution.

Transcript of First Session

Therapist: Welcome. I'm glad you've both come in. I know a bit about your situation from Natalie's call, and in a moment I'd like to hear from you, David, about your views. First, I'd like to know if you know about the confidentiality issues on the informed consent form before you sign it, and any question you have about the forms I sent out to you.

I've previously sent them the informed consent form for couples, a modified symptom checklist (SC) for each, the Couples Pre-counseling Inventory (CPCI), and the Dyadic Adjustment Scale (DAS).

Natalie: Those are very clear.

David: Will you be giving us our tests?

Therapist: I will give you the results during the next session as soon as I complete my review. So David, what are the issues that concern you?

David: I'd like Natalie to get over what I did and start to trust me again.

Natalie: How can I trust you when you won't really admit you were involved with her? I've seen this happen before, and I don't want to be a part of it again.

Here, Natalie's social learning from previous experiences in college extends to David's emotional affair, which is understandable. Yet she needs to view David as a different individual who may be capable of trust again.

Therapist: Natalie, is what David did similar to how your previous boyfriends cheated on you?

Natalie: No, not really, but I'm afraid it will turn into that.

Again, perhaps understandably, Natalie is generalizing and catastrophizing out of fear and cognitive distortion, providing the therapist an opportunity for cognitive restructuring.

Therapist: Natalie, can you tell David how he is different from your previous boyfriends and ways you have been able to trust him during your marriage?

Natalie: (*turning to David)* David, you really have a lot of great qualities I admire that my boyfriends didn't have, and I've been able to trust you in every way to support me until this incident came up.

David: (*turning to Natalie*) Thank you, Natalie, and I want to show you that I am trustworthy, even though I slipped, and will continue to support you.

> *This intervention allows Natalie to* ***partialize****, or see the affair as a mistake and not as representative of who David is in their relationship. The objective is for her to view David's behavior in context, and not to engage in "negative sentiment override," viewing him as a generally untrustworthy person. It's also a beginning step in repairing the injury to Natalie and restoring David's view of himself as a good person capable of stumbling. When the affair is explored fully in a later session, Natalie will be prompted to "trust, but verify" in continuing to observe David's behavior.*

David: I want you to know, Natalie, that it started out as a fun thing with this person, and OK, we became involved over the internet, never in person, and it was a time when you admitted we were distant from each other, but I'm totally responsible for letting it get this far.

Therapist: So Natalie, without approving of it, can you understand what David is saying in relation to this woman?

Natalie: Yes, I do, but I don't want him to feel he's blaming me for it, and I would never have done what he did.

Therapist: Natalie, would you please restate in your own words what you understood David was saying?

> *Here the therapist is attempting to have them clarify and understand the other's point of view and to foster listening skills and acceptance of the intellectual and emotional perceptions they each bring to the session. This is not to justify the affair or to imply that it is behind them.*

Natalie: David, I hear that you became involved only over the internet at a time when we were distant from each other and are taking responsibility for what you did.

Therapist: You both seem to have some understanding of the circumstances of what went on, and Natalie said she would never have done it. So David, what do you know about yourself that led you to do what you did?

David: I'm not sure. I guess I can't tolerate frustration easily and I've always been impulsive.

Therapist: Has this been true in other areas of your life as well?

David: Yes, I suppose so.

> *Therapist is searching for generalization to other activities.*

Natalie: He is impatient, can't stand in lines, and is always pushing for things to happen on his schedule.

At this point there is some mutuality and potential for support.

Therapist: So you both agree on David's impulsivity and that Natalie does not have that same tendency. Of course, you are both aware that a tendency does not inevitably lead to action.

The therapist seeks awareness in David through psycho-education and self-discovery.

David: I guess I've never thought of it that way.

Therapist: We may explore that further in an individual session, or I may suggest you see an individual therapist to work on that if needed. Before we discuss the affair more, I'd like to cover a few other areas about your relationship if that's ok.

Here the therapist attempts to shift the couple's mindset from the affair as their primary focus, to a broader perspective of their strengths and challenges together.

Natalie and David: Sure.

Therapist: I've observed so far that you listen to each other well, make good eye contact, and seem to have an understanding of each other.

Here the therapist validates their current behaviors.

Therapist: How would you say your communication is usually?

David: It's usually pretty good, though. When Natalie goes quiet I don't know what's going on with her.

Natalie: Sometimes it's annoying when he keeps asking me if I'm ok over and over. We discuss most things ok, but I can hardly ever get David to talk about his feelings.

Therapist: I'll note that and we'll work on some basic communication exercises. Would each of you tell me what happens when you're trying to solve a problem together?

Natalie: David will often try something and give up when he can't easily come up with a solution; then when I suggest a solution, he'll usually just say "ok, that's good."

Therapist: It sounds as though you're very compliant, David, in solving problems. What's it like for you when you give up, then agree to Natalie's solution?

David: I guess it's my impatience when I give up, and it's easier for me to do what Natalie suggests.

Therapist: I'd like to ask you, David, to plan a nice outing together this weekend, aside from errands or chores; just something enjoyable for the two of you to do.

David hesitates and Natalie looks at him. This simple task demonstrates various critical sub-processes: the ability to collaborate on problem-solving, relative degree of contribution, their ability to accept each other's influence, and to assert individual preferences.

David: I can't think of anything just now. OK, what if we go river rafting?
Natalie: You know I get seasick easily, and the water levels have been low all year! What if we go hiking in the park Saturday afternoon and stop at that little café for a snack?
David: OK, sounds good to me.

Here, David gives up and just goes along with what Natalie suggests. As part of the assessment package, this brief exercise provides another indication of David's tendency toward impulsivity and passivity, and I hypothesize that his easy compliance leads to resentment and acting out, indicating that assertion training and more prompting is needed for David in order for him to contribute more to the relationship.

Therapist: David, I bet there is something you would like to ask Natalie to do with you that you may not have brought up before.
David: Yes, but she often pushes to get what she wants.
Therapist: This is a time for you to say what you want in a convincing manner, and to hang in there so you each are satisfied with your plans.
David: OK, Natalie, would you like to try that new rock climbing place with me?
Natalie: I never knew you were interested in that; sure, that sounds like fun.
Therapist: David, I hope you continue to tell Natalie what you want and how you feel in this way, and realize that you may be on the same page and feel more in synch with each other.
Natalie: I really like that you spoke up more, David—I see more of you coming through.

Through prompting, assertion, and validation, David has been reinforced not only for speaking up, but for who he is as a person.

Therapist: I'd like to check with you now on how you share the basic tasks of your relationship: social engagements, household chores, relating to each other's families, and so on.
David: Well, I take care of most of the yard work, and pay the bills.
Natalie: I do all of the housework, keep in touch with both of our families and friends, and plan our social outings.

Therapist: Do you feel you share responsibilities equally?

Natalie: Early in our marriage I did everything I'm doing now and he promised he'd do more when he got situated in his job, but it hasn't turned out that way and I feel I'm doing 75% of everything that needs to be done.

David: I thought we shared things pretty equally; I didn't know you felt that way.

Here is another clue to the distance they have been experiencing for some time: their communication was deficient in that David did not know how Natalie felt, she did not communicate it, and she feels resentful.

Therapist: So initially, in looking at the foundations of your marriage, it looks like we need to pay attention to:

- More emotional expression on both sides, particularly by David
- Active listening and feedback by both of you
- More equally sharing your common tasks
- David's more active participation in problem-solving
- David's impulsivity
- Natalie's general issues with trust

The reason I point these out is that problems in these basic areas can undermine your intimacy and feelings of satisfaction with each other. Are you both open to working on these together?

David and Natalie: Yes, that sounds good.

In the above exchange the therapist continues to explore the basic Behavioral Couple Therapy foundations of their marriage, as delineated by Jacobson and Margolin (1979). This connects their pre-affair status to possible antecedents of David's acting out and offers them a potential context for the affair, without suggesting cause and effect. It also allows them to see a pathway to increase the intimacy they are lacking. Next, acceptance and commitment are explored.

Therapist: I'd like to review two other basic areas in your relationship before we make a plan for further sessions, and we'll cover them more extensively in the Couples Pre-counseling Inventory in the next session. But I'd like to ask you both how you feel about the permanence of your marriage. Have either of you ever consulted a divorce attorney or deliberately had a period of separation from each other?

David and Natalie: No, neither of us has done that.

David: Although I thought about it, I've always wanted our marriage to work.

Natalie: I have too, but I came here to try to work things out.

Therapist: Good. So both of you are committed to remaining in your marriage, save perhaps for an ongoing affair or another really major offense?

David and Natalie: Yes, that's correct.

Therapist: Let me take that a bit farther. There are traits or behaviors in each other that you admire, others that may irritate you, and others that you will absolutely not accept. What do you feel you've had to compromise about with each other?

David: Natalie doesn't like being with my family, so I usually go to their house by myself. It disappoints me, but I can manage it.

Natalie: David doesn't pay attention to his diet, and I always insist on buying healthy foods, so it irritates me, but I just let him eat what he wants; I know I need to lose weight just as he does.

Therapist: So you each have things that you'd prefer to have the other change, but you've come to accept it.

David and Natalie: Yes.

Therapist: So have you each thought of things that would cause you to not stay together?

David: Nothing for me, except that if she decides never to have children, that would be a deal-breaker for me.

Natalie: If he has another affair or if he ever hit me, I'd be out of here.

Therapist: So you each have pretty good acceptance of each other and are committed to stay together, except for affairs, abuse, and children, is that correct.

David and Natalie: Yes.

Therapist: I appreciate your taking the time to help me to understand more about your relationship in general, and I know the crisis of the affair is what brought you here, and we'll make that priority number one. I'm also wondering what you know about the other issues we've discussed so far that may have played into the distance and resentment that was part of the affair. In other words, you were both somewhat dissatisfied with your relationship and perhaps David's impulsivity and your resentment over his not expressing his feelings contributed to it. Are you both open to exploring these issues in the next session?

David and Natalie: Yes, if you feel that's important.

Therapist: So I would first like to ask you not to discuss the affair during the next week until we meet since it hasn't gone well thus far when you've done it by yourselves, and to reflect on what was going on prior to the affair that created distance between you. Is that something you will both agree to?

The request to not discuss the affair outside of therapy is based on observation during assessment that the hurt, hostility, defensiveness, and resentment it has engendered has been reinforced each time it comes up, and they do not yet have the tools to communicate about it effectively. Further assessment is also needed to evaluate the reason for attacks regarding weight and other issues that may require attention through individual therapy.

David and Natalie: It will be hard, but we will do it.

Therapist: Finally, I'd like to schedule an extended session with you next time. I'll see David first for thirty minutes, then Natalie individually for the same time, and then bring you both together for thirty minutes. I do that to get to know each of you better as individuals and to allow you to talk freely. Please recall the issue we discussed in the informed consent about any critical secrets you might bring up that we would have to find a way to disclose to the other person, as therapy is most effective when there is openness about anything that might impede progress.

Next time I will discuss any new information I find in the inventories and individual sessions with you, and give you feedback on how we might focus in moving forward, and I'll ask for your preferences on priorities, frequency, and scheduling of sessions. We'll lay the groundwork for exploring the affair *[see Allen et al.,* 2005*; Spring,* 2012*]* so that you can move ahead and it does not have to interfere with your relationship in the future. To do that, it will be important for you, Natalie, to be able to ask any questions you want and for you, David, to agree to be completely open and honest. Is that agreeable to you both?

David: I figured that would be important, and I believe I can do that.

Natalie: That would be such a relief for me.

Therapist: Of course, the issue is your ability to rebuild trust, and I look forward to working with you to do that.

David and Natalie: We look forward to that as well.

Summary

This session attends to numerous common factors in effective couple therapy such as understanding their history together, attending to the therapist's relationship with the couple jointly and with each individual, balancing attention and acknowledging priorities of each individual, empathic listening and feedback, obtaining "buy in" to specific tasks and plans, and providing structure for the couple to understand and follow. These aspects are essential in CBCT as well as in other models, and create the context for specific techniques to be implemented effectively. It is especially important to continue *reinforcing* and *validating* skills and concepts the couple brought to therapy as well as their acquisition of new ones in order to maintain their momentum and hopefulness.

Natalie's Symptom Checklist revealed some mild depressive elements, insomnia, concern with her weight, and conflict with her family-of-origin. David endorsed his impulsivity, excessive alcohol, tobacco, and eating habits. These will be considered in treatment planning, and assessed further if they appear to impede the couple therapy. In that case, a referral will be made for individual treatment.

The CPCI (Stuart, 1996) comprises thirteen extensive categories, and Natalie and David's thoroughness in completing them is considered to be a strong indication of their commitment to work through their difficulties; this was reinforced throughout the initial and subsequent sessions, and is also considered a positive sign in that couples often view seeking therapy as an acknowledgement of failure rather than an indication of their hopefulness to repair the relationship. A unique feature of the CPCI is that each person endorses an item (e.g. intimacy, communication, sexual interaction) and how they believe their partner would endorse that item. The three areas mentioned above predictably reflected significant distress for this couple, and most notably, there was a great deal of discrepancy in the way each believed the other would respond. The following is a summary of results from the major categories of the CPCI:

- Intimacy and support
  Both were dissatisfied with their level of general intimacy, while David's discontent was at a much higher level. He indicated that he felt Natalie was more satisfied than she indicated in her report.
- Caring behaviors
  As resentment continued to build and their intimacy declined, David and Natalie lost the desire to show caring behaviors, small and large, to each other. Natalie reported David doing much less to support her than he indicated.
- Communication patterns
  David indicated he and Natalie were mostly satisfied with their communication, while Natalie indicated great dissatisfaction for herself and that David was satisfied at the level he actually endorsed.
- Conflict
  Both indicated high levels of conflict. David and Natalie's different trajectories with his moving across the country made the basic conflict (the emotional affair) a crisis without a foundation to rely upon and a chronic, contentious issue which brought out each other's vulnerabilities.
- Sexual interaction
  On the item about frequency of initiating intercourse, David stated that he does so four times per month, while Natalie said he initiates only once per month. Their sexual interaction is definitely dysfunctional, and at a low ebb.
- Personal style
  David's impulsivity and both of their recollection of issues from their families-of-origin led them to revert to accustomed ways of thinking and behaving, and to project negative attributes onto each other. David's alcohol abuse fueled his tendency to act out.
- The relationship now and at other times
  Aside from a few months during their courtship and some normalcy earlier in their marriage, there were few times when their communication, problem-solving, and equity in sharing together was highly functional. They both

indicated high levels of current dissatisfaction now and less at the beginning of their relationship.

- Past relationships
  David's history of numerous relationships seems to have created the precedent for him to look elsewhere when things weren't working out; Natalie had little experience to draw upon regarding past relationships.
- Current mood
  Both were depressed and anxious, with anger and lashing out as their characteristic defensive reactions to each other. David reported a lower level of depression for himself than Natalie indicated for him.
- The DAS assesses the domains of cohesion, satisfaction, consensus, and affection. Natalie and David scored at a low range on all of these measures, indicating a level of distress that inevitably affects their functioning both as a couple and individually.

Use of these and other measures is common in CBCT and are a valuable means of collecting empirical data, combined with information about individual and couple histories, observation, in-session exercises, and assignments outside the session. This type of multi-level assessment is considered vital to effective treatment planning and to determine progress that is being made throughout the course of therapy. The model presented also explored the fundamental areas of communication, problem solving, and behavior exchange (Jacobson & Margolin, 1979), essential to the behavioral activation aspect of CBCT. Cognitive introjects and projections were apparent in the couple's distorted thinking from their families-of-origin and from their experiences with each other (Epstein & Baucom, 2002; Weiss, 1980). It was also illustrated how common factors in all of psychotherapy such as the therapeutic relationship itself and "third wave" CBT approaches such as *acceptance* and *commitment* can be appropriately integrated into the process, similar to other philosophical and therapeutic procedures that are consistent with principles of social learning and contingency management.

Termination in CBCT focuses upon the key elements explored in assessment and throughout treatment: *the processes of communication, problem-solving, and behavior exchange*, and the concepts of *acceptance* and *commitment*. In this first session, Natalie and David are offered a glimpse of clear, authentic, non-hostile communication, and a view of solving the problem of the affair. If Natalie can begin to view David as a trustworthy person again and he proves himself worthy of her trust, the hostility and resentment can subside. If they show signs of accepting each other as they are, without name-calling and pointing out each other's past, their relationship can be stabilized, and the return of caring behaviors and sexual activity would be an indication that termination is imminent. In the area of *Self-Regulation* (the over-arching concept), if David can manage his impulsivity and Natalie can decrease her cognitive and emotional reactions to past family experiences, the current conflict in their marriage can cease and termination would be indicated.

Readers are encouraged to appreciate both the value of the systematic, principle-based approach of this model and the general concept that effective treatment begins with a thorough grounding in an established, empirically based approach to couple therapy and the possibilities that exist to incorporate other congruent concepts and methods. In actual contemporary practice, a true diversity exists among most CBT models and few are monolithic in everyday practice.

Note

1 Acknowledging that the term "CBT" includes diverse models, the case discussion in this chapter is the clinical approach used by the author in treating couples, and is drawn from the principles and techniques described from models described herein, particularly Helford's *Self Regulation Couple Therapy* (SRCT).

References

Allen, E. S., Atkins, D. C., Baucom, D. H., Snyder, D. K., Gordon, K. C., & Glass, S. C. (2005). Intrapersonal, interpersonal, and contextual factors in engaging in and responding to extramarital involvement. *Clinical Psychology: Science and Practice, 12*(2), 101–130. doi:10.1093/clipsy.bpi014.

Azrin, N. H., Naster, B. J., & Jone, R. (1973). Reciprocity counseling: A rapid learning-based procedure for martial counseling. *Behavior Research and Therapy, 11*(4), 365–382.

Bandura, A. (1965). Influence of models' reinforcement contingencies on the acquisition of imitative response. *Journal of Personality and Social Psychology, 1*, 589–595.

Bandura, A., Ross, D., & Ross, S. A. (1961). Transmission of aggression through imitation of aggressive models. *Journal of Abnormal and Social Psychology, 63*, 575–582.

Barfield, G. S. (2004). A personal odyssey—Shaping political and feminist principles in the person-centered approach. In G. Proctor & M. B. Napier (Eds.), *Encountering feminism: Intersections between feminism and the person-centered approach* (pp. 39–58). Ross-on-Wye, UK: PCCS Books.

Beck, A. T. (1967). *The diagnosis and management of depression*. Philadelphia, PA: University of Pennsylvania Press.

Bradbury, T. N., & Fincham, F. D. (1987). Assessing the effects of behavioral marital therapy: Assumptions and measurement strategies. *Clinical Psychology Review*, 7(5), 525–538.

Burns, D. D. (1980). *Feeling good: The new mood*. New York, NY: Morrow and Co.

Bussod, N., & Jacobson, N. S. (1983). Cognitive behavioral marital therapy. *Counseling Psychologist, 11*(3), 57–63.

Butler, A. C., Chapman, J. E., Forman, E. M., & Beck, A. T. (2006). The empirical status of cognitive-behavioral therapy: A review of meta-analyses. *Clinical Psychology Review, 26*(1), 17–31. doi:10.1016/j.cpr.2005.07.003

Dattilio, F. M. (1989). A guide to cognitive marital therapy. In P. A. Keller & S. R. Heyman (Eds.), *Innovations in clinical practice: A source book* (pp. 27–42). Sarasota, FL: Professional Resource Exchange.

Dobson, K. S. (Ed.). (2009). *Handbook of cognitive-behavioral therapies.* New York, NY: Guilford Press.

Ellis, A. (2004). *Rational emotive behavior therapy: It works for me – It can work for you.* Amherst, NY: Prometheus Books.

Epstein, N., & Baucom, D. (1990). *Cognitive behavioral marital therapy.* Levittown, PA: Brunner/Mazel.

Epstein, N. B., & Baucom, D. H. (2002). *Enhanced cognitive-behavioral therapy for couples: A contextual approach.* Washington, DC: American Psychological Association Books.

Epstein, N. H., Baucom, D. H., & Daiuto, A. (1997). Cognitive-Behavioral couples therapy. In W. K. Halford & H. Markman (Eds.), *Clinical handbook of marriage and couples interventions* (pp. 415–450). New York, NY: Wiley.

Fincham, F. D., & Bradbury, T. N. (1993). Marital satisfaction, depression, and attributions: A longitudinal analysis. *Journal of Personality and Social Psychology*, *64*(3), 442–452.

Gotlib, I. H., & Ruscher, S. M. (1988). Marital interaction patterns of couples with and without a depressed partner. *Behavior Therapy*, *19*(3), 455–470.

Gotlib, I. H., & Beach, S. R. H. (1995). A marital/family discord model of depression: Implications of therapeutic intervention. In N. S. Jacobson & A. S. Gurman (Eds.), *Clinical handbook of marital therapy* (pp. 411–436). New York, NY: Guilford Press.

Gottman, J. M. (1979). *Marital interaction: Experimental investigations.* New York, NY: Academic Press.

Gottman, J. M. (2002). A multidimensional approach to couples. In T. Patterson (Ed.), *Comprehensive handbook of couple therapy: Vol. II—Cognitive behavioral approaches* (pp. 355–372). New York, NY: John Wiley & Sons.

Gottman, J. M. (2015). Relationship check up. Retrieved from https://checkup.gottman.com/

Halford, W. K. (2003). *Brief therapy for couples.* New York, NY: Guilford.

Hayes, S. C., Strosahl, K. D., & Wilson, K. G. (1999). *Acceptance and commitment therapy: An experiential approach to behavior change.* New York, NY: Guilford Press.

Jacobson, N. S., & Christensen, A. (1996). *Acceptance and change in couple therapy.* New York, NY: Norton.

Jacobson, N. S., & Margolin, G. (1979). *Marital therapy: Strategies based on social learning and behavior exchange principles.* New York, NY: Brunner/Mazel.

Jacobson, N. S., Christensen, A., Prince, S. E., Cordova, J., & Eldridge, K. (2000). Integrative behavioral couple therapy: An acceptance-based, promising new treatment for couple discord. *Journal of Consulting and Clinical Psychology*, *68*(2), 351–355.

Jacobson, N. S., Follette, W. C., Revenstorf, D., Baucom, D. H., Hahlweg, K., & Margolin, G. (1984). Variability in outcome and clinical significance of behavioral marital therapy: A reanalysis of outcome data. *Journal of Consulting and Clinical Psychology*, *52*(4), 497–504.

Jacobson, N. S., Follette, W. C., Revenstorf, D., Baucom, D. H., Hahlweg, K., & Margolin, G. (2000). Variability in outcome and clinical significance of behavioral marital therapy: A reanalysis of outcome data. *Prevention and Treatment*, *3*, np.

Kelly, A. B., & Halford, W. K. (1993). Adapting behavioural marital therapy to the needs of a secondary marriage: A case evaluation. *Behavioural and Cognitive Psychotherapy*, *21*(2), 115–125.

Lazarus, A. (1981). *The practice of multimodal therapy.* New York, NY: McGraw-Hill.

Lebow, J. L. (2014). *Couple and family therapy.* Washington, DC: American Psychological Association.

Liberman, R. P. (1970). Behavioral approaches to family and couple therapy. *American Journal of Orthopsychiatry*, *40*(1), 106–118.

Liberman, R., Wheeler, E., de Visser, L., Kuehnel, J., & Kuehnel, T. (1980). *Handbook of marital therapy: A positive approach to helping troubled relationships.* New York, NY: Plenum.

Madanes, C. (1981). *Strategic family therapy.* San Francisco, CA: Jossey-Bass.

McGoldrick, M., & Giordano, J. (1996). Overview: Ethnicity and family therapy. In M. McGoldrick, J. Giordano, & J. K. Pearce (Eds.), *Ethnicity and family therapy* (2nd ed., pp. 1–27). New York, NY: Guilford Press.

Mahoney, M. J., & Thoresen, C. E. (Eds.). (1974). *Self-control: Power to the person.* Monterey, CA: Brooks/Cole.

Meichenbaum, D. (1996). Stress inoculation training for coping with stressors. *The Clinical Psychologist, 69,* 4–7.

Meichenbaum, D. (2008). *Core tasks of psychotherapy/counseling: What "expert" therapists do.* Presentation at the 12th annual Melissa Institute conference.

Minuchin, S. (1974). *Families and family therapy.* Cambridge, MA: Harvard University Press.

Neisser, U. (1967). *Cognitive psychology.* Englewood Cliffs, NJ: Prentice Hall.

Patterson, G. R. (1971). *Families: Application of social learning to family life.* Champaign, IL: Research Press.

Patterson, G. R. (1982). *A social learning approach: Coercive family process.* Eugene, OR: Castalia.

Patterson, G. R., & Chamberlain, P. (1994). A functional analysis of resistance during parent training therapy. *Clinical Psychology: Science and Practice, 1*(1), 53–70.

Patterson, T. E. (1997). Theoretical unity and technical eclecticism. *The American Journal of Family Therapy, 25*(2), 97–109.

Pinsof, W. M., & Chambers, A. L. (2010). Empirically informed systemic psychotherapy: Tracking client change and therapist behavior during therapy. In J. H. Bray & M. Stanton (Eds.), *The Wiley-Blackwell handbook of family psychology* (pp. 431–446). Malden, MA: Blackwell. doi: 10.1002/9781444310238

Seligman, M., & Csikszentmihalyi, M. (2000). Positive psychology: An introduction. *American Psychologist, 55*(1), 5–14.

Snyder, D. K. (1979). *Marital satisfaction inventory.* Los Angeles, CA: Western Psychological Services.

Spanier, G. B. (1976). Measuring dyadic adjustment: New scales for assessing the quality of marriage and similar dyads. *Journal of Marriage and the Family, 38*(1), 15–28.

Spiegel, M. D., & Guevremont, D. C. (2010). *Contemporary behavior therapy* (5th ed.). Belmont, CA: Wadsworth Cengage.

Spring, J. A. (2012). *After the affair.* New York, NY: Harper Collins.

Stuart, R. B. (1969). Operant-interpersonal treatment of marital discord. *Journal of Consulting and Clinical Psychology, 33*(6), 675–682.

Stuart, R. B. (1980). *Helping couples change: A social learning approach to marital therapy.* New York, NY: Guilford Press.

Stuart, R. B. (1996). *The Couple's Precounseling Inventory.* Champaign, IL: Research Press.

Stuart, R. B., & Jacobson, B. (1987). *Couples Pre-Counseling Inventory counselors guide.* Champaign, IL: Research Press Company.

Sue, D. (1994). Incorporating cultural diversity in family therapy. *The Family Psychologist, 10*(2), 19–21.

Waring, E. M., Stalker, C. A., Carver, C. M., & Gitta, M. Z. (1991). Waiting list controlled trial of cognitive marital therapy in severe marital discord. *Journal of Marital and Family Therapy, 17*(3), 243–256.

Watzlawick, P., Weakland, P. H., & Fisch, R. (1974). *Change: Principles of problem formation and problem resolution.* New York, NY: W. W. Norton & Co.

Weakland, J. H., Fisch, R., Watzlawick, P., & Bodin, A. (1974). Brief therapy: Focused problem resolution. *Family Process, 13*(2), 141–168.

Weiss, R. (1980). Strategic behavioral marital therapy: Toward a model for assessment and intervention. In J. P. Vincent (Ed.), *Advances in family assessment and theory* (Vol. 1, pp. 229–271). Greenwich, CT: JAI Press.

Whisman, M. A., & Weinstock, L. M. (2002). Cognitive therapy with couples. In T. Patterson (Ed.), *Comprehensive handbook of couple therapy Vol. II—Cognitive behavioral approaches* (pp. 373–394). New York, NY: John Wiley & Sons.

Wills, R. M., Faitler, S. L., & Snyder, D. K. (1987). Distinctiveness of behavioral versus insight-oriented marital therapy: An empirical analysis. *Journal of Consulting and Clinical Psychology, 55*, 685–690.

Wolpe, J. (1958). *Psychotherapy by reciprocal inhibition. Conditioned Reflex: A Pavlovian Journal of Research and Therapy, 3*(4), 234–240.

6

GOTTMAN METHOD COUPLES THERAPY

Vagdevi Meunier

History of the Model

One day, in the mid-1970s, two young researchers and professors at Indiana University, John Gottman and Robert Levenson, were commiserating about their mutual difficulties in romantic relationships. Bob said, "You know, John, I think we may be better at studying relationships than having them" (Gottman, 2014). Those prophetic words signaled the beginning of a four-decade collaboration that has produced the most prolific and comprehensive longitudinal scientific study of healthy and unhealthy relationships. Gottman began a collaboration with Levenson with the idea that studying emotion and physiology might yield some understanding of internal subjective experiences that would provide more predictive power to their intervention research. In the first few trials of this collaboration, Gottman and Levenson knew very little about what to look for and what they were going to find, and as Gottman notes,

> We didn't realize that it would be a contribution to couples therapy just to observe happy, as well as unhappy marriages. Our samples, rather than using extreme groups, employed uniform samples throughout the happiness spectrum, from marital happiness to complete misery.
>
> *(Gottman, 2015, p. 10)*

Starting in 1976, Gottman and Levenson systematically observed, coded, and documented the repeating patterns in the development and demise of relationships across spans of twenty years or more. Based on more than twelve studies, seven of whom were the primary nonintervention longitudinal studies that followed groups of couples from newlyweds to couples in their late sixties, the research followed more than 3500 couples from representative samples across the US (Gottman & Navarra, 2011). The seven foundational studies replicated their results and taught them how to predict with over 94 percent accuracy whether a married couple would be together six years later or be divorced (Gottman, 1994).

Gottman (2015) writes about being inspired by a 1969 paper by Goldfriend and D'Zurilla that suggested observing how "masters" solve a problem that "disasters" (i.e. the clinical population) had not yet solved. This became the basis of his research approach and Gottman and his colleagues designed multimethod multidimensional studies that systematically analyzed the differences between happy stable couples (**The Masters of Marriage**) and unhappy failing (**The Disasters of Marriage**) as well as unhappy stable couples. When John Gottman started teaching at the University of Washington, he was offered an apartment lab that came to be known as "**the Love Lab**," where couples were invited to come and spend a whole day with each other while being observed. The studio apartment had a big picture window overlooking a lake, living and dining areas, and a small kitchenette. Couples participating in the research would be asked to either spend time with each other in the lab while wearing halter monitors that tracked physiology, video monitors that recorded their activity, and researchers observing and rating their positive and negative interactions through a one-way mirror, or they may be asked to sit facing each other in chairs that measured fidgeting (called the Jiggleometer), wearing earlobe and finger devices that measured heart rate, blood velocity, and galvanic skin response, and asked to have dialogues on positive and negative topics. Along with observation and direct measures of their physiology, couples were also interviewed using a research protocol that traced the trajectory of their relationship, evaluated their perceptions and experiences of several variables in the relationship, and completed surveys on marital satisfaction, psychological distress, and other self-report measures. In some studies couples were asked to watch their own discussions, and using a rating dial, rate their perceptions of their own and their partner's emotional state. Many of these measures were synchronized to the video recording so analyses of emotion, physiology, or perception could be tied to specific events in the discussion. The wealth of data that was collected over forty years provided a unique glimpse into the inner and outer experiences of couples in happy as well as unhappy relationships and gave the researchers the power to successfully predict the outcome of a relationship with over 94 percent accuracy from a fifteen-minute conflict conversation.

The first article that was published on the initial research was a 1976 article in the *Journal of Personality and Social Psychology* called "Behavior exchange theory and marital decision making" (Gottman, Notarius, Markman, Bank, Yoppi, & Rubin, 1976). The article discussed the first two studies conducted on distressed and non-distressed couples, evaluating the intent and the impact of messages received. The findings described in this paper mirrored later studies showing that distressed couples often perceive messages as more negative than intended. Gottman's background in mathematics was prominent in the early research as he explored how to conduct time series, repeated measures, and covariant analyses. His first book, *Marital interactions: Experimental investigations*, which was published in 1979, was a primer on how to conduct statistically sound research on couples using coding systems for affect, behavior, and physiology. The research findings from the primary studies on heterosexual married couples was finally made available to the public through his first book for the general public titled *Why marriages succeed or fail* (1995), where he outlined the significant results from the seven primary studies. It was not until 1999 that his book *The marriage clinic* gave students, researchers, as well as clinicians a glimpse into the methodology, the measures, and the techniques that were developed not only to observe couples but also to redirect or prevent distress.

In 1987, John Gottman married Julie Schwartz, a psychologist with many years of clinical experience working with challenging populations. She began to collaborate with John and his research team to translate his basic research into theory and then his theory into practice. John quips that as a researcher he was fascinated with simply observing couples deteriorate in front of his eyes while Julie wanted to do something about it (Schwartz-Gottman & Gottman, 2015). Through this husband–wife collaboration as well as working with other expert researchers in the field of emotion, couples, and psychotherapy such as Robert Levenson, Neil Jacobsen, Paul Ekman, Howard Markman, Paul Poluso, Julia Babcock, and others, the Gottmans were able to learn from and influence the direction of many research studies on relationships.

In 1996, Gottman and his research team conducted some "**proximal change studies**," where they tried to change the trajectory of a couple's conflict discussion by intervening with a brief technique, and they realized that some couples showed improvement while others did not (Gottman, 2014). One reason for the within-group difference was the way in which the couple handled the technique. For example, one group of couples was asked to pick three adjectives that described a positive quality in their partner and tell them about the adjective with a story that illustrated that quality. Another group was asked to pick three concerns that they wanted to give their partner feedback about. A third group was asked to read a magazine article. In the first group some couples turned the positive adjective checklist into a concerns list and created a negative feedback experience out of it. In the second group, some couples turned the concerns list into a positive experience by giving gentle feedback and inviting their partners to consider changes. So how the couple approached the technique seemed to better predict the second half of their conflict conversation.

Many years of systematic observational research yielded rich data on happy stable couples and what they did that predicted relationship success and also data on unhappy couples in failing relationships. At that point in the research they had two rich checklists of successful and unsuccessful behaviors. They realized they needed a larger framework, or a theory that would help provide a causal explanation or a blueprint for how couples developed and maintained successful relationships as well as what goes awry in relationships that don't succeed. The dissemination of the Gottman research to the public and the training of clinicians began with the development of the **Sound Relationship House theory**, which then led to the development of a clinical intervention method, a training program for clinicians, and also a two-day seminar called The Art and Science of Love workshop for couples (Schwartz-Gottman & Gottman, 2015).

The findings from more than four decades of research are so varied and complex that this chapter cannot do justice to the depth and breadth of work that was accomplished. In order to understand the treatment model that was developed from the decades of multidimensional observational research, it is important to know the primary findings from the research that evolved into the Sound Relationship House theory of healthy relationships.

Primary Research Findings

The 5:1 Ratio of Positive to Negative Moments

Master couples demonstrated a consistent pattern during conflict discussions of a 5:1 ratio of positive to negative moments. Distressed couples had a .8 to 1.0 ratio when they were fighting. This ratio was present regardless of whether the conflict management style of the couple was conflict minimizing or volatile. The ratio of positive to negative is important because it suggests that healthy relationships have a very high level of positive interactions (Gottman, 1995). In fact, when a master couple was observed simply spending time with each other in the apartment lab, in other words not being asked specifically to discuss a conflict topic, their ratio was closer to 20:1 suggesting that happy relationships are a rich environment of fun, easy interaction, positive appreciation, and admiration.

Perpetual, Gridlocked, and Solvable Problems

The research showed that across all couples, happy or unhappy, 69 percent of the problems were perpetual and unsolvable (Gottman, 1995). These problems usually represented personality styles, preferred ways of doing things, or values that each partner was fighting to maintain in the relationship. Perpetual problems were not predictive of distress if the couple was able to maintain a dialogue on the issue and both feel heard and understood by the other. A small percentage, about 16 percent, of the perpetual problems were labeled **gridlocked perpetual problems**. Gridlocked conflicts were characterized by several aspects that made them entrenched and distressing impasses in a relationship. In gridlocked perpetual conflict, each partner in the relationship felt rejected by the other, the arguments repeated many times but they never seemed to make progress, both felt entrenched and polarized in their positions on the conflict, over time they began to vilify their partner's position on the issue, and after repeated failures at discussing the issue, both partners felt flooded or physiologically activated each time they discussed the topic and would begin to avoid talking about it. The research found that changing gridlock to dialogue was a critical skill that all distressed couples needed to learn.

Preferred Conflict Style and Meta-Emotion Discrepancy

Gottman found three preferred conflict styles that he called conflict minimizing, validating, and volatile (Gottman, 1995). Couples with any of the three styles of conflict could have happy stable relationships if they had matched preferred conflict styles and the positive to negative ratio of 5:1 was present during conflict. Descriptions of each style can be found in his book *Why marriages succeed or fail* (Gottman, 1995). Preferred conflict styles are closely associated with a person's meta-emotion philosophy: this is how they feel about feelings. Often, childhood experiences, cultural socialization, and gender socialization can influence one's meta-emotion philosophy (Gottman & Silver, 2015).

The Four Horsemen and their Antidotes

Not all conflict was predictive of relationship distress. Gottman (1995) found four behaviors that when present repeatedly or early in a conflict discussion, were highly predictive of relationship deterioration. Escalated arguments that included the **Four Horsemen of the Apocalypse** which are Criticism, Defensiveness, Contempt, and Stonewalling, were found to be highly predictive of conversations that deteriorated and if repeated often, relationships that were headed towards dissolution. Criticism and defensiveness were common behaviors found during disagreements between partners and even master couples were found to fall into them. **Criticism** was defined as an attack or blaming statement when a problem that exists in the relationship was projected on to one partner. **Defensiveness** was defined as a counter-attack characterized by a sense of righteous indignation or innocent victimhood. Defensiveness was marked by an absence of taking responsibility for even a small part of the problem. Contempt was the most toxic of the four horsemen and was the single best predictor of deterioration in the conversation or relationship. **Contempt** was defined as any statement or behavior that communicates superiority or shows one person talking down to another. Examples of contempt included name-calling, swearing, correcting the partner's grammar or facts, or nonverbal facial expressions like a sneer along with an eye-roll. When contempt was present repeatedly in the first fifteen minutes of a conversation, not only did this predict the end of the relationship, it also correlated with the number of infectious illnesses in the recipient over the next four years. Gottman (2015) believed that contempt was absent in master couples because they had a rich climate of fondness and appreciation, that is, "The masters seemed to have a habit of mind in which they scanned their social environments for things to appreciate" (p. 21). The fourth horseman was **Stonewalling** which was defined as nonverbal behaviors which communicated that the partner had stopped participating in the conversation and had in effect become like a stone wall. Gottman found that stonewallers were usually physiologically flooded and were engaged in suppressing their responses in an ineffective attempt to avoid making things worse. In the samples studied, 85 percent of the stonewallers were men. However, stonewalling was also present in lesbian relationships.

It is important to note that one or two instances of using a four horsemen strategy was not necessarily a sign of relationship demise. Typically, these four horsemen were part of a larger framework of an isolation and distance cascade (described in the second section) and would show up repeatedly and early in conflict conversations.

Physiological Arousal

Couples engaged in a conflict discussion showed physiological activation very similar to soldiers in a combat zone (Gottman, 1999). Inside their bodies, the sympathetic nervous system was activated, causing **Diffuse Physiological Arousal** (**DPA**) as if the organism was in danger, which included a heart rate over 100 beats per minute, rising blood velocity, narrowing of the visual field to reduce distraction from the periphery, narrowing of the auditory spectrum, and the movement of blood away from the extremities to the core to prepare the body to take action to escape the danger. DPA can result if there is escalating negativity and can predispose the partner to take actions that escalate the argument, shut down the argument, or typically engage in the four horsemen strategies, which are verbal analogues to fight, flight, or freeze. It was found that a high heart rate predicted stonewalling within ten seconds.

Repair Attempts

Gottman's observations of master couples found that repair both during a difficult conversation as well as after a fight or regrettable incident were of prime importance in maintaining the friendship and goodwill in the relationship. Master couples were found to be sensitive to signals of escalation and DPA and used repair attempts to diffuse or lower the negativity. **Repair attempts** were any gestures, words, or nonverbal signals from one partner to another that invited or suggested an apology, an acknowledgement, or a redirection. Distressed couples, on the other hand, had a higher threshold for negativity, did not repair often or effectively (typically they brushed unresolved arguments under the rug and tried to move on), and even when they attempted to repair, the partner did not accept their repair. The reason for this discrepancy was related to the overall atmosphere or "weather" of the relationship.

At the end of four decades of systematic research, Gottman and his collaborators were able to both predict relationships that were likely to fail with over 94 percent accuracy as well as understand the valid and reliable differences between the masters and disasters of relationship. Through the collaboration with his wife, Julie Schwartz Gottman, the research findings were transformed into a theory that had explanatory power as well as utility in the clinical practice of couples therapy. This theory was the Sound Relationship House theory (SRH).

Theory of Problem Formation

The Sound Relationship House (SRH) (see Figure 6.1) provides a phenomenological understanding of what healthy relationships look like when compared to distressed relationships and the model was developed as a way of understanding of how problems developed and became entrenched in distressed relationships.

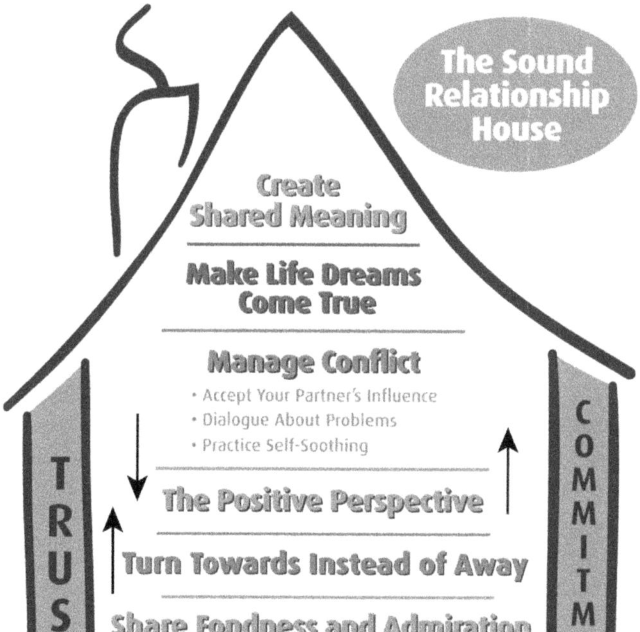

FIGURE 6.1 Sound Relationship House.
Reprinted with permission from Dr John Gottman and The Gottman Institute (www.gottman.com).

The Sound Relationship House model has seven levels and two walls. The seven levels were the basis for John Gottman's *New York Times* Bestseller book, *The seven principles for making marriage work* (Gottman & Silver, 2015). The seven levels can be classified into three dimensions, namely, the friendship, conflict, and shared meaning dimensions. These three dimensions form the basis for the assessment as well as the treatment plan in Gottman method couples therapy.

Friendship Dimension

Friendship is seen as the foundation of the relationship in the beginning (Gottman & Silver, 2015). The components of friendship are the first three levels of the SRH. First, **Love Maps** refers to the mental map each partner has of their partner's world including preferences, interests, childhood experiences, priorities, stressors, and dreams. In healthy relationships, each partner makes an effort to keep these love maps updated as the relationship grows and life experiences impact each person. Second, **fondness** and **admiration** refer to the amount of gratitude and appreciation that is shown and expressed between the partners. The third level is **Turning Towards**, which stands for the frequency with which partners in a couple respond to each other's bids for attention with positive and supportive gestures. Jani Driver (Gottman, 2014), an associate of John Gottman, defined the fundamental unit of intimacy as the bid and the turn where the **bid** is a gesture or statement inviting the partner's attention and the **turn** is the response from the partner. In response to a bid, the partner can turn towards or respond positively, turn away or ignore the bid, or turn against or respond harshly to the bid. Turning towards increased intimacy and safety, turning away increased distance and loneliness, while turning against increased resentment and anger. In the newlyweds study (Gottman, 1995), couples in stable relationships were turning towards each other 86 percent of the time while couples headed for separation were turning towards each other 33 percent of the time (Gottman, Coan, Swanson, & Carrere, 1998). In the case of Natalie and David Johnson, the couple did engage in building love maps and turning towards each other early in the relationship. They showed enthusiasm as they talked about their shared interests in movies, Dallas Cowboys games, their sex life, and restaurant experiences. Both agree that they have not maintained this early dating behavior after marriage. David traveled more often to Texas to be with Natalie while they were dating, a gesture that she could interpret as David cherishing her, turning towards her, and building a bond with her.

The Conflict Dimension

The fourth level of the SRH is the **Positive Perspective** and is adapted from Robert Weiss's work on Positive or Negative Sentiment Override (Hawkins, Carrere, & Gottman, 2002). Couples in **positive sentiment override** had a general sense of trust and positivity in the relationship and were likely to interpret ambiguous signals with positive intent. Couples in **negative sentiment override** were likely to interpret neutral or ambiguous signals with negative intent.

Gottman (1995) found conflict was inevitable in all couples and reciprocal anger was not predictive of ailing relationships. In the example case, David and Natalie discovered more differences and points of contention in the relationship in the third year of marriage and they began to argue more often. When conflict included escalating negativity, the presence of the four horsemen, and failures in repair, the negativity impacted the functioning of the relationship at a high level. Distressed couples were likely to fall into negative arguments easily, struggle to solve even the simplest of problems, and did not have exit strategies from negative interactions. During the first session, this was evident in the Johnson couple. They had difficulty having a respectful conversation that lasted more than a minute because of the underlying negative tension between them that cast a pall over their attachment. Major disagreements were likely to end in gridlocked impasses where each partner felt vilified, rejected, and reactive to each other. Satisfied couples, on the other hand, had a gentle approach to conflict, a low threshold for negativity, frequent repair and recovery from arguments, and a sense of humor that created the positive to negative ratio of 5:1 during disagreements. David and Natalie describe several major disagreements that have become gridlocked conflict, such as having a baby, David's smoking, and their sex life, and over time they have gone from a positive to a negative sentiment override in their communications with each other.

Shared Meaning Dimension

The final two levels of the SRH comprise the **shared meaning dimension**. The sixth level, **Making Life Dreams Come True**, is both about supporting each other's existential agendas and attachment needs during conflict as well as more generally supporting each other's life dreams. In intimate relationships some conflicts have a hidden agenda, often relating to one or both partner's emotional needs, values, or deeply felt longings, that can make simple solutions challenging. Since 69 percent of all problems are unsolvable, master couples seemed to understand that in perpetual conflict, maintaining dialogue and seeking partial or temporary compromises that supported each other's existential or attachment needs were important. Similarly, when couples experienced the relationship as supporting their life dreams, they were more willing to sacrifice for each other and build a sense of family with each other. As David and Natalie began to perceive each other as not supporting their individual dreams (for example, having a baby), the shared meaning dimension of the relationship was negatively affected.

The last level, **Creating Shared Meaning**, refers to the fact that the adult romantic bond is about creating shared experiences, new values and life dreams, and building memories of special events and experiences with each other. This is often referred to as the "**attic**" of the SRH where couples create a sense of purpose, home, family, and shared culture and memories with each other through repeated events and activities that have special meaning in their lives. The couple builds rituals of connection, where they have repeated activities or experience they can count on. The key to shared meaning is that small gestures, rituals, habits, or events done on a regular and frequent basis can change the trajectory of the relationship.

Distance and Isolation Cascade

As a result of the early results from the seven primary studies, Gottman identified how relationships deteriorate and end up at the brink of dissolution (Gottman et al, 2005). He called it the "**distance and isolation cascade**" (p. 253) because the outcome of a relationship that is ailing is a feeling of isolation and alienation from each other. There were two types of divorcing couples that emerged in the research. **Early divorcers** who divorced an average of 5.6 years after marriage were characterized by rapidly escalating and distressing conflict that included frequent arguments and an absorbing negative affect state. **Late divorcers**, who divorced an average of 16.2 years after marriage, were characterized by detachment, emotional disengagement, suppression of positive as well as negative affect, and a lack of connection or empathy for each other. David and Natalie have begun their descent on the distance and isolation cascade as they turn away from each other, judge each other's motives, and begin to drift apart from each other both physically as well as emotionally. Since their difficulties emerged within three years of marriage, and their profile is characterized by hostile conflict and reactivity, they match the early divorcing profile.

Trust and Commitment: The Walls of the Sound Relationship House

Trust and commitment as two important variables in a healthy relationship were added to the SRH model in recent years as a result of observing that teaching couples the skills associated with the seven levels of the model did not guarantee that all couples could have a happy stable relationship (Gottman, 2011). The key elements seemed to rest in how trust was built and preserved in the relationship through the three phases of love and how much each partner was invested in the relationship. In his book, *Principia amoris*, Gottman (2014) describes the three stages of falling in love.

Phase 1: Limerence

The first stage is characterized by **limerence** which has been described as the intoxication caused by a cocktail of hormones and neurotransmitters that surge through the body when one person is attracted to another. During this phase there is excitement, obsessive preoccupation with one another, impulsivity, lust, and physical symptoms such as flushing, trembling, and adrenalin when in proximity to the other person. During this phase, it seems effortless to dream about a future together, to want to know everything about the other person, and to happily take risks (for example, sexually) or give our trust and heart to the other person.

This first phase is strengthened when the couple engages in building love maps and expressing fondness and admiration for each other in frequent and meaningful ways. We see this occurring naturally in the beginning of Natalie and David's relationship. Their excitement and sense of compatibility of interests and activities, their attraction to each other, and shared enjoyment of mutual experiences made for a strong emotional bond. As the adrenalin and excitement start to lessen, other hormones and chemicals such as oxytocin helps build a sense of comfort, bonding, attachment, receptivity, pleasure, and a motivation to deepen the relationship. Friendship, safety, intimacy, and eroticism function together to create a foundation for the love the couple feels for each other. As phase one is navigated, the couple is drawn into a more intimate and personal relationship with each other.

Phase 2: Building Trust

Trust in the first phase may be more gifted than earned. In the second stage, the chemicals have faded and the reality of the complexity or rough edges of the relationship may begin to surface. Couples in this stage may have some experiences of doubt, fear, or disappointment that disperse the rosy glow. Traits and behaviors that seemed charming before may become sources of irritation or annoyance. Gottman (2014) found that most fights occurring in the first two years of a relationship are a result of this disillusionment experience. Relationships cannot survive this stage if the partners are not actively engaged in gaining trust and credibility with each other.

Trust is built through small and large experiences in the relationship where each partner demonstrates that they value the other, prioritize the other's needs or interests, and will work towards building intimacy and commitment (Gottman, 2011). Each partner in the relationship looks for evidence that their partner will be there for them especially during emotionally significant moments and will care enough to "have their back." Building trust at this stage is about setting aside one's self-interest and holding the partner's best interests in heart and mind. When this occurs, each partner experiences fairness and justice in relationship negotiations or decisions. Trust cannot be built when negotiations are based on each person trying to achieve their own self-interest (Gottman, 2014). In distressed relationships, competitiveness over getting one's way not only creates impasses, it also erodes trust and safety in the emotional bond. We see the tension between trust and mistrust in Natalie and David's relationship in the second year. As small and large differences emerge and conflict communication is not successful, both partners begin to lose faith in their partner's emotional availability as well as care for them. This is the time that David begins to spend more nights with friends, at bars and sporting events, and eventually online chatting with a woman outside the marriage.

When trust and commitment are present, the relationship progresses from dating to engagement and then to exchanging vows in a marriage or commitment ceremony.

Phase 3: Building Commitment and Loyalty

Gottman's contribution to the understanding of trust and betrayal is unique and very useful for clinical practice with couples. He suggests that building and losing trust in a relationship is not the same as betrayal (Gottman, 2011). The process of building trust versus mistrust happens in all relationships. Trust is gained when partners are attuned and emotionally present for each other. Mistrust is created when mis-attunement or turning away takes place but can be restored through the repair process. Betrayal, on the other hand, is related to failures in investment, true commitment, and loyalty.

Gottman (2014) found that during this third phase of **building commitment and loyalty**, the couple is faced with significant choices. The first choice is to nourish gratitude and cherish the partner, focusing on what they have gained in being with their partner. The second choice is whether to nourish resentment and focus on what they have lost or sacrificed in the relationship. If the couple focuses on cherishing their relationship and being grateful, they work together towards a lifetime commitment and deep loyalty. If the couple focuses on resentment and the gaps in the relationship, they work in their self-interest and are likely to move towards betrayal. Gottman describes a twenty-four-step cascade (Gottman, 2011) towards betrayal that begins with repeated experiences of one partner reaching for the other during moments of pain or need and the responding partner turning away with negative internal thoughts such as "who needs this negativity or this demand, I can do better." Gottman suggests that betrayal in a relationship can be predicted if one observes the twenty-four steps moving in an orderly fashion towards one partner harboring resentment, negative comparisons, and ultimately justifying starting liaisons outside the primary relationship. This kind of betrayal does not define all affairs or betrayals but is found in love relationships where there is an avoidance of conflict, repeated experiences of turning away during moments of pain leading to suppression of self-disclosure; especially of unmet emotional needs. The key elements of betrayal and erosion of trust in Natalie and David's marriage are the avoidance of conflict, suppression of self-disclosure, and the nurturing of resentment. Both partners appear to have suppressed their frustration towards each other in the second year of marriage while spending time away from each other. At the same time, internally, both of them began to build judgment, resentment, and negative attributions towards the other partner. They probably began to lose compassion and empathy for each other's needs and saw the partner's behavior as selfish or harmful on purpose. Natalie demonstrates this assumption in her argument with David about his smoking as well as her contempt and disrespectful manner of talking to David about his conversations with Devyn.

When the couple enters counseling, the Gottman trained therapist carefully evaluates the strengths and challenges of the relationship using the Sound Relationship House model and judges whether the distance and isolation cascade or the cascade towards betrayal is in play in the relationship to create a treatment plan that addresses the specific causes of the distress and reverses the negative trajectory.

Theory of Problem Resolution

In Gottman method couples therapy the targets of change are: 1) to increase positivity when the couple is not fighting; 2) to reduce negativity during fights, and 3) to increase positivity during fights (Gottman, Driver, & Tabares, 2002). Changing positivity during the non-conflict context takes place through small positive behaviors repeated on a daily basis and thus is the easiest aspect to improve. Positive affect that creates a general atmosphere of fondness and admiration reduces negativity during fights and also contributes to successful repair. The hardest goal to impact through counseling is the third goal of increasing positivity during fights because when negative sentiment override is present it is difficult to convince partners to see the good in their relationship or to practice compassion and generosity (Gottman, 1999). This is very evident in the conversations David and Natalie have in session where each of them was harsh and reactive towards each other and failed to see the other person's perspective. However, if a couple can make improvements in the first goal of increasing positivity outside of disagreements, the likelihood of achieving the second and third goals are greatly increased. If an affair or betrayal has taken place or is imminent, the counselor will implement the three-stage counseling model for affair recovery with three steps: Atone, Attune, Attach. In the third step, work on rebuilding the primary relationship will be integrated into the counseling process.

The Assessment of the Couple

Gottman method couples counseling begins with a three-session assessment process based on the research protocol, which is used to identify the strengths and challenges of the couple in counseling by mapping their relationship on to the Sound Relationship House. When betrayal has occurred, the assessment will focus at first on the impact of the betrayal on each partner, rebuilding trust and commitment, and then helping the couple establish a strong relationship based on the SRH model (Gottman & Silver, 2013).

In the first session, the counselor conducts a semi-structured clinical interview that includes understanding the couple's narrative and reasons for seeking counseling, followed by an oral history interview where the trajectory of the relationship is traced from the very first moment of meeting each other to the critical moments and transitions in the relationship, adjustment to each other after commitment or marriage, and adjusting to life challenges such as becoming parents, health challenges, or outside influences (Gottman, 1999). This is where the counselor would track the sequence of events leading to Natalie and David deciding to move in together and eventually get married. Challenges they faced included adjusting to living with each other, David finding a new job in Texas, adjusting to married life, and the move towards wanting to become parents (which they did not agree on). Towards the end of the first session, the couple is invited to discuss a conflict topic while the counselor observes and codes the conflict dimensions that had predictive power such as the presence of the four horsemen, physiological arousal (by measuring the heart rate), escalating negativity, low positive to negative ratio, and the failure of repair. The conflict sample that Natalie and David demonstrated in session confirmed the presence of the four horsemen behaviors: Natalie showed contempt towards David, David showed defensiveness and both were highly critical of each other. They also showed a tendency towards escalating negativity, inability to exit negative states, and an inability to repair or accept repair from each other. While it is not possible in the clinical context to predict the outcome of a single relationship, the research provides a framework for evaluating the danger signals that could lead to the end of the relationship.

The second session is split into two individual sessions of forty-five minutes each and each partner is interviewed for their wishes for the counseling, their complaints about the relationship, and their commitment level. The individual session also gives the counselor an opportunity to ask questions about domestic violence, secrets, betrayals, and other aspects of the relationship that may not be disclosed in a joint session with the caveat that whatever is shared in the individual session becomes part of the couples counseling process.

The couple is given a set of surveys that give each of them an opportunity to separately rate the strengths and challenges in the relationship. The surveys are analyzed and combined with the clinical interviews to form a detailed profile of the couple's individual wishes and dreams, the relationship strengths and growth edges, and the priorities for treatment.

The Gottman Treatment Plan

Once the counselor has gathered the information from the assessment interviews and surveys, the treatment plan is developed with goals identified in the friendship, conflict, and shared meaning dimensions of the relationship (Schwartz-Gottman & Gottman, 2015). Since the interviews and surveys help the counselor map the couple's relationship on to the Sound Relationship House model, the treatment plan is fairly straightforward to create and share with the couple using the model as a template. When co-morbidities such as violence, betrayal, addictions, or individual psychological disorders are present, the treatment plan incorporates a focus on the co-morbidities during couples counseling as well as adjunct services such as individual therapy, addiction treatment, or psychiatric treatment (Schwartz-Gottman & Gottman, 2015).

A typical treatment plan will include helping the couple establish skills for managing conflict, rebuilding the friendship and shared meaning systems, and strengthening trust and commitment by building a couple system with responsiveness, attunement, and cherishing each other (Gottman & Silver, 2013). Couples learn the Sound Relationship House model and how couples counseling will reinforce their strengths and transform their challenges. Couples are encouraged to put time and energy into their relationship at home with a focus on friendship and shared meaning. In the case of Natalie and David, the couple has repeatedly turned away from each other and neglected the positive friendship and shared meaning dimensions of their relationship in the past two years. Although a focus on affair recovery will be primary, the Gottman trained therapist will also encourage the couple to begin to put time and energy into building positivity with each other from the very beginning.

Conflict management is the primary focus of early counseling sessions in order to reduce and diffuse the escalating negativity, stabilize the relationship, help the couple re-invest in each other, and build hope and optimism for the future (Gottman, Schwartz-Gottman, & DeClaire, 2007). Friendship and shared meaning are brought into the counseling sessions as examples of homework and the couple is encouraged to focus their efforts at home on building positivity outside the conflict context. The conflict blueprint provides a four-step framework for understanding and managing conflict discussions (Gottman, 2014). Step one is a communication exercise that includes listening, validation, acceptance of two subjective realities, and building understanding through postponing persuasion. In these first sessions, all techniques are set aside if the four horsemen behaviors of criticism, defensiveness, contempt, or stonewalling enter the discussion or if one of the partners becomes physiologically activated. The couple is coached to implement the antidotes to the four horsemen, learn self-soothing, and learn how to redirect a conversation away from gridlock and escalation. As the safety and stability in the couple increases, step two in conflict management helps a couple dialogue about perpetual problems by understanding each partner's inner world, dreams, values, needs, longings, and building empathy for each partner's position on the major problems in the relationship. The **Dreams within Conflict technique** is the foundational exercise in Gottman couples counseling because it embodies the spirit and structure of the existential, relational, and narrative focus of the Gottman approach (Schwartz-Gottman & Gottman, 2015). Couples learn to not only understand but also begin to nurture admiration and cherish each other's contribution to the richness in the relationship and understand how their inner dreams as well as childhood experiences impact and inform their coping strategies during emotional moments. Step three is the compromise process where their part in reducing intimacy or loyalty and increases the thoughts of cherishing versus trashing in their internal dialogue. The important aspects of the prior relationship that need to be transformed through counseling are the avoidance of conflict and the turning away from each other. David will be guided to turn back towards Natalie, share more of his thoughts, feelings, and experiences with Natalie, to reduce or eliminate focus on outside relationships, and to rebuild the friendship base with his wife. Natalie will be coached to also work on reversing the conflict avoidance and to become more open to David's efforts to turn towards her. The couple begins to dialogue about their relationship prior to the betrayal and whether that was meeting each of their needs and starts the process of deeper conversations to understand and validate each other's emotional needs, dreams, and values. As Gottman and Silver (2013) note, "A deep sense of feeling 'known' and knowing the partner is the ultimate shield against disloyalty" (p. 170). During this phase issues such as shame, childhood trauma, vulnerabilities, and loneliness are explored and understood in terms of how this relationship can help heal and nurture their opposites. This may be the phase of counseling when David explores and addresses the emotional ruptures he has experienced in his family, the trauma or wounding he experienced in the incident with his sister, his cut-off from his father, and any other childhood experiences that have left him with "enduring vulnerabilities" (Gottman, 2011). Natalie's ruptures with male members of her family might also be a focus of exploration during this stage of treatment. The conflict blueprint is used to help the couple learn and practice new conflict management skills that reverse their tendency to avoid conflict in the past. Specific exercises in session and at home to build trustworthiness, transparency, courage, and loyalty are discussed and implemented to form new patterns of relating to each other that serve to cement a strong emotional bond. For example, asking David and Natalie to self-disclose and share their vulnerable needs around rituals of connection (Schwartz-Gottman & Gottman, 2015) might be a part of helping them overcome childhood wounds and build a strong intimacy with each other.

Phase 3: Attach

In this phase the couple dialogues about marriage number two (i.e. the new marital contract they will forge with each other, the previous relationship that led to betrayal being seen as relationship number one) with each other, having let go of the past unhealthy habits that put them on the betrayal cascade, and begin to implement and reinforce new habits of intimacy and honesty. Natalie and David would use this time in treatment to explore how they might have both contributed to early gridlocked arguments about having a baby, David's smoking, or disagreements around minor activities in terms of their expectations of each other, how they both handled disillusionment, and how they might have lashed out at each other instead of learning how to build bridges with each other through mutually respectful communication. Sexual and emotional intimacy are addressed as the couple moves towards attunement in the bedroom as well as the rest of the house. For Natalie and David it will be important that a discussion around sex also addresses their tendency to avoid difficult communication. Helping them build rituals to initiate and refuse sex might help them build safety and comfort with each other. A conversation about sexual attraction towards each other, encouraging and supporting each other to move towards greater physical health and positive body image might also feature in this part of the counseling. The focus on sex, passion, and romance utilizes the dreams within conflict technique as well as the compromise process to help each partner ask for and receive what they need and find pleasurable. Both partners are helped to explore and articulate their longings for healthy interdependency, emotional connection, and reciprocal support for their life dreams and personal values.

At the end of this three-phase trust recovery process, the couple may wish to take stock of their strengths and challenges on the Sound Relationship House model without the distraction and impact of a betrayal. Any conflict management skills or issues that are not related to the betrayal may be addressed and worked through. Shared meaning may become the focus of the sessions as the couple works on building new life dreams, goals, or existential values that were suppressed in relationship number one. The couple is now ready for a strong healthy relationship with trust, commitment, and loyalty that enriches the friendship and shared meaning dimensions. When Natalie and David are able to get past the hurt of the betrayal, they might discover the original compatibility and trust that brought them together across hundreds of miles.

Relapse Prevention

Couples counseling cannot be considered successful or completed without some consideration of relapse prevention. Natalie and David are relatively early in their intimate relationship with each other and fit a pattern for early divorcers, which includes rapid escalating conflict. This pattern also has a better prognosis if the escalation is stopped and reversed. The early attraction, bond, and interest in each other may still be available to resurrect (Gottman, 2014). Research shows that couples tend to relapse to pre-intervention levels of distress within two years if there is no ongoing effort to maintain gains (Gottman, Driver, & Tabares, 2002). Relapse prevention is addressed in the Gottman approach in several ways. First, the couple is coached to expect relapse and to learn what triggers or variables put them on the road to relapse. These triggers and variables are explored in session and agreements made about how they will address it with each other. Second, the couples counseling is faded over time with increasing gaps between sessions to help the couple transfer the gains to their home life and practice the skills on their own to ensure that they are changing their habits and behavior rather than just knowing what needs to change. Third, relapse is addressed through specific guidelines for weekly activities and time together that will maintain a focus on the health of the relationship. Finally, the couple is encouraged to continue building their relationship through periodic booster sessions of counseling, couples retreats and workshops, or establishing joint interests and activities such as dancing, outdoor activities, or community efforts that will bring them together as a team (Schwartz-Gottman & Gottman, 2015).

Case Transcript

Therapist: Hello, thank you for coming in today. This first session is an opportunity for us to meet each other and for me to learn what you would like to get out of couples therapy and for us to see if I am a good fit for you as a couples therapist. Does that make sense? Let's start with, if you don't mind, the two of you telling me what brings you to couples therapy today, whoever wants to go first.

This is the couple's narrative. The therapist observes what the couple says and how the story is told, who dominates the conversation, whether there is connection or interaction between the partners, and the emotional tone of the narrative.

Natalie: I found out that David is cheating on me and I really was thinking about getting a divorce if we had not started coming to couples therapy.

Therapist: So tell me about that, tell me how you came to discover it? How long ago did you find out?

The therapist is trying to build rapport with both partners and not appear to take sides with the hurt partner's subjective reality too quickly. The therapist is establishing the timeline of the discovery of the affair.

Natalie: Recently, I discovered this internet affair for the past six months, so…

Therapist: So, this internet relationship has been going on for six months?

Natalie: Yes, I just happened to be looking at the history section on David's laptop and I found these personal messages between David and this woman Devyn.

Therapist: Then what happened?

Natalie: Well, I mean, David was saying on these messages that he was going to divorce me and move across country to live with this lady. And then when I confronted him about the affair, he denied it. So then I made him open up the emails and there they were and then he tried to explain that he was just conversing with this woman and that it wasn't serious and he was just saying things to keep her talking to him.

Therapist: What was that like for you Natalie, to find out this information out?

The therapist moves into exploring the impact of the betrayal on the hurt partner and evaluate any PTSD symptoms.

Natalie: That was devastating. I mean, you know, you don't expect to find your husband cheating on you and I don't care if you don't have the perfect relationship right now or not, he doesn't have the right to be cheating on me. It's not something that you would expect from your husband.

Therapist: So you asked him about it, and it sounds like David, you denied it at first? What was going on for you?

The therapist is making sure to maintain equal focus on both partners and to explore what the discovery of the betrayal triggered in both of them.

David: I didn't really see it as denying it, because I didn't see it as an affair. I just, was just having a conversation with this woman online for six months.

The husband is reacting to the therapist's choice of words, i.e. denial and rationalizing his behavior.

Natalie: Huh (*snide laugh*), really you don't think this as an affair, this is ridiculous for you to even say that…

Natalie's reaction would be coded as a contemptuous statement because she is talking down to David. Again, because this is an assessment, the therapist observes and takes note, without intervening.

David: Ha, I never had sex with her!

Therapist: It appears that it's really hard for you to hear him say that it was not an affair.

Natalie: Yes, I mean really, even now he sounds like he's in denial or he's not fessing up to this, that fact that he was doing this deceptive thing for six months.

At this point, Natalie is likely becoming emotional and escalated in her reaction to David. There may be signs of physiological activation as she tries to confront his denial herself. The therapist might decide to take both of their heart rates with a pulse oximeter if the physiological arousal seems clear.

Therapist: Can you stay open for a little bit, to just hear what his experience was at first? Is that okay? So David, you were thinking, you were just having fun with this woman online. How did you get into it? How did you get into talking to her?

The therapist encourages Natalie to stay open and hear David's explanation of how he got into the relationship with Devyn. If Natalie becomes hostile or attacking, the therapist might choose not to go into the story of the affair just yet. So far Natalie is sending nonverbal signals that she is willing to hear David's side of the story and so the therapist continues.

David: Well (*clears throat*), it is somebody that I see at work, somebody I know through work. And so we had, I wouldn't call it a relationship, I would call it a collegial relationship with each other, and then we just started emailing back and forth.

Therapist: And then? Do you understand what makes Natalie sees this as a betrayal?

The therapist is attempting to build a consensus between the partners that a betrayal has taken place and that Natalie's emotional reaction is understandable in these circumstances.

David: Well, I think one of the things that she saw was that I had written that I loved this woman. That I had written to Devyn telling her I loved her.

Therapist: Tell me how that came to be?

David: Well, you know, I didn't mean it, but I thought if I just said something like that, it would keep us talking. And you know it was just something fun to do. You hear about catfishing all the time, so I thought I would just play this on.

David is still denying that his choice to tell Devyn he loved her might be construed as an affair. The therapist does not confront this because at this point, it is important for both partners to agree on why they are in counseling and what they would like to get out of it.

Therapist: So it sounds like the immediate reason to come for counseling is because this relationship on the internet came out, and Natalie, you were pretty upset?

Natalie: Right, exactly.

Therapist: And how about you David, are you feeling upset too or emotional?

David: (*looking at Natalie*) Well, I'm not as upset as you are, but I do feel sad that our relationship is not what it was, because we used to have a lot of fun and that's what I looked forward to in our relationship. But, as things got more tense, we got more distant.

David's statement indicates the couple was on the twenty-four-step cascade towards betrayal.

Therapist: I get the impression this affair got revealed very recently, like a week or two weeks ago. Is that right? So have you done any work to recover from the betrayal, have you talked to each other or seen another counselor.

Natalie: I would say we are, because we, like you pointed out, we're not in agreement that it was an affair or not. One of the words you used was betrayal. It certainly was a betrayal. Can you actually agree that it was a betrayal at least?

David: Yeah, I can see how you might have felt that way.

The therapist is observing that the couple is able to talk to each other without using the four horsemen. That Natalie is building consensus with David and that David is taking some responsibility by accepting that her subjective experience of betrayal makes sense. These are good signs that predict that couples therapy could help this couple rebuild trust and safety with each other.

Therapist: So you know sometimes when an affair is discovered, couples can go into an emotional crisis and also physical and mental crisis. People can have symptoms of trauma or symptoms of being in acute stress. Have either of you been struggling with any kinds of symptoms.

Natalie: Yeah, I mean I can't trust him now. I don't know what he's doing when he is on his computer.

Therapist: How does that show up, in terms of your behavior?

The therapist is inquiring about Natalie's emotional and psychological functioning. If she is experiencing symptoms of stress, that might become the focus of the session even at this early stage in order to make sure there is no risk to either partner and that Natalie's symptoms are evaluated and addressed right away.

Natalie: I just feel real edgy, irritable.

Therapist: Okay, anything else? Are you having any other symptoms? Any difficulties with daily functioning?

Natalie: I'm having some difficulty staying asleep, kind of tossing and turning and thinking. My head just keeps on twirling. I feel like I can't stop thinking about this issue.

Natalie's symptoms sound reasonable and understandable. She does not appear to be in acute crisis that needs immediate action.

Therapist: Okay. How about you David? Any symptoms, or any difficulties you are struggling with?

David: I get along pretty well at work, because I feel separated from it, but as soon as I get home, I tense up. I feel uptight, just waiting for the next shoe to fall. Waiting for her to say something about it.

Therapist: So when you have conflict, how bad does it get?

David: Bad enough that I go to the guest room to sleep at night.

Therapist: If I was a fly on the wall, and you were having a really bad fight, what are some things I would see?

The therapist is evaluating the level of risk from conflict at home. The couple has not escalated in the session but conflict at home may be different.

Natalie: I mean it escalates, because I feel like he just doesn't hear what I'm talking about. Like I'm talking to the wall or something. He just kind of sits and or walks away or goes to the other bedroom. (*Natalie makes an exasperated sound.*) It is very frustrating.

Natalie is describing what sounds like one of the four horsemen, stonewalling. Although the hurt spouse is encouraged to express their feelings and ask questions of the betraying partner, the therapist will intervene and coach the hurt partner not to use any of the four horsemen behaviors.

Therapist: But, in terms of the escalation, it appears to be mostly it's talking and yelling, is that right?

Natalie and David (respectively): Yes, it's verbal.

Therapist: So, it's mostly verbal, anybody throw anything, break anything?

Natalie and David (respectively): No!

Therapist: Good, good, so you've been able to keep it regulated, or managed. I mean the conflict conversations. Certainly the internal emotions are very intense. I can imagine that you're both feeling very tense and on edge about it. And it seems to be affecting your sleep, Natalie? Is it also affecting other aspects of your life, in terms of your daily functioning?

Natalie: I guess when I'm at work, I'm able to pretty much function. I guess it's really in my downtimes…

Therapist: Okay, so that's good news actually, because it sounds like you are both functioning. You're both able to go to work and stay productive at work. So certainly I would say you are in an emotional crisis, but it doesn't sound like there is a mental health crisis going on that requires us to take emergency action. Would you agree with that?

The therapist is providing positive feedback to the couple about their ability to maintain emotional regulation despite the crisis of discovering a betrayal. The therapist is also clarifying and validating that both partners are experiencing an emotional crisis but it is not at an emergency level.

Natalie and David (respectively): Yes.

Therapist: I'm really glad you came to couples counseling. I think couples counseling is a great way to work on this issue to resolve this experience, or overcome this experience of betrayal in your relationship. And one thing that the two of you may have already been struggling with before that is a kind of disengagement or detachment from each other, lack of intimacy, and inability to communicate without conflict. So we may be able to work on that as well and maybe help you preserve this marriage, if that's what both of you want. Although I would also say, once you've worked through the affair or betrayal and then you've worked through some of the conflict that was happening before, you will also be in a better place to see what you both want out of this marriage. Does that make sense?

The therapist is describing the relationship in terms of before and after the betrayal so the couple can see the problem as starting before the betrayal. This is done to frame the problem as a larger issue of the relationship deteriorating and not just the betrayal as a blame or fault of David. While the work of affair recovery will focus on David accepting responsibility for his choices and help him earn Natalie's forgiveness, the therapist is making sure not to pass any moral judgments (explicit or implied) about David's affair. In the Gottman approach, affairs are seen as a common although devastating crisis in a relationship and one that does not reflect a moral or psychological failing on the part of the betraying partner.

Therapist: What I would like to do is take a few minutes if you don't mind and go back to the very beginning of your relationship. So tell me about the very first time the two of you met, what some of your impressions were of each other, what you remember about this meeting, what stood out to you about each other, and how the two of you got together?

The therapist switches into the ***oral history interview****. The emotional tone (positive or negative), the nostalgia, the specific memories, and the way the couple interacts with each other during this part of the story all have predictive value. Couples who re-tell their story of coming together with a positive frame are more likely to preserve their relationship.*

Natalie: It was online actually. It was an online dating service and I was living here in Texas and David was across the country so we just kind of went back and forth with these communications via email and chat for quite some time, probably about three months.

Therapist: So do you remember when you first saw his profile or who initiated the contact? David or Natalie?

David: I guess I did. I saw her picture and thought she was pretty and I liked what she wrote on the profile.

Therapist: Do you remember any of it? What was it that stood out to you about her profile?

The therapist is probing further to see if David can remember any specific things about Natalie that he found positive. One reason for this probing is to see if David has any positive feelings or memories associated with meeting Natalie. Another reason is that David re-telling his impressions of Natalie in a positive light helps lighten the tension and sadness in the relationship during the session.

David: You know, she said that she liked to have fun and go out and do different things together, and she wasn't just a couch potato. It sounded like we would have a good time together no matter what we were doing and I was intrigued about that.

Therapist: How about you, Natalie? Do you remember when he first initiated contact, what your impressions of him were? You probably looked at his profile too, right? What did you think about it? What stood out to you?

Natalie: He sounded like he was somebody who had some depth to him, that he could hold a relationship. So I was kind of looking for somebody who had some kind maturity. I really haven't had very long-term relationships, so that was something I was looking for at the time. And so the fact that he took the initiative really stood out for me.

Therapist: Great, so then you started chatting or emailing back and forth right, and…

David: We started calling each other.

Therapist: Oh okay, were you in communication every day or…

David: Several times a week, we talked on the phone, we had long conversations.

Therapist: Okay, what were some of the high points of that, do you remember?

Now the therapist is moving on to understanding the high points and the low points of the dating experience for this couple. Since this relationship started as an online relationship, the therapist is interested to learn if there were hiccups in the long-distance relationship before they ever met or if it was very positive.

David: Well, for me, we found we had so much in common. You know, we enjoyed so many similar things. It seemed like we could talk about things that were just superficial and laugh about it. We could also talk about things that were really deep that really meant something. I really was impressed with that. I mean, I don't have those conversations with everybody.

Therapist: Okay, how about you?

The style of the oral history interview is to let the couple take center stage and not direct the action too much unless there was negativity or escalation that needed to be managed. By being less directive, the therapist gets a glimpse of how the couple responds more to each other's narrative than to the therapist's questions.

Natalie: Yeah, I would agree with that. And the other thing is that you really made me laugh. And I really enjoyed being on the phone. I felt like he was lighthearted and could kind of grow with things. What I really wanted was to be with someone who didn't have a bad temper or anything like that. He talked about different things he enjoyed doing. Which was very intriguing to me, because I wanted to do things too and not just sit on the couch. It seemed we would get along very well. We did for a period of time.

Natalie is now directing her conversation to David rather than the therapist. Her compliments are likely to help him feel hope and a sense of connection with Natalie which is likely to increase his motivation to work on the affair recovery with her.

Therapist: Good, then did you have a face to face at some point, maybe?

David: Yeah, I flew down to Texas from Maine and we spent four days together (*chuckle*).

Therapist: Nice, and, tell me about that.

David: It can be a comical response between us. Before the week was up we were in bed together and the sex was good.

Therapist: Let me slow it down some, you're already getting to the good stuff. Let me slow it down to when you came here, you flew down, right? Did she come pick you up at the airport? So your very first meeting, when you set eyes on each other was at the airport, what do you remember about that very first meeting? What are some of the highlights?

This is another first impressions moment so the therapist wants to capture their impressions and memories of each other when they first met.

David: She had such a warm face. I mean she was so welcoming, she had a great body, and I saw that, you know you don't catch that on profiles on internet dating sites. I was very pleased, visually pleased with what I saw.

Therapist: Okay and what about you, what did you think about your first meeting at the airport, what do you remember?

Natalie: He was handsome and tall and I was just like (*Natalie makes an excited noise that sounds like "woof"*) and you know the very fact that you came across the country because that is just what I wanted. I don't exactly have words for someone taking that much initiative. I was very pleased already, but when I saw him, I was pleasantly surprised. He looked very nice and kind and he looked like he had a very good persona about him.

Therapist: So then he came to stay with you and it sounds like the chemistry was instant like you said that by the end of that four days you were having sex already. Any highlights or anything special you discovered of each other in those first four days?

David: We got along great. There was very little conflict. I don't remember disagreeing with you much that weekend, we just clicked on so many levels.

Therapist: So you both have very positive memories of those first four days, sort of a sense of magic. Like the time you spent together was magical. You didn't disagree with each other, you did really fun things together. And then you flew back to Maine. And then how did you continue with the relationship?

The level of positivity in the room as the couple retells their memories of the first four days is heightened. Couples rarely have gray or ambiguous feelings about this time in the relationship.

David: Well, we started flying back and forth. We saw each other about once a month when we could and that was kind of difficult for me because I wanted to be with her more and I couldn't. You know when you start seeing each other once a month, it's like a honeymoon all over again. Because you don't want to have any conflicts, you don't want to leave anybody feeling let down at the end of a weekend trip.

Therapist: So you'd have these long separations and these intense coming togethers where you were together once a month. Sounds like some of that honeymoon continued and when you were not fighting, you were really getting along. Well at what point did you decide to take if further? Of all the people in the world, what made you decide that you wanted to spend the rest of your life with this person. What was it about him or her?

The therapist is tracking the ups and downs in the trajectory of the relationship looking for "moments of brightening" as well as moments of disconnection or when perpetual problems first became obvious.

Natalie: Well, you know, our conversations were very fulfilling, even though we enjoyed each other's company going and doing stuff. I felt we really enjoyed each other's company just sitting around and talking and having a conversation. It was such a peaceful and really loving time.

Natalie is describing how they began building love maps and the fondness and admiration early in the relationship through learning about each other and building admiration and appreciation. Considering that Natalie is the hurt spouse, her ability to go back into their history and share these memories with a warm glow is indicative of her attachment to David and the possibility that affair recovery work will be successful.

Therapist: Did you have a sense of greater vision or purpose when you thought about deciding to get married to each other?

Natalie: Well, I think so, because I did find myself going there in my thoughts and my dreams as to how it would be if David came down to Texas to be with me.

Therapist: Okay. David, of all the people in the world, what made you pick Natalie as your life partner?

David: You know because we got along so well on so many levels, I really wanted to move to Texas to see where is this going. Is it going somewhere serious can we make this work as a marriage?

Therapist: What was it about her, about this relationship that made it feel right, that made it feel like it was worth investing in?

Both Natalie and David are answering the questions in a concrete way so the therapist attempts to elicit the existential or deeper symbolic bond between them that may have existed.

David: I was just smitten with her. I just liked laughing with her, liked holding her. We just seemed to fit together like a glove on a hand. You know the things that I was weak in, she was strong in. And that was a good thing. I'm not perfect and I don't think she thought I was.

Natalie: Well come to find out, David likes to drink. Hello!

Natalie is making a sarcastic comment here that exposes David's drinking but in a harsh manner. The therapist notices that Natalie has feelings of anger that tend to come out as four horsemen behaviors. As the therapist makes a note of this, the treatment approach later on will be to help Natalie apply the antidote to criticism which is to express her feelings without blame and making a positive request.

Therapist: So now, we're talking about when you started to live together. Did you live together before marriage or did you live together only after you were married?

David: We lived together for about a year and then we decided to get married.

Therapist: So did you begin to notice some trouble in the beginning like when you were living together or did that start out later?

In a typical oral history interview, the couple's story of their relationship will include places and times when they got into arguments or had to face hardships. The therapist tracks these both as hard times in the relationship but also as examples of perpetual or gridlocked problems in the relationship.

David: I don't know. I'd say later, because in the beginning we were having a great time.

Natalie: Yeah, the first year was really good.

Therapist: So what was your adjustment? What did you each have to adjust to in living with the other person?

David: I don't know, everybody has their quirks. How they hang their clothes up, whether they do the dishes, or whether they leave the dishes in the sink.

Natalie: He wasn't working at first. So he moved in with me and even though that really did cause a lot problems, we moved forward with the marriage. I guess today people would call them red flags. But I didn't think much of them, the drinking and the smoking part of it. I really didn't put much weight on them at first. It looked like it kind of slowly came into our worldview.

Therapist: We found in the research done by John Gottman, that all couples have certain issues that are like perpetual issues. These are issues that don't ever get solved, because they are really about conflict or tension between the two of you because you are different people with different backgrounds. Do you remember what some of your perpetual issues were, as you began to learn about each other and get adjusted to each other?

The therapist defines perpetual issues to help orient the couple towards disagreements that may be ongoing in their relationship. Again the couple is minimizing their areas of conflict although Natalie hinted there were a lot of problems when David moved in.

David: I know now that Natalie wanted children right away and I wasn't wanting children right away because I thought it was important to have fun as couple first. I mean we have friends that have babies, and I just saw the difficulties in their family. When you bring a baby into that situation it just changes things. And I wasn't ready to give her up for that yet. I wanted her to myself.

Therapist: Did you have conflicts around that and discussions around that?

Typically conflict about whether to have children or not can be a deal-breaker issue in couples. This couple appears to have talked about it without breaking up which could be a good sign of the strength of their bond.

David: Yeah, we talked about it quite a bit.

Therapist: Okay, any other perpetual issues? Sounds like maybe his drinking? Was there conflict around as to how much was too much or whether or not it was problematic or not a problem?

Natalie: Yeah, and the smoking as well. It seemed like at first he wasn't smoking that much, but then he kept going more and more and I kept talking to him about his health. He said there was nothing wrong with his health. Then I said, what about me, you're smoking in the house. You know it smells in here, it's staining things. It just got bad, because it all started out very slowly because at first we just started disagreeing on real small things, like where to go to dinner, what movie to see. I don't know why we just couldn't figure that out. Started to have such small little issues and then over time it felt like we just could not agree on most things.

Natalie is describing the common pattern of growing disagreements in a conflict-minimizing couple. In an effort to minimize tension, the couple avoids confrontations and has many indirect or tentative conversations that never result in an agreement or outcome. This means the conflict is simply ignored or put on a back burner only to be brought up again when it gets triggered by something else. David's smoking appears to be one such issue.

Therapist: It sounds like that was exactly the kind of thing that you felt you really agreed with each other on at the beginning of the relationship. So it sounds like there was some lack of trust or safety with each other and then all these other things, that at one time were not problems, became problems. But the big ones were having a baby or not having one, the drinking, and smoking. Would you agree David that those were perpetual problems?

The therapist is clarifying that small issues can become perpetual problems when the trust or safety in the relationship is not being built. From Natalie's description of David's smoking, it appears that she may have begun to experience him as not being there for her and not caring about her interests or values.

David: Oh yeah, they surfaced several times, I agree with that.

Therapist: Okay, so one of the things we like to do is actually have the two of you have a conflict discussion and then for me to just watch and video tape it so I can really watch how the two of you discuss your disagreements. So I was wondering based on what all you've talked about, the very first conflict you brought up was whether or not what David did with this woman was an affair or not. And I wonder if that might be a topic you can discuss. If you can turn around and face each other and have a discussion and try to solve it. I want to see how you solve it and what you are like as a couple when you're having conflict. I'm just going to watch and not intervene. Go ahead and start talking to each other whenever you're ready.

The conflict sample is a part of the first assessment session when a therapist does not intervene or ask questions and allows the couple to talk for about ten minutes on a conflictual topic of their choice. As the therapist observes the conflict discussion, she is looking for glimpses of the couple's conflict management style.

Natalie: So, what I'm wondering is, you know, I'm calling this an affair and you're really not even calling this an affair, but why were you communicating with this woman? So what is going on between you and this Devyn woman?

(This is a harsh start-up where Natalie has opened the conversation with a blaming statement.)

David: Nothing, I told you before, nothing!

(David responds immediately with defensiveness, not taking responsibility for any part of it.)

Natalie: Then why all the emails saying that you love her?
David: What are you talking about?
Natalie: David, I've seen all the emails, don't play stupid...

(As the accusations continue, Natalie begins to show contempt. Telling David not to play stupid is a way of talking from a superior place.)

David: Okay, I'm talking to someone but it's not what you think.
Natalie: It's not that you love her, don't love me, and are going to divorce me and move in with her?
David: I might have said something like that, but I didn't mean it. I was just playing, just trying to keep talking with her, it was just something fun to do, kind of like "catfishing."
Natalie: David, I'm not an idiot. If you want to be with her then admit it and leave, but if you want any chance with me then you better start by telling me the truth.

(Natalie continues to be harsh and contemptuous. Although hurt partners who have recently discovered their partner's infidelity are typically much more angry and attacking than Natalie is showing here, her behavior still has elements of the four horsemen that will need to be addressed in treatment.)

David: Okay, okay, look you know things between you and me haven't been great recently. When was the last time we had sex? Huh?
Natalie: And do you think that's my fault?
David: Do you think it's mine?
Natalie: I'm not the one that's an alcoholic.

(Natalie expresses contempt not only by ambushing David, but also by labeling his behavior with a diagnosis that implies that he is inferior to her.)

David: Oh, I forget you're perfect.

(David responds with sarcasm that escalates Natalie's contempt with a contemptuous statement of his own.)

Natalie: I'm not perfect, but I'm not having an affair with someone on the internet. Have you ever met her?
David: No, it's only been email conversations.
Natalie: You've never skyped her? Don't bullshit me.

David: Fine, we video chatted.

Natalie: Did you talk naked and have sex online?

David: What does it matter? Do you think you've done everything to make this marriage work?

Natalie: I haven't led anyone else on.

David: But you thought about divorce before that, didn't you?

Natalie: I have, but I wanted to try and make things work out first.

David: Of course, otherwise I would have left you a long time ago.

Natalie: You know I have never done anything so harsh to our marriage that could not be forgiven such as a divorce. But yet you think it's okay to have this email affair or whatever you want to call it and think nothing of it basically and when you're not really being accountable for it.

David: I told you about it. I admitted finally what I did, is that not being accountable?

Natalie: So are you saying yes, you had an affair?

David: No, I'm saying I had conversations with her and yes we skyped.

Natalie: How can you say this is not an affair when you are over there you are saying you loved her.

Therapist: So let me interrupt for a second and just check in with you both and see how's this feeling, are you in the middle of the conflict that you're usually are at home?

Natalie: Yes, he's getting me really angry. He's making me madder and madder because again, his not even taking responsibility just makes me angry.

Therapist: So David I know that you had said earlier, you could call it a betrayal. That felt more reasonable. So can you help Natalie understand how you see it as a betrayal?

David: I see it as a betrayal, because I was, I did say things to her that I should not have said, like I love you.

Therapist: So the betrayal part is the fact that you lied to Devyn about loving her, and somehow gave her something that really is more true of your relationship with Natalie. How does that sit with you?

Sometimes couples get really caught up in arguing about what the relationship between David and Devyn was. That's actually a distraction, because I'm working with David and Natalie. I want David and Natalie to agree on something that they can work on repairing. As he repairs the betrayal of the marriage, he may change his mind on whether that was an affair or not.

Natalie: It's still aggravating, but you know at least he can admit it was a betrayal.

Therapist: Yeah, that feels more reassuring or validating somehow. Listening to the two you talk about this relationship that you had with Devyn, I think that is where we need to start. I'm going to be giving you some questionnaires to take home with you as you walk out the door. I'm going to ask you to complete those separately and bring it in when you come to see me by yourself. The next thing I want to do is meet with each of you individually, if that's okay with you. I'd like to do that and just get a sense of how you are doing and what you would like to get out of therapy. And then I would like all of us to come together in the same room for a third session, where I will share with you my impressions of the strengths and challenges in your relationship. Does that make sense?

David: Yeah, that makes sense.

Therapist: Well thank you so much for coming to see me and for agreeing to do this. I will see you both next week.

References

Gottman, J. (1979). *Marital interaction: Experimental investigations.* New York, NY: Academic Press.

Gottman, J. M. (1994). *What predicts divorce: The relationship between marital processes and marital outcomes.* Hillsdale, NJ: Lawrence Erlbaum Associates, Inc.

Gottman, J. M. (1995). *Why marriages succeed or fail and how you can makes yours last.* New York, NY: Simon and Schuster.

Gottman, J. M. (1999). *The marriage clinic.* New York, NY: Norton.

Gottman, J. M. (2011). *The science of trust: Emotional attunement for couples.* New York, NY: Norton.

Gottman, J. M. (2014). *Bridging the couple chasm: Level 1 training in Gottman method couples therapy.* Workshop presented in Chicago, IL, September 12 and 13.

Gottman, J. M. (2015). *Principia amoris: The new science of love.* New York, NY: Routledge.

Gottman, J. M., & Navarra, R. J. (2011). Gottman method couples therapy: From theory to practice. In D. K. Carson & M. Kasado-Kehoe (Eds.), *Case studies in couples therapy: Research-based approaches* (pp. 331–344). New York, NY: Routledge Press.

Gottman, J. M., & Silver, N. (2013). *What makes love last: How to build trust and avoid betrayal.* New York, NY: Simon & Schuster.

Gottman, J. M., & Silver, N. (2015). *The seven principles for making marriages work: A practical guide from the nations foremost relationship expert.* New York, NY: Harmony Press.

Gottman, J., Coan, J., Swanson, C., & Carrère, S. (1998). Predicting marital happiness and stability from newlywed interactions. *Journal of Marriage and the Family, 60*(1), 5–22.

Gottman, J., Driver, J., & Tabares, A. (2002). Building the Sound Marital House: An empirically-derived couple therapy. In A. S. Gurman & N. S. Jacobson (Eds.), *Clinical handbook of couple therapy* (3rd ed., pp. 373–399). New York, NY: Guilford Press.

Gottman, J. M., Notarius, C., Markman, H., Bank, S., Yoppi, B., & Rubin, M. E. (1976). Behavior exchange theory and marital decision making. *Journal of Personality and Social Psychology, 34,* 14–23.

Gottman, J., Ryan, K., Swanson, C., & Swanson, K. (2005). Proximal change experiments with couples: A methodology for empirically building a science of effective interventions for changing couples' interaction. *Journal of Family Communication, 5*(3), 163–190.

Gottman, J. M., Schwartz-Gottman, J., & DeClaire, J. (2007). *Ten lessons to transform your marriage: America's love lab experts share their strategies for strengthening your marriage.* New York, NY: Three Rivers Press.

Hawkins, M. W., Carrere, S., & Gottman, J. M. (2002). Marital sentiment override: Does it influence couples' perceptions? *Journal of Marriage and Family, 64*(1), 193–201.

Navarra, R. J., Gottman, J. M., & Schwartz-Gottman, J. (2015). Sound Relationship House theory and relationship and marriage education. In J. J. Ponzetti, Jr. (Ed.), *Evidence based approaches to relationship and marriage education.* New York, NY: Routledge.

Schwartz-Gottman, J., & Gottman, J. M. (2015). *10 principles for doing effective couples therapy* (Norton Series on Interpersonal Neurobiology). New York: W. W. Norton.

7

IMAGO RELATIONSHIP THERAPY

Wade Luquet

Brief History of the Model

Imago Relationship Therapy (IRT) was co-created in the relationship of Harville Hendrix and Helen LaKelly Hunt. In an attempt to understand their own relationship, as well as those of couple clients, Hendrix and Hunt developed theories and processes that eventually became IRT and resulted in Hendrix's popular book *Getting the love you want: A guide for couples* in 1988. A synthesis of psychoanalytic theory, attachment theory, Gestalt, Rogerian, Transactional Analysis, and other theories for which Hendrix received training, IRT began to come together as its own theory of relationality through a series of lectures Hendrix was asked to give in classes, workshops, and churches (Hendrix, 2005). A former minister and professor, he began to draw adherents and students to his ideas and established the Institute for Imago Relationship Therapy in New York City in the 1980s where he began a certification program in IRT that has resulted in over 2000 certified therapists in thirty-three countries worldwide.

IRT was given a boost by Hendrix's frequent appearances on the *Oprah Winfrey Show*—one episode even won Oprah an Emmy—which accelerated sales of his book and placed it on the *New York Times* bestsellers list. Hendrix would become Winfrey's most frequent guest with more than sixteen appearances. With millions of copies of the book in print in more than fifty languages, Hendrix and Hunt have since written several other popular books including *Keeping the love you find: A guide for singles* (1993) and *Giving the love that heals: A guide for parents* (1998).

In 1996, the first book for professional therapists, *Short-term couples therapy: The Imago model in action*, was written by Wade Luquet (1996/2007), followed by an edited casebook, *Healing in the relational paradigm* (Luquet & Hannah, 1998) and a theory book, *Imago relationship therapy: Perspectives on theory* (Hendrix, Hunt,

Hannah, & Luquet, 2005). There have also been numerous peer-reviewed articles and dissertations on IRT (Muro & Holliman, 2014; Muro, Holliman, & Luquet, 2016a; Schmidt, Luquet, & Gehlert, 2016) and the recent completion of the first randomly controlled clinical trial of Imago in an out-patient setting that indicated statistically significant improvement in marital satisfaction as measured by the Marital Adjustment Test (Gehlert, Schmidt, Gingerich, & Luquet, submitted).

Multicultural therapists report the appeal of IRT with various American cultures including African American couples who report liking that they, rather than the therapist, control the session (Weiser & Thompson, 1998). Hispanic couples find appeal in IRT's emphasis on connectedness (Bain, 1998; Muro & Holliman, 2014), while gay and lesbian couples like the idea of being mirrored and validated by another—something often lacking for them in the hetero-centric culture (Kleinberg & Zorn, 1998). In a workshop format IRT has been shown effective in increasing relationship satisfaction in low-income diverse populations (Muro, Holliman, & Luquet, 2016b). IRT also has international cross-cultural peer-reviewed publications reporting positive outcomes from Korea, Iran, Israel, and other countries outside the United States (Aram & Shlak, 2008; Etemadi, Navabinejad, Ahmadi, & Farzad, 2006; Oh, 2010).

Imago, the Latin word for image, names the basic premise in IRT, which is that individuals are attracted to persons who have both positive and negative characteristics of their early childhood caretakers—their attraction system (Hendrix, 1988). Couples are drawn to each other for a reason. Intimate relationships that begin in romantic love have an unconscious purpose to bring two people together who are "wounded" in the same place developmentally so they can heal those wounds through the relationship. Frustrations in relationships are signs of disconnection in that healing process, and in fact, re-wound couples often to the point of deep resentment and separateness. Through the use of a dialogue process that includes mirroring the partner, validating him or her from his or her point of view, and empathizing with their partner's emotional state, the couple is able to reconnect on an empathic level and understand the other. In a psychoeducational model of treatment delivery, couples are taught the theory and processes of IRT and coached by the therapist in various dialogical processes that increase understanding, appreciation, and caring behaviors while decreasing negative interactions between the couple.

Theory of Problem Formation

It is important for any model to be able to engage in the therapeutic relationship with a conceptualization of how problems form and are resolved (Reiter, 2013; Sperry, 2005). Case conceptualizations guide the therapy, determine next steps, and ultimately guides the client toward a successful resolution of the problem. If the couple therapist has a model of how a problem is formed, they typically have an idea for how to reverse the problem or resolve the issue. These conceptual frames are the base of therapist competency (Sperry, 2010).

IRT has a conceptual framework that begins before the couple even meets. Individuals seem to be imprinted with an image of their early childhood caretakers and utilize that image to seek an appropriate love partner—what is referred to as the **Imago** (Hendrix, 1988). This image is really a pattern of behaviors, both positive and negative, that seems familiar to each of the partners and is unconsciously attractive when seeking a mate. Frustrations in relationships can be linked to an unconscious effort to resolve problems from the past as they appear as behaviors in the present relationship.

Unfortunately, couples tend to utilize similar coping skills they have used in the past—yelling, getting quiet, sarcasm, being distant—that only seem to increase frustration and resentment between the partners (Hendrix, 1988; Luquet, 2007). IRT therapists use this framework to teach skills that help the couple understand how their individual past has affected their present relationship and exacerbates their present power struggles with their partners. The therapists then teach the couple skills to help them understand their own, and their partner's, past needs, or wounds, and help them experience an empathic response, as opposed to a reactionary response. The case of David and Natalie Johnson will help illustrate this process.

End of Romantic Love

David and Natalie's relationship started like most others—in the spell of romantic love. Meeting online like many modern-day couples, they found that after getting to know each other they had a desire to be together on a regular basis. So great was their desire for each other that they were willing to travel to be together on a monthly basis. At that time, their love was no doubt real. But what was this great pull to be with each other and the giddy exuberance often seen in young couples? And why does it so often end? Neuroscience is now unlocking some of the mysteries of romantic love, and most of these changes can be attributed to a drug reaction triggered by the presence of the significant other and the chemical effect on the pleasure center of the brain (Tarlaci, 2012).

fMRI studies by Fisher, Aron, and Brown (2006) found that subjects who were intensely in love had a response in their dopaminergic reward system when exposed to photographs of their beloved. They felt good in the presence of their romantic partner. Fisher and her collaborators believe there are three primary neural systems that direct romantic love with the intention of reproduction. A person's sex drive motivates them to seek a range of partners for mating; their attraction system draws the person to specific partners; and the attachment system motivates the person to stay together long enough to reproduce and perform parenting duties specific to the species (Fisher, Aron, & Brown, 2006). While this scientific explanation is a rather unromantic view of romantic love, it is relevant to how

Imago relationship therapy views the process of mate selection and future problems in relationships.

Initially, the lovers only see the positive traits because the dopaminergic reward system keeps them anaesthetized to the negative traits. Eventually, the brain gets used to the chemical bath of phenylethylamine, norepinephrine, and dopamine, responding less to their effects. Consequently, the couple is able to see and experience the negative characteristics of their partner, often reporting they have "fallen out of love." David and Natalie's three-year relationship is right on time in this developmental model of romantic love relationships. The drugs have worn off and now they have to begin the real work of relationship—to understand why the attraction system brought them together and how to work with the struggles brought forth in an effort to increase their attachment and love for each other.

The Purpose of Relationships

With our cultural "happily ever after" mentality, it is difficult for young couples to think about the future realities that relationships are work. With the extravagance of modern weddings, one would think that relationships will remain forever in bliss till death do they part. However, as stated earlier, the bliss of relationships does end, and couples must find their purpose for being together. IRT views the purpose of the love relationship as maintaining a connection with the significant other while resolving issues that occurred during the developmental processes of childhood that are playing out in the marriage through recurring frustrations (Hendrix, 1988). Connection with the other can be maintained by empathically understanding the source of childhood frustrations and growing past the issues that will surface until understood and acted upon. Healing and resolution will occur within the safety of a committed relationship with an understanding and empathic partner—all wounding occurs in relationship and all healing occurs in relationship.

For David and Natalie, the process of developing empathy and understanding of their partner will take place with a dialogue skill taught to them by the Imago therapist and practiced in the sessions and at home. But for David and Natalie to fully understand the need for this dialogue process, they must understand the healing purpose of their relationship. The purpose of their relationship is brought to consciousness through psychoeducational dialogue processes and by a writing exercise called **the Imago Workup** (Hendrix, 1988; Luquet, 2007). The Imago Workup is a paper-and-pencil exercise in which the couple sits quietly and recalls as much as they can about their early childhood caretakers. They will list positive attributes of their early childhood caretakers—*always there, warm, caring*, and negative attributes of those same caretakers—*never there, mean, too quiet*. They will finish the sentence, "What I always wanted and needed as a child was..."—*to be told I did things right, to be told I was loved, to be visible in the family*. The couple will also list their recurring frustrations as a child and what they did when they got frustrated—*cried, screamed and yelled, got quiet, walked away*. Finally, they will list how they wished they could have felt—*happy, special, competent*. The information they recalled about their caretakers will be placed in a series of sentence stems, not about their caretakers, but about their partner whom they are frustrated with; for example, I am trying to get a person who is... *never there, mean, and too quiet*... to always be... *always there, warm and caring*... So that I can get... *to be told that I did things right*... and feel... *happy, special and competent*. I stop myself from getting this sometimes by... *crying, screaming and walking away*.

Typically, a couple will react to this exercise with surprise as they realize that the frustrations they experience with their partner relate directly to the frustrations they experienced with their early childhood caretakers. They begin to understand that problems form when each of them bring old childhood issues into their present relationship and fight them out in similar ways they did in their youth. However, this understanding is not enough to end the frustrations; it is an enlightenment that starts the process of comprehending the need to change their behavior with one another. Often times when couples are presented with the need to change a behavior, they will quickly revert back to old behaviors because they do not see the point of doing things differently. Without context, partners feel coerced. When they can understand that their present behavior affects their partner because of their partner's past wounding and present needs, they are more likely to stick with a behavior change because they understand on a deeper level the need for the change. And a change can only stick when it is practiced over time and becomes a regular, habitual behavior.

Role of the Therapist

It should be noted at this point that Imago has a different view of the role of the therapist. The Imago therapist acts as a coach and facilitator of the process rather than a transferential object or a behavioral change agent. As can be seen through the Imago Workup, partners already are transferential objects for each other, so there is no need for the therapist to take on that role. Couples marry each other *because of* the similarities between the partner and the early childhood caretaker. Through a series of informational sessions, as well as learning and practicing skills, the therapist teaches the couple how to gently and intentionally deal with their frustrations, thus giving each of them a different experience of the outcome of the past that has made itself present. The therapist also assigns weekly homework to reinforce and practice what is learned in the session. Certainly this process does not always go smoothly, but given enough positive experiences and a supportive therapist facilitating the process, the brain begins to re-interpret and reconsolidate past volatile issues into less volatile issues. The energy behind the frustration lessens as it is heard and validated and connection can be restored.

Why Do Problems Arise?

Most couples, like David and Natalie, have experienced the minor problems of two people living together such as putting their things away, trying to decide where to eat, or what to do for the day. While important and can accumulate into resentments over time, these frustrations are more annoying than relationship-ending. Couples may typically brush off the frustrating interaction or talk until there is at least some resolution. One or the other may not be happy with the results, but they adjust to the agreement in various ways and the couple can go about their day. These interactions can benefit by using simple communication skills such as active listening and brainstorming (Markman, Stanley, & Blumberg, 2010). It is the intense core issue arguments that affect couples the most and often result in furious fights or unsettling silence and distance. These interactions are what Imago theorist Randy Mason refers to as the "relationship nightmare" (Mason, Mason, & Hannah, 2005, p. 193).

The **relationship nightmare**, according to Mason et al. (2005), occurs when an unconscious precipitant meets a conscious precipitant, or what we also call the power struggle. In other words, if a partner makes a shaming statement and that statement triggers past shaming wounds stored in the unconscious, a disconnect between the partners will occur that can trigger intense reactions. The couple can quickly go from connection to chaos and feel disengaged from each other. Disconnection can lead to retaliatory comments or retorts that can intensify the shaming leading to a further disengagement and fragmentation, rather than the relationship cohesion experienced when a couple is in sync (Mason et al., 2005). Power struggles will either end in reconnection and understanding if the couple can listen and validate the core scene being activated, or it will end in a rupture that may build up, causing an alienation that will lead to a distant or parallel relationship. So while tapping the relationship nightmare can be uncomfortable to the couple, it also presents an opportunity for growth and understanding of the other that brings about a deeper connection if the couple is able to fully hear the core scene that triggered the event.

There are several places David and Natalie's relationship nightmare, or core issues, may be being triggered. Being the youngest of three and the only male in a family that really wanted a boy, David may have been a special child in the family. However, David was also a bit of a disappointment to his father, who was a very good athlete, due to his short, pudgy stature and lack of athletic ability. It is possible that he is carrying shame for his lack of athletic ability as well as a lack of recognition for what he does do well from his father whom he rarely talks to at this time in his life.

Likewise, Natalie was also affected and shaped by her youth. The divorce of her parents, her mother's remarriage, and the lack of contact from the males in her life has shaped her ideas of relationships. She also bore the weight of being a parentified child but was not acknowledged for her efforts. Her father seemed caring when he was around but did not initiate contact with her and as a result she developed a "love/hate" relationship with him and became "infuriated" with both her father and stepfather for their lack of involvement in her life. For both David and Natalie, these interactions with their early childhood caretakers have shaped their view of relationships and are at play in their present marriage. For the IRT therapist, helping couples understand how their childhood affects their relationship is essential.

Case Conceptualization and the Imago Developmental Model

An exploration into a couple's past reveals that relationship patterns can be traced to early childhood development. This information is useful for the couple but also for the therapist who can use it for assessment purposes, assist in case conceptualization, and understanding couple relationship types. Individuals tend to fall in love with and marry others who are developmentally wounded in the same place they are wounded. In the romantic phase, outward beauty and intense, intimate conversations are not the only aspect couples are attracted to in the other. What couples are unable to see is there is also an attraction to a similar developmental need. This attraction is an unconscious process being masked by the dopamine reaction of romantic love but is revealed in the frustrations experienced in the power struggle stage of the relationship.

When conceptualizing a case, IRT therapists use this developmental model to target treatment to the developmental wound. IRT defines five developmental stages of childhood that affect romantic relationships (Hendrix, 1988; Luquet, 2007). They are briefly described here:

Attachment Stage (0–2 Years)

Infant needs at this time are parents and caretakers who are warm, available, and consistent. The infant needs someone who takes care of their basic needs of feeding, changing, holding, loving, and being a consistent figure in their lives. Those who do not get their needs fulfilled may become clingy in future relationships, looking for someone to be available and dependable, or they may become avoidant of relationships because their early experiences were too painful and did not provide them the reliable relationship they needed as an infant.

The **clinger-avoider couple** is the result of early attachment deficits and consequently may have the most difficulty finding relationship satisfaction following therapy. There is often a desperate quality to this couple as the partner who clings tries to make contact with the partner who has a very difficult time maintaining contact in the relationship. There tends to be a constant approach and avoidance with this couple, and while they can make some progress in the therapy, they can just as easily fall back into old patterns of clinging and isolation (Fein, 1998). Such couples often stay together unhappily because they still need each other and have difficulty finding alternate partners to satisfy their needs.

Exploration Stage (1–3 Years)

This is a period of infancy where the child can now move around on its own through walking and crawling. The toddler is curious and enjoys the freedom of moving around freely, but also still needs the security of a consistent parent getting excited about their discoveries. Children at this age can often be observed exploring a new room or a toy, and then looking up to their parent for a smile or reassurance that what they are doing is ok and that someone is still there watching over them. Sometimes they have parents who are too strict, or the children were "groomed" to act a certain way and they are not able to explore. Others do not get the assuring feedback or a nod of approval needed to develop a curiosity. Sometimes these children will become loud in order to be noticed or approved, and this behavior pattern will often follow them into their adulthood and relationships. Others who were restricted or groomed might become defiant and do what they want to do without consideration for the other. They may become narcissistic in their ways, feeling they deserve to do what they want when they want.

This stage is a very early period of personality development and the results of this developmental wounding may be the **fuser-isolator couple**. The fuser looks for the attention they did not get as a child and will become quite verbal when they do not get the attention they are seeking. They are often attracted to the isolator who seeks to do things on his or her own unencumbered by most relationships. This is a volatile couple who often get into loud arguments. They can be calmed down by teaching the isolator to listen to and validate the other's point of view—no easy task when isolators are so sure they are right (Luquet & Chadwick, 1998; Solomon, 1998).

Identity Stage (3–5 Years)

Play and imagination are not only fun for children, these activities are also how they try on different parts of their emerging selves. Whether they are pretending to be a doctor, Superman, dog, cat or playing house, children are developing parts of what will be their future identity. Children need mirroring from their parents through such statements as "You are Superman!," "What a cute puppy you are!" In other words, children need to feel as if they are being what they think they are being in order to develop a solid, yet flexible personality as adults. When they do not get that, or in some way they are shamed for their "silly play," they may develop a rigid personality feeling as if there is only one way to be and it is my way. Or they may not have a solid sense of self since their play and imagination was not acknowledged by their caretaker and they become insecure and unsure of themselves. They may have difficulty making decisions and often rely on others to make decisions for them.

This wounding often results in the **rigid-diffuse couple**—a perfect match since the rigid partner loves telling the diffuse partner what to do. When the diffuse partner tries to make decisions, their choices are often met with reasons why they will not work and this is the best way to do things. The rigid partner likes things the way he or she has set them up, and there is little room for flexibility. This relationship can work for a period of time until the diffuse partner decides to develop a sense of self and become independent which can result in confusion for the rigid partner who thought they were doing everything right and the relationship was good. The rigid partner has to learn to adjust to the diffuse partner's emerging self, loosen the reins, and be able to validate the evolution of their mate (Luquet & Chadwick, 1998).

Power and Competence Stage (4–6 Years)

Children at this age have an interest in using their newfound motor skills to complete various task. Similar to the task of Erikson's industry versus inferiority stage (Erikson, 1950), the child at this stage seeks activities that develop some beginning skills such as coloring, painting, helping to cook, or fix something. What they need from parents is praise, affirmation, and mirroring. They need to be told how great what they are working on has turned out: "Beautiful picture!" or "Thanks for helping me out painting that door. You did a terrific job!" Unfortunately, what children sometimes get is shaming or partial mirroring: "You drew outside the lines here," or "You really made a mess of that door!" They will develop a feeling of being less than competent and capable and may adapt to that by developing a competitive personality to be seen, noticed, or praised. Or they may develop a passive personality and feel they cannot do anything right: "I can't do that. Can you do that for me?"

A wound at this stage results in the **competitive/passive couple**—possibly the most common of couple types seen in private practice settings. These couples often have a member who is competitive in their jobs or in sports and is constantly seeking validation from others. They become the "Type A" go-getters and become frustrated by their partners who cannot seem to keep up, or worse, they do not view as being as competent as they are. The passive partner may not be as concerned about goals of success or making money. Their goals may be parenting, spirituality, or self-development which are important activities that do not seek external validation from the world at large. This frustrates the competitive partner who does not see this as purposeful or particularly useful. The competitive partner has a difficult time validating what they consider trivial interest, yet feel they themselves should be validated regularly for what they do. But still, this couple is often composed of well-developed individuals who are able to attach to others; they are curious, and have strong identities through their work or parenting responsibilities. Their dissatisfaction often comes from not being noticed and appreciated for what they do (Hannah, 1998).

Concern Stage (6–9 Years)

At this stage, children are in school and are making friends. They are working toward understanding relationships outside the family and often go through the positives and negatives of being part of a peer group. Some of these children will not be able to find a peer group; they may have different interests or cannot afford the latest fashions and they are shunned. As adults, they may prefer being by themselves and become loners. Others may have difficulty making friends and compensate by taking care of others so they are liked by the person or group. As adults, they may become caretakers of others and work overly hard at being liked.

The **loner-caretaker couple** is an interesting pairing of one partner who prefers to be by him- or herself and the other who wants to take care of others. The caretaker seems to have boundless energy and is constantly on the go, looking for ways to help others and to be thanked for his or her ability to help. While they are modest and humble, they do like the acknowledgement. This acknowledgement is often hard to come by at home with the loner who just does not think to be thankful to his or her partner. The loner is often awkward in social situations and counts on the caretaker to be the face of the family and relationship. When others see this couple, they will think about the caretaker's energy and the loner's "support" of his/her need to help others. In reality, the caretaker is tired and could use some validation from the loner partner.

It is important to note that the couple types identified by the Imago developmental model are typologies and are meant to be general in nature. In practice, there is variety within each of these couple types. Some will be more or less extreme in their behavior while others will be more or less intense in their emotion. While they may show traits of other developmental stages, typically one stage, and the needs associated with that stage, is dominate. The purpose of the developmental model is for the therapist to be able to conceptualize the case and the course of treatment for the particular couple. Like any diagnosis, it is also possible that as more information becomes available, the therapist may have to reassess and change initial assumptions and adjust the treatment as needed. Because IRT is transparent and informative, the couple is presented with a short lecture that explains developmental wounds and helps them find where they may be as a couple on the developmental scale (Luquet, 1996). This information helps them see their purpose in each other's lives and helps develop empathy between them.

With the limited information provided in the case, we might initially consider that David and Natalie are wounded at the power and competence stage and are a competitive-passive couple. This assessment is based on the history of David's father being disappointed in him while Natalie's family was distant and gave her the role of parentified child without much positive feedback. Natalie went on to a successful career in the competitive world of real estate while David admirably took a job as a teacher in her home town. David seems low key in his dealings with others and seems to take on a passive role with others with Natalie seemingly much more assertive from the information we have.

Another area assessed by the IRT therapist is how couples express or repress energy in the relationship, or what Imago refers to as **minimizing** and **maximizing** (Hendrix, 1988; Luquet, 2007). In every couple, there is one partner who tends to maximize problems while one tends to minimize the situation. The partner who maximizes may say, "You are always late!" while the other who minimizes responds, "I was late two times and you make it seem like it is every time." Infuriated by that response, the maximizer has to respond, "Only twice! Are you kidding me? You were even late to our wedding!" to which the minimizer may respond, "Oh, you keep bringing that up. Didn't we talk about that already? You really need to let that one go." At that, the maximizer is set off and the usual argument begins as the minimizer smugly listens and rolls his or her eyes at the level of emotion. Though the maximizer may look like the "crazy one" in this situation, it is really the minimizer that set all of this in motion by not listening carefully and understanding what being late means to his or her partner.

Looking at the dialogue between the Johnsons, it seems apparent that David is the minimizer and Natalie is the maximizer. Though their levels of energy expression can change from time to time when David gets pushed to the point of needing to vent, the two dialogue examples presented (see Chapter 2) show Natalie rightfully having great concern about the affair and David's smoking, and David minimizing her concern. This communication style can only lead to an escalation and eventual disconnect between the couple as they do not feel heard and understood by the other. The Johnsons are in real trouble here and they need a means to understand each other and develop a connection where both feel understood and validated.

Theory of Problem Resolution

If couple problems can be attributed to disconnection, then resolution begins with connection. All healing for couples occurs when partners are in sync and understand the other; this does not mean agreement but understanding and validation of the other. Couples learning to understand each other is achieved in IRT through a process called **Couples Dialogue** (Hendrix, 1988; Luquet, 2007). In the first few sessions, couples are taught the two most important aspects of the therapy model: how to create a safe space so they are not reactive to each other and how to listen to each other using the couples dialogue: a three-step process that involves mirroring the words of the partner, validating his or her partner from his or her partner's point of view, and showing empathy by imagining how the other may be feeling. To dialogue with an emotional connection will require some intentional behavior changes from the couple and the facilitation of the therapist since this way of listening is not natural or congruent with how they have been communicating with each other, but given enough practice and reinforcement, they can learn to use dialogue in conflictual situations.

Creating a safe space is essential in this work. Frustrations and arguments are a neurological response to negativity and a sense of danger; we have no choice but to defend ourselves through fight or flight tactics in threatening situations. Humans in defensive posture cannot hear one other. Cut off from our emotional neural system, we are not able to be empathetic with the person speaking.

Cognitive and affective neural systems have difficulty working at the same time because one system turns off the other (Anthony et al., 2013). To stay out of the defensive brain, David and Natalie will be taught some simple meditative skills such as breathing and visualizing to prevent them from becoming flooded with negativity (Goleman, 2012; Gottman, 2002) and to focus on their partner—what the neurosciences call becoming attuned (Gottman, 2011; Schore, 1994; Siegel, 1999). They would also be asked to look into each other's eyes for one minute prior to beginning the dialogue—a process known to decrease feelings of threat as pupils enlarge and signal safety to the other (Goldstein, Kilroy, & Van de Voort, 1976; Hess, 1965).

Couples Dialogue

From this place of safety, David and Natalie will be able to hear and respond to each other more fully and respond to what they heard. They would be taught the main skill of IRT: the couples dialogue. The couples dialogue is a three-part process of mirroring the partner's words, validating what is said from the partner's point of view, and taking a guess or empathizing about what they have expressed. In the initial sessions the listener would be coached to respond to the partner through sentence stems, validating responses, and questions inviting more information such as "If I heard you right, you said...," "Did I get that?," "Is there more?," "Let me see if I got all of that," "It makes sense to me that you see things that way," "What makes sense about that to me is...," "I imagine that might make you feel...," Eventually through homework and in-session practice, the couple will be able to utilize this process on their own to work through conflicts.

For many, this exercise may sound like the usual active listening, and in many ways it is. IRT takes active listening further by adding the validation and empathy component. The couples dialogue deepens the conversation and often evokes an emotional connection between partners. While most couples practitioners know that active listening is a good way for couples to hear each other, it is only recently that we are understanding the neurological processes that are occurring as humans are empathic with each other. The recent discovery of mirror neurons seems to indicate that the receiver of the message is able to feel the feelings of the other, without falling into the other's internal state. Conversely, the sender of the message also *feels felt* by the receiver of the message when they are listened to empathically (Carr et al., 2003; Siegel, 2012). Recent research of individuals discussing a social conflict while in an fMRI with an experimenter listening and responding empathically at times and un-empathically at other times shed light on the usefulness of empathic listening. The results indicate that cognitive empathy such as that displayed in dialogue has a "... positive effect on feelings and emotions in social conflict situations" (Seehaussen et al., 2014, p. 959) for the person being listened to in the fMRI. The empathic connection is calming and healing.

As an example, here is what may have happened if David listened to Natalie in dialogue about his smoking rather than the reactive way they talked in the initial case. Notice that Natalie asks if he is available to talk about the issue. This allows David to prepare himself for this conversation and not feel ambushed thus setting off his defensive brain.

Natalie: Are you feeling safe so we can talk?
David: Yes, I can hear you now.
Natalie: It really bothers me when you smoke. It is really smelly, and I worry about your health.
David: So if I am hearing you, it bothers you when I smoke. You find it smelly and you worry about how it is affecting my health. Did I get that?
Natalie: You did.
David: Is there more about that?
Natalie: Yes, I get really scared that you will get sick from your smoking—a heart attack or lung cancer or something. That would be really bad, and I don't want that to happen.
David: So you are scared that I might get sick from my smoking. You are worried that I might have a heart attack or get lung cancer and that scares you, and you don't want that to happen. Did I get that?
Natalie: Yes.
David: Is there more?
Natalie: Not right now.
David: I can see that it scares you, and it makes sense to me that you would worry about that. Those things certainly can happen. And I imagine you feel scared, concerned, and worried about our future. Did I get that?
Natalie: You did. Thank you.

At this point, there is no solution to the frustration, just hearing and validation between the couple. David was able to hear that Natalie was concerned about his smoking, mostly for health reasons. He was able to validate her knowing that health reasons are a real concern for smokers. Natalie feels heard, and he is not being asked to agree with her, so there is no need for either of them to escalate. However, there may be a deeper meaning for her concern that they may want to explore as a couple to understand the origin of the intensity of her emotions around this issue. In the therapy session, the therapist guides them into a deeper level of dialogue (Hendrix, Hunt, Luquet, & Carlson, 2015). **Deeper dialogues** can occur when couples are guided by the therapist to take emotions to a deeper level of understanding: "Natalie, can you tell David more about feeling scared? David, you listen to Natalie and mirror her." The therapist can also help the couple understand the childhood origins of their frustrations.

Therapist: Natalie, I hear that you are scared and worried about David's smoking and weight, and that makes a lot of sense to me, too. When you think about it, does this fear and worry remind you of anything from your childhood?

Natalie: I think it does.

Therapist: Can you tell David about that?

Natalie: Yes. I think that I worry that if something happens to you, I will be left alone again. My dad was not there for me when I really needed him. I worry that you might not be there when I need you.

David: So if I am getting it, you are worried that I might get sick, and I won't be there for you just like your dad who was not there for you as a child. Did I get that? Tell me more about that?

Natalie: I really needed him there with me. My mom put a lot of responsibility on me because she was trying to make ends meet by working and she was living her own life, so I always wished he was there for me and my mom. It just did not feel fair. I was doing a lot of parenting of my siblings, and there was no one there and no one telling me if I was doing a good job or not. I felt so alone in my house.

David: So you are saying you felt like no one was there for you. Your dad left and you had to be responsible for the others while your mom worked and had her own life. You had to be so grown up, and you did not get any feedback from your parents on how you were doing. You were very alone. Did I get that and is there more?

Natalie: Yes, you got it. I think that's why I worry so much about your weight and smoking. I really don't want to be left alone again to figure everything out. I need a partner with me.

David: You're saying you need a partner with you, and you don't want to be on your own again to figure things out. That's why you worry so much about my weight and smoking. Well, that makes so much sense to me. I can see why that is a concern for you. I imagine you do feel scared and worried about being left again to fend for yourself.

At this point, David has heard Natalie on a deeper, more emotional level and is receptive to her emotions and thoughts around this issue. Expanding a couple's level of emotional connection increases empathy levels and allows partners to respond to each other's needs (Johnson, 2004). In this instance, David is not in the defensive posture he was in the original conversation about his smoking and at this point may be open to change. Certainly, he may have a response, and he will get his chance to talk about this in dialogue, but at the moment he is focused on Natalie and what this means to her. In IRT, hearing and understanding the other comes first which makes a request for change feel less coercive and easier to enact. IRT utilizes a process called Behavior Change Request to make changes in the relationship (Hendrix, 1988).

Behavior Change Request

In IRT, frustrations are viewed as desires stated negatively. When he says he hates when she is late, what he desires is for her to be on time. When she says she hates going to visit his family, she is saying that she wishes things were different when they visit. The IRT therapist teaches couples to transform their frustrations into desires so they are more easily heard by the receiving partner. When frustrations are stated negatively, the reactive brain is activated and the receiver goes on the defensive.

To help in this process, couples are encouraged to make a list of their frustrations and are then coached to change them to desires. The desires are taken one step further by being transformed into a specific, measurable, doable **Behavior Change Request** (BCR) (Hendrix, 1988; Luquet, 2007). These requests are very specific, typically naming the behavior and time frame. Much like a mental health treatment plan, one partner writes what is needed from the other which typically is the area the other most needs to grow in to. For example: "You never listen to how I'm feeling about this issue!" becomes the desire "I need you to listen to how I feel" and is transformed into a specific, positive, and measureable BCR, "Twice this week, I would like you to sit down with me in the family room for fifteen minutes and dialogue about going to your family reunion. I would like to hear your thoughts fully, and I would like for you to understand how I feel about the visit by using the dialogue process." The important part of this request is to get the partner who is probably defending the family visits with logical statements to sit and listen to the emotions behind the concern or anxiety and understand the validity of those emotions for the partner making the request.

Interestingly, a request asking one partner to listen to the feelings of the other is usually given to the partner who most needs to develop their ability to experience emotion. Conversely, a request for a partner to think through an issue before reacting is usually presented to a typically emotional partner who needs to develop cognitive means to handle problems. For example, a request such as: "Once this week, I would like for you to sit and make a list of three ways we can work together to lessen the stress of Christmas visits for you and the family and we can discuss it using dialogue for twenty minutes" is usually made to the partner who is more emotional than cognitive and this request asks them to take a moment to think through the situation before reacting. A line often told to couples in IRT is: "Your partner has the blueprint for your growth." It is not that one partner has what the other needs and is just refusing to give it to them, but what one partner needs is what the other partner most needs to develop in their personality. Listening and responding to a partner's needs through a BCR becomes a growth process for those willing to stretch into new or little used behaviors.

For David and Natalie, a Behavior Change Request session might go like this.

Natalie: Thank you for hearing my concern about your smoking and weight gain. I really think it has to do with feeling I will be left alone and feel responsible. Can I make a Behavior Change Request about this?

David: Sure, I can hear you now if you'd like.

Natalie: I know asking someone to stop smoking or lose weight is not a fair request. It's what I would like, but I understand it is not as easy as just making a request.

David: So you understand that is a big request to ask me to just stop smoking or lose weight, even though it is something you would like to see happen. Did I get that?

Natalie: Yes, you did. So what I would like within two weeks, I would like for you to schedule an appointment with your doctor to have a complete physical and to just talk to him about ways to quit smoking.

David: So you would like for me to call my doctor within two weeks to schedule an appointment to get a physical and to talk to him about quitting smoking. You are not asking me to stop, just to get information. Did I get that?

Natalie: You did.

David: Is there more?

Natalie: Yes. For a second request, twice a week, I would like for you to come to me and say something like "I will be here for you. You are not alone and you are doing a good job."

David: So you would like for me to come to you twice a week and let you know that I will be there for you and that you are not alone. And you want to know that you are doing a good job. Did I get that?

Natalie: You got it. That would really help me a lot. It would help my wound of feeling alone and worrying that I was doing something wrong even though I was doing my best. When I found out you were having the affair and what you said to that woman about leaving me, I felt devastated. I tried to act tough, but I was really scared. I need to know that you will be there for me.

David: So you need to know that I will be there for you, and the affair really scared you making you feel that you would be alone again. It really devastated you. You really want to know that I will be there for you. That makes so much sense to me. I can see how that would have made you feel scared, worried, and angry. Working on these requests would help you feel less alone and worried. I would like for you to have that, and I will make an effort to work on these requests.

Natalie: Thanks for hearing that.

David: You're welcome.

If this were done in a therapy session, the therapist could assist the couple in creating a safe space for David to respond without taking away the importance of Natalie's request, or they could request that David hold his response for another day so Natalie can feel fully heard and understood. At that point, it might be easier for Natalie to hear David because he was responsive to her request. It is also likely that David's request may seem opposite of Natalie's, for example "Twice this week, I would like for you to give me thirty minutes to myself after I come home from work." This may help him with a wound of feeling smothered by his parents as a child.

Closing Exits

For David and Natalie to continue their relationship, they will have to do something IRT refers to as **closing exits** (Hendrix, 1988). When frustrations appear in relationships, couples will often begin to find ways to spend less time with each other in an effort to avoid conflictual emotions. This distancing can take place in commonly used exits, such as hobbies, spending time with friends, or overworking, or it can take place in more relationship destructive forms like substance abuse or straying outside the relationship. While each individual in the relationship deserves and should have time away from each other, there comes a point where it becomes distancing and possibly catastrophic, as in the case of Natalie and David with the affair and possible alcoholism. If the Johnsons hope to continue their relationship, these will be issues that have to be addressed early in the therapy. These serious issues cannot be ignored or addressed insufficiently lest the issues will make a return either by repeating the actions or simmering resentments. If the internet affair and other issues are addressed thoroughly in dialogue, the couple will be able to move past these issues and continue their relationship.

Eaker-Weil and Tuttle (1998) utilizes the Imago Couples Dialogue to work with couples that have had affairs. Through a procedure using the three-part dialogue process that allows the betrayed to ask questions and feel emotions about the betrayal, she finds the validation of the betrayed by the betrayer is the most important healing element (Eaker-Weil & Tuttle, 1998). The early work of healing from an affair is filled with "obsessing, dart throwing, and working through the rage" (Eaker-Weil & Tuttle, 1998, p. 243). The betrayed will ask a lot of questions, and there will be periods of time when the rage and obsession will seemingly show itself out of nowhere. The betrayer may be tempted to want to move on and quit discussing the matter, but it is best that the couple continue with the discussion until both feel fully heard and understood. Affairs are not so much about the need for sex, but, according to Eaker-Weil and Tuttle, "... a product of mutual emptiness in a relationship, and lack of intimacy is a core problem that the affair is masking" (p. 241). To prevent an affair from re-occuring, this emptiness must be discussed and intimacy and connection restored.

Imago therapist and sex counselor Tammy Nelson (2013) utilizes the Imago dialogue to help couples who have gotten past the rage to have conversations about the affair. She works with couples to make sure the dialogues are kind and compassionate toward both the betrayed and the betrayer. Couples can use the dialogue to discuss what happened in their relationship that interfered with their communication and decreased their appreciation for each other that led to the affair. The couple would also have a deep and frank dialogue about the status of their present sexual relationship including possible problems that led the partner to stray (Nelson, 2013). Nelson encourages couples to create a new relationship agreement about sexuality in their marriage since the original agreement made at the beginning of their relationship has been broken and needs to be renegotiated understanding the needs of both partners and given the present culture. With the proliferation of pornography, internet chat rooms, online dating services, strip clubs, and other arenas that may pull partners out of their original marital agreement, the couple is encouraged to look at what would be acceptable in a new agreement to prevent misunderstandings later; if an issue comes up, it should all be in the agreement. This new agreement needs to be adhered to, looked at periodically, and renegotiated as needed. The important part is that this sexual relationship discussion is done openly and in dialogue (Nelson, 2013).

Bruce Wood (1998) uses dialogue in conjunction with the twelve-step program. Comparing the dialogue process to the acceptance and validation of a good twelve-step program, the addicted person is able to talk about the problem with substances in a safe and accepting setting with their partner. Couples are guided to listen without judgment and validate the difficulty the partner may be having that requires self-medicating, as well as how difficult it would be to give up their substance of choice. This listening helps couples to hear the underlying issues of the addiction and avoids the confrontation of the addicted person that has sometimes been used in treatment settings with little effect in the recovery process (Wood, 1998).

The Johnsons will have to take a long look at both the affair and the possible alcohol problem to progress in their relationship. If David is having a problem with alcohol, he will need to make a commitment to decrease his intake, go to a twelve-step program, or if severe, go to an alcohol program. It is near impossible to deal with marital problems when one or both members of the couple are alcoholics. If it is determined that David's drinking is more of a social type, then it would be good to explore Natalie's concern to determine if it has its origin with one of her caretakers. Certainly individuals whose young lives have been impacted by alcohol or drugs may have a sensitivity toward drinking and drug use, and David will have to become aware of Natalie's sensitivity to alcohol use if that is the case. The Johnsons will also have to address the internet affair and negotiate a new relationship contract. David was already meeting women on the internet prior to their relationship. Now that they are married, is any type of internet contact with other women acceptable? Is it ok to go to a strip club instead of a sports bar with his friends when they are out? What constitutes an infidelity for both Natalie and David? What behaviors are acceptable or unacceptable in regards to relationships with others? In their new contract, there should be no surprises.

David and Natalie will also have to look at other exits that may be draining energy from their relationship. Does Natalie's real estate job have her out of the house several nights a week and on the weekends when David is home? Is there a way she can consolidate her time so they are together more often? Is David out with his friends so often that it interferes with time he could be spending with Natalie? The couple needs to look at all of the activities and obligations that keep them apart and decide what is necessary and what can be altered so they can spend more time together creating the relationship intimacy they need.

Increasing Caring Behaviors and Decreasing Negativity

As the exits are being closed, the couple interaction may become more intense. After all, the exits were created as a way to avoid issues in the relationship. When issues emerge, couples are encouraged to use dialogue to work through them and understand that things may get worse before they get better. While these issues are being brought forth and dealt with, they need to be replaced by behaviors of happy and stable couples. In IRT, we do this by increasing caring behaviors and decreasing negative interactions (Gottman, 2002; *Clinical instructors manual*, 2015). From the first session in IRT, couples are encouraged to increase behaviors pleasurable to both and to become intentional with their words to reduce negativity in the relationship. Caring behaviors increase pleasure which in turn increases the feeling of safety and connection. Negative interactions have the opposite effect and cause the brain to go into a protective mode where distrust and disconnection are prominent in the relationship. Increasing the positive while decreasing the negative can foster neurological changes that increase trust and allow couples to connect on a deeper, more intimate level (Siegel, 2012). Rather than couples approaching each other in a defensive posture waiting for a negative comment, couples can learn to create safety, curiosity, and pleasure by practicing some intentional behaviors.

Research from John Gottman (Buehlman, Gottman, & Katz, 1992) revealed that happy and stable couples have a five-to-one caring behavior ratio in their daily interactions. In other words, happy and stable couples flood each other with caring and kindness. They speak pleasantly with each other. They say "please" and "thank you" and are appreciative of each other. Couples in IRT are taught that if they want to be a happy and stable couple, they need to start acting like one (Clinical Training Manual, 2015). IRT therapists have couples make a list of pleasurable behaviors that their partner can do for them that would be caring such as making dinner reservations, going to a movie they both want to see, or a walk in the park. They are also coached to be kind to each other in their interactions—to say please and thank you, and to tell each other nice things. This kindness begins to change the temperature of the relationship as the couple, even if they are faking it at first, begins to see the good in the relationship and in each other.

When couples have fun and decrease negativity, they are working against an evolutionary process known as the **negativity bias** (Baumeister, Bratslavsky, Finkenauer, & Vohs, 2001). The negativity bias evolved as a way to keep humans from rushing into situations that might be dangerous. Those early humans who rushed in to pet the lion may have been eaten; thus by natural selection, we are left with a brain that judges negatively before positively in most situations (Ito & Cacioppo, 2005; Ito, Larsen, Smith, Kyle, & Cacioppo, 1998). The negativity bias can only be overridden by positive offsets—positive experiences that convince the brain that the situation is safe. As couples learn to communicate with dialogue to work through the negative issues, they must simultaneously learn to experience fun in their relationship. Fun creates pleasure and pleasure is interpreted as safety by the always protective brain.

Distressed couples cease to have fun or have joyous experiences as they did at the beginning of their relationship. Of course, it was easy in the beginning because of the dopamine rush they were experiencing and the newness of the relationship. If couples want to experience a little of that rush, they need to do things that both find fun and exciting like watching a comedian they both like, climbing a mountain with a great view, watching children play, or going to hear music they both like. If they are able to have a sustained belly laugh with each other, that is even better since a belly laugh also releases chemicals that produce a euphoric feeling similar to romantic love.

Recently, some IRT therapist have begun to ask couples to make a **zero negativity contract** with each other (Hendrix, H., personal communication, October, 2013). In other words, couples will eliminate all negativity in the relationship. While an interesting idea, a danger exists in that it can be construed as meaning never to ask for change and to always be positive. In previous studies, this has not always turned out well, especially for women (Baucom et al., 2006; Shilling et al., 2003). It seems that in couples that were asked to cease all negativity, women's relationship satisfaction went down while men's improved according to the two studies. This may be because zero negativity may be confused with no request for change. According to IRT co-founder Helen Hunt, what zero negativity should mean is talking in such a way that does not "cause an ouch!" (Hunt, H., personal communication, October, 2013). In other words, saying "You never take out the garbage!' causes a pain and is negative. Rewording the request to "I am feeling upset that the garbage is in the kitchen" makes the point, but with less negativity attached. IRT therapists work with couples on how to choose their words so they do not activate defensive postures. Lessening negativity means being intentional in word choices and eliminating sarcasm, slights, eye rolls, and bringing up past actions to prove a point.

Termination

IRT tends to be a short-term model of couples therapy, lasting about twelve to twenty sessions (*Clinical instructors manual*, 2015). This is typically an adequate amount of time for moderately distressed couples to learn about and experience Imago Relationship Therapy and be able to practice it on their own with only occasional contact with the therapist as needed for follow-up. Of course, more distressed couples or couples who want to have a therapist available for their work will stay longer. Sometimes sessions can be spaced out over longer periods of time for financial reasons or so the couple can become independent of the counseling process.

The goal of the therapy, aside from relieving marital distress and increasing relationship satisfaction, is for couples to learn a new way to think about relationships. The IRT therapy process will teach the couple that their relationship has a purpose that may have its roots in their childhood, teach them the basic couples skill of dialogue, and how to use it in various situations. Couples will learn how to bring fun and positivity back into the relationship and use the sessions to develop a deeper understanding and emotional connection with each other as well as root out resentments that are causing them to be defensive and disconnected. They will participate in activities together that are fun and create a new vision for their lives together. Most importantly for termination purposes, they will be able to utilize the skills they have learned in session at home on their own. Couples will know that they can return to the therapy at any time, but they can also use the tools presented and practiced in the sessions at home to bring the relationship back to a connected and calm state.

Imago Relationship Therapy may not be for everyone. Those looking only to fix a problem may lose patience with the dialogue process; the therapy process of understanding what is behind the issue may be frustrating and too slow for them. Those looking to prove a partner wrong and be right may not find this method satisfying since validation supports both sides of an argument. But for those looking for a new way to think about relationships and learn skills for empathy, caring, and understanding their behaviors and how their past impacts their present relationship, Imago Relationship Therapy offers an opportunity to learn about themselves and their partner. IRT does more than save marriages—it expands them.

Case Transcript of the First Session

Natalie and David Johnson bring multiple issues into the therapy room. What will be most important for this first session is making a connection with them and to start the process of teaching couples dialogue. IRT is a psychoeducational therapy process that will give them the tools and experience they need to work on present concerns and future situations as they emerge.

Therapist: It's nice to meet you both. Did you have any trouble finding the place?

Natalie: No problem. We live pretty close, so we knew where we were going.

David: We did not know where to park, so we are out front. I hope that is ok.

Therapist: That's fine. No problem at all. So tell me how you two met?

Researchers found they could predict with 94% accuracy if a couple would stay together or divorce if they told their "how we met" story fondly and with details (Buehlman, Gottman, & Katz, 1992). This question is diagnostic in nature and the answer tells a lot about how difficult the case will be.

Natalie: Unfortunately, we met online. We communicated for a few months before we actually saw each other. I should have known better, but I took a chance, and we met at my house in Texas. It was a little awkward when we first actually met, and I felt obligated to sleep with him since he came so far to see me. Sometimes I regret the whole thing.

David: Well it was much harder on me. I was the one who did most of the traveling. After a while, it was just easier to move to Texas than to commute.

Based on this description of how they met, it can be assumed that this will be a difficult case. When couples are doing poorly, they tend to rewrite their history toward the negative. It is a good idea to reframe the story toward the positive as hopefully the story will change as the couple finds more relationship satisfaction. In the end, you want them to leave with a better story.

Therapist: Wow, so you are one of the growing number of couples who met online! Isn't that amazing how people can do that nowadays! So many couples are meeting that way. And David, you went to great pains and expense to be with Natalie. Do you all remember that time? What made that time happy for you both?

David: It was new and exciting. I found her attractive. We did a lot of fun things. The sex was great, and we just seemed to care for each other back then. It's much different now.

Natalie: Yeah, things really changed. We did have fun back then and it all seemed like the right thing to do. It was exciting and new. But I guess the newness wore off. I don't know if we will ever get that back again.

Therapist: Well, you are probably right about that part. When couples are newly in love, there is a drug reaction that happens in our brain that makes it seem so exciting. Did you know that?

Natalie: No.

Therapist: Sure, there is a chemical mix of dopamine, norepinephrine, and phenylethylamine that is released when we are in the presence of our new partner. It's a pretty heavy-duty reaction that makes us feel vital and alive. But like most drugs, our bodies get used to it and the reaction to the drug lessens leaving most couples wondering "What happened?"

David: That makes sense because I am wondering what happened!

Therapist: Well, lots of things have happened since you met. But the one thing you need to know is things won't be like that again. It can, however, be different and maybe even better. I would like to teach you a few things about relationships and show you some skills that you can use to make things much better than they are now if you learn to use them in your relationship. Does that sound ok to you?

It is good to be realistic with couples in these situations. Only very rarely do you find couples who live in the blissful state of new romance through the relationship. Most couples are left wondering what changed. It is also important to give them hope of something better, but not the same. One of the most important ways of determining outcomes in a therapy situation is if the client feels hope and trusts the therapist to help them. The first session should be spent building trust, hope, and leaving the couple with some usable skills they can practice during the week (Norcross, 2009).

Natalie: Yes, we need something better than we have now. That would work for us.

Therapist: Great. Let's see if we can do that. First, I'd like to see how you usually do things. Can I get the two of you to talk to each other about what brings you both here today?

This is done so the therapist can get an idea of how the couple interacts with each other in as naturalistic a setting as possible. This also becomes a segment of communication that can be referred back to when talking about the brain's defenses and maximizing and minimizing. It gives the therapist an idea of what the communication problem is between the couple, as well as a point of reference to illustrate the psychoeducational aspects of IRT. Typically, these interactions should go on for no longer than three minutes.

Natalie: You want us to talk to each other. Not you.

Therapist: That's right. I'll jump in after a few minutes.

Natalie: You better because this could get ugly. David, I can't believe you were talking with that Devyn woman on the internet. That really pisses me off knowing you were doing that in the basement, and naked at that!

David: Oh are we going to start with that?! I thought we talked about that, and I told you I would not do it again. Can't you get past it?

Natalie: I'm really hurt and angry about that! I can't just get past it. You told her you were going to leave me and marry her!

David: I was just messing with her. I wasn't going to leave you. You took that too seriously.

Natalie: *(angrily)* How the hell was I supposed to take it? You said you would leave me! Leave me!

David: You weren't supposed to see that.

Natalie: You…

Therapist: OK, let me stop you there for a minute. Take a breath. Is this how your arguments go at home?

Natalie: Yes, but sometimes louder.

David: She is always on me about things.

Therapist: OK, so let me talk to you both a little bit about what could be going on here when you talk to each other like this. First of all, I can see why you are both upset, and rightfully so. Natalie, I can imagine you are really angry and hurt about what was going on with David and the woman he was talking to. You must have felt very deceived by this.

Natalie: Oh I did!

Therapist: And David, I can see how you think this issue should be done and over and you are tired of talking about it. And I guess if it keeps coming up, it's not fully done yet, yes?

David: Seems that way.

Therapist: OK, so let's talk about what's happening and then give you something better to work with so you both feel fully heard.

The short interaction between the couple shows that this is not only a live issue, but the couple is not hearing each other fully. This interaction would just escalate with no connection or resolution. At this point, the IRT therapist would talk to the couple about the defenses used by the brain to protect them and look at how those defenses were actually used in that interaction and other heated frustrations and arguments. When animals from reptiles on up feel endangered, they will use various modes of fight, flight, playing dead, hiding or submitting. To anchor this idea, the therapist will ask them if they can remember times where they did fight, leave a room, freeze, stay at work, or just give in to stop an argument. Most will recognize that they have done all of these things at one time or another. The therapist reminds them that because these defenses are hard-wired in the brain, they have no choice but to use these defensive postures. They need a different way to hear so they can hear each other without these defenses. The therapist will talk to the couple about creating a safe space for their dialogues by teaching them simple visualization, centering, and breathing techniques.

It was also important for the therapist to validate both of them so they understand the therapist will not be taking sides. It is easy to feel for Natalie and take her side against David because of the internet affair, but it would not be useful for their therapy as David would feel ganged up on. Also, the therapist using the dialogue process with the couple lets them know that the process is important and gives them an example of its effectiveness. The session resumes after the therapist talks to them about ways to calm their reactive brain.

Therapist: I'm going to take you through the three-part process of couples dialogue. We are going to start with mirroring, and David, you are basically going to say back to Natalie what she says to you from your place of safety. You will say something like, "If I got that...." or "If I heard you right, you said..." OK?

David: I'll give it a try.

Therapist: Natalie, can you ask David if he can hear what you have to say now? This gives him a chance to get himself safe.

Natalie: David, I'd like to talk to you about what happened. Can you hear me now?

David: Give me a second to get ready. *(David closes his eyes and takes a deep breath. He visions himself sitting in a boat on his favorite lake and fishing. He knows to come back to the boat if something Natalie says triggers him to respond. David is faced toward Natalie. He opens his eyes and looks into hers for one minute.)* OK, I can hear you now.

Natalie: I was so upset and shocked when I found those texts between you and this Devyn woman. I know things were bad between us, but I never thought you would stoop to this.

Therapist: David, can you mirror that?

David: If I got that, you were very upset when you saw the text between Devyn and myself. You knew things were bad between us, but you never thought I would stoop that low.

Therapist: OK, now ask her "Did I get that?"

David: Did I get that?

Natalie: You did.

Therapist: Now ask her "Is there more about that?"

It is important that the sender is heard correctly and how they want to be heard. Many times the receiver will mirror back incorrectly or the way they wanted something to be said. The therapist is there to facilitate that process. If David does not get it right, the therapist would have Natalie say it again and have David check his level of safety so he can hear Natalie, and not his own desires for the conversation. Also, the "Is there more?" question invites more from the sender who in a non-dialogical conversation probably would have been cut off by receiver who would be trying to defend themselves.

David: Is there more about that?

Natalie: Yes, I was really crushed by this. And I think you made it worse by blowing it off as nothing. It really is something. My whole life could be changed by this and I really need you to see that.

Therapist: Can you mirror that, David?

David: So you were really crushed by this. And what made it worse is that I said it was no big deal and for you it is not only a big deal, but your whole life may change because of this. Did I get that?

Natalie: *(crying)* Yes, you got it.

David: Is there more?

Natalie: I need you to see how tough this is for me. I'm not sure about our future and what is going to happen to us.

David: We'll be O…

Therapist: *(stops David)* Ah Ah… David you need to hear Natalie first. You'll have your chance later. Right now, this is about her concerns. Go back to your safe place and mirror that again.

The IRT therapist cuts off attempts to defend an action or make light of a situation until the sender is fully heard. Natalie needs to talk about the deep hurt this has caused her and David needs to learn how to listen deeply. Repairs will come later when they both feel fully understood.

David: *(takes a breath)* So if I am hearing you correctly, you need for me to see how tough this is for you, and you are not sure what is going to happen to us. Did I get that?

Natalie: You did.

Therapist: David, I want to teach you the second part of dialogue called validation. Validation is not agreeing. It is saying that if you were sitting in Natalie's seat looking at the world through her eyes, you could see how this makes sense to her. Can you see that? Does she make sense to you? And respond to her.

The therapist requests the response be made to Natalie so the therapist does not become the center of the dialogue.

David: (*thinking for a second*) Yes, I can see that. That makes sense to me.

Therapist: So she makes sense. David can you say to her "What makes sense about that to me is…" and let her know what makes sense?

David: What makes sense about that to me is that we aren't doing well, and I can see how my communication with Devyn would make that worse for you. You were not thinking this was going on, and I can see how you would wonder about our future now that you know I did this. Yes, it makes sense to me that you would be so upset.

Therapist: David, the third part of the process is empathy. Put yourself in her shoes for a minute and take a guess at how Natalie might be feeling right now about this? Say something like "I can imagine this might make you feel…"

David: I can imagine this might make you feel deceived, scared, and angry.

Therapist: Ask her "Did I get that?"

David: Did I get that?

Natalie: You did.

Therapist: So he got it. That's good. Let's stop for a second and think about this. What was different about what just happened for the two of you? We're not done yet, but let's take a look at what was different about that short, but important, interaction.

It is good to have both an experiential and cognitive experience with a new behavior. Most of the IRT therapy will be experiential in nature with the couple having many discussions in dialogue, but it helps for them to think about what was different.

Natalie: Well, he heard me. It felt like for a second he could see how this upset me and how his actions made me look differently at our relationship.

David: It was hard. I wanted to say something, but you would not let me. Do people really talk like this?

Therapist: You're right, it is hard. And it does not seem natural at first. People do learn how to talk like this in conflictual situations, but it takes practice. I could see it was hard and you were wanting to respond. And what did you notice when you let Natalie talk?

David: Well, I noticed that I could hear her, and I felt for her.

Therapist: That's right. Were there any fight or flight responses?

David: Part of me wanted to, but I kept thinking about that safe place and breathing.

Therapist: Good. That is something you have to work at for a while, but it will get easier. Natalie, David gave you three feelings he thought you might be feeling. Can we return to the dialogue, and can you talk about one of those feelings?

Natalie: Yes, I'd like to do that.

Therapist: David, can you get yourself safe again.

David: I'm there.

Natalie: David, I'm feeling scared about us. I don't know about our future....

Natalie continued to talk about how scared she was about the future of the relationship. David, with coaching from the therapist, was able to listen to her in dialogue. At the end, she looked visibly relieved that he heard her, and he seemed to understand her angst about this situation. They reversed the process for a few minutes and rather than David defending his actions, he talked instead about how he had not realized how much this hurt her, and he talked to her about how he was not happy in the marriage either, and how he hoped they could work on things. Natalie was able to hear David in dialogue.

The IRT therapist gives Natalie and David homework to practice the dialogue for a half an hour three times per week, as a way of learning the process. They were given written material with the dialogue explained. They were also asked to say one nice thing to the other at least one time a day and do something that is mutually fun together twice before the next session. It is important that homework is given and checked each session so the couple knows that the real work takes place day-to-day at home and not only under the guidance of the therapist.

References

Anthony, J. I., Dawson, A., Begany, K. L., Leckie, R. L., Barry, K. P., Ciccia, A. H., & Snyder, A. Z. (2013). fMRI reveals reciprocal inhibition between social and physical cognitive domains. *NeuroImage, 66*, 385–401.

Aram, D., & Shlak, M. (2008). The safe kindergarten: Promotion of communication and social skills among kindergartners. *Early Education & Development, 19*(6), 865–884. doi:10.1080/10409280802516090

Bain, H. (1998). Imago therapy with Hispanic couples. In W. Luquet & M. T. Hannah (Eds.), *Healing in the relational paradigm: The Imago relationship therapy casebook* (pp. 113–124). New York, NY: Routledge.

Baucom, D. H., Hahlweg, K., Atkins, D. C., Joachim, E., & Thurmaier, F. (2006). Long-term prediction of marital quality following a relationship education program: Being positive in a constructive way. *Journal of Family Psychology, 20*(3), 448–455.

Baumeister, R. F., Bratslavsky, E., Finkenauer, C., & Vohs, K. D. (2001). Bad is stronger than good. *Review of General Psychology, 5*(4), 323–370.

Brainert, G., & Luquet, W. (1998). The rigid/diffuse couple. In W. Luquet & M. T. Hannah (Eds.), *Healing in the relational paradigm: The Imago relationship therapy casebook* (pp. 55–76). New York, NY: Routledge.

Buehlman, K. T., Gottman, J. M., & Katz, L. F. (1992). How a couple views their past predicts their future: Predicting divorce from an oral history interview. *Journal of Family Psychology, 5*(3), 295–318.

Carr, L., Iacoboni, M., Dubeau, M.-C., Maziotta, K. C., & Lenzi, G. I. (2003). Neural mechanisms of empathy in humans: A relay from neural systems from imitation to limbic areas. *Proceedings of the National Academy of Sciences, 100*(9), 5497–5502.

Clinical instructor's manual for Imago Relationship Therapy. (2015). Lexington, KY: Imago Relationships International.

Eaker-Weil, B., & Tuttle, L. K. (1998). Validation as a facilitator of forgiveness for adultery. In W. Luquet & M. T. Hannah (Eds.), *Healing in the relational paradigm: The imago relationship therapy casebook* (pp. 241–250). New York, NY: Routledge.

Erikson, E. H. (1950). *Childhood and society*. New York, NY: Norton.

Etemadi, O., Navabinejad, S., Ahmadi, S. A, & Farzad, V. (2006). The effect of couples therapy by method of Imago therapy in increasing marital intimacy referred to counseling center in the Isfahan city. *News and Research Counseling, 5*(19), 9–22.

Fein, J. M. (1998). Couples wounded at the attachment phase. In W. Luquet & M. T. Hannah (Eds.), *Healing in the relational paradigm: The Imago relationship therapy casebook* (pp. 19–36). New York, NY: Routledge.

Fisher, H., Aron, A., & Brown, L. L. (2005). Romantic love: An fMRI study of a neural mechanism for mate choice. *The Journal of Comparative Neurology, 493*(1), 58–62. doi:10.1002/cne.20772

Fisher, H. E., Aron, A., & Brown, L. L. (2006). Romantic love: A mammalian brain system for mate choice. *Philosophical Transactions of the Royal Society B: Biological Sciences, 361*(1476), 2173–2186. doi:10.1098/rstb.2006.1938

Gehlert, N., Schmidt, C., Geigerich, V., & Luquet, W. (submitted). Randomized controlled trial of Imago Relationship Therapy: Exploring statistical and clinical significance. Submitted to *The Journal of Marital and Family Therapy.*

Goldstein, M. A., Kilroy, M. C., & Van de Voort, D. (1976). Gaze as a function of conversation and degree of love. *The Journal of Psychology, 92*, 227–234.

Goleman, D. (2012). *Emotional intelligence* (2nd ed.). New York, NY: Random House.

Gottman, J. (2002). *The seven principles of making marriage work*. New York, NY: Random House.

Gottman, J. M. (2011). *The science of trust: Emotional attunement for couples*. New York, NY: W. W. Norton.

Hannah, M. (1998). Therapist heal thyself: A passive/competitive couple. In W. Luquet & M. T. Hannah (Eds.), *Healing in the relational paradigm: The Imago relationship therapy casebook* (pp. 77–98). New York, NY: Routledge.

Hendrix, H. (1988). *Getting the love you want: A guide for couples.* New York, NY: Holt.
Hendrix, H. (1993). *Keeping the love you find: A personal guide.* New York, NY: Simon & Schuster.
Hendrix, H. (2005). The evolution of Imago Relationship Therapy. In H. Hendrix, H. Hunt, M. T. Hannah, & W. Luquet (Eds.), *Imago relationship therapy: Perspectives on theory* (pp. 13–34). San Francisco, CA: Jossey-Bass.
Hendrix, H., & Hunt, H. (1998). *Giving the love that heals.* New York, NY: Simon & Schuster.
Hendrix, H., Hunt, H., Hannah, M.T., & Luquet, W. (Eds.) (2005). *Imago relationship therapy: Perspectives on theory.* San Francisco, CA: Jossey-Bass.
Hendrix, H., Hunt, H., Luquet, W., & Carson, J. (2015). Using the Imago dialogue to deepen couples therapy. *Journal of Individual Psychology, 17*(3), 253–272.
Hess, E. K. (1965). The role of pupil size in communication. *Scientific American, 233,* 110–119.
Ito, T. A., & Cacioppo, J. T. (2005). Variations on a human universal: Individual differences in positivity offset and negativity bias. *Cognition and Emotion, 19*(1), 1–26.
Ito, T. S., Larsen, J. T., Smith, N. Kyle, & Cacioppo, J. T. (1998). Negative information weighs more heavily on the brain: The Negativity Bias in evaluative categorization. *Journal of Personality and Social Psychology, 75*(4), 887–900.
Johnson, S. (2004). *The practice of Emotionally Focused Couple Therapy: Creating connection.* New York, NY: Routledge.
Kleinberg, S., & Zorn, P. (1998). Multiple mirroring with gay and lesbian couples: From Peoria to P-town. In W. Luquet & M. T. Hannah (Eds.), *Healing in the relational paradigm: The Imago relationship therapy casebook* (pp. 135–150). New York, NY: Routledge.
Luquet, W. (1996). To what end: Couples therapy. *Journal of Couples Therapy, 6*(1–2), 13–30.
Luquet, W. (2007). *Short-term couples therapy: The Imago model in action* (2nd ed.). New York, NY: Routledge.
Luquet, W., & Chadwick, B. (1998). The exploratory wounded couple. In W. Luquet & M. T. Hannah (Eds.), *Healing in the relational paradigm: The Imago relationship therapy casebook* (pp. 37–54). New York, NY: Routledge.
Luquet, W., & Hannah, M. T. (1998). *Healing in the relational paradigm: The Imago relationship therapy casebook.* New York, NY: Brunner/Routledge.
Markman, H. J., Stanley, S. M., & Blumberg, S. L. (2010). *Fighting for your marriage* (3rd ed.). New York, NY: Jossey-Bass.
Mason, R. C., Mason, M., & Hannah, M. T. (2005). The relationship nightmare as an expression of disconnection. In H. Hendrix, H. Hunt, M.T. Hannah, & W. Luquet (Eds.), *Imago relationship therapy: Perspectives on theory* (pp. 193–200). San Francisco, CA: Jossey-Bass.
Muro, L., & Holliman, R. (2014). Relationship workshop with high-risk, Hispanic couples. *North Carolina Perspectives, 9,* 51–62.
Muro, L., Holliman, R., & Luquet, W. (2016a). Imago Relationship Therapy and accurate empathy development. *Journal of Couple and Relationship Therapy, 15*(3), 232–246.
Muro, L., Holliman, R., & Luquet, W. (2016b). The impact of the Safe Conversations workshop with diverse, low income couples. *The American Journal of Family Therapy, 44*(3), 155–167.
Nelson, T. (2013). *The new monogamy: Redefining your relationship after infidelity.* Oakland, CA: New Harbinger.
Norcross, J. (2009). The therapeutic relationship. In B. Duncan, S. Miller, B. Wampold, & M. Hubble (Eds.), *The heart and soul of change* (2nd ed., pp. 113–142). Washington, DC: American Psychological Association Press.

Oh, J. (2010). Psychosocial development in South Korean couples and its effects on marital relationships. *Journal of Human Understanding and Counseling, 31*(1), 47–63.
Reiter, M. D. (2013). *Case conceptualizations in family therapy*. New York, NY: Pearson.
Schmidt, C., Luquet, W., & Gehlert, N. (2016). Evaluating the impact of the Getting the Love You Want Couples workshop on relational satisfaction and communication patterns. *Journal of Couple and Relationship Therapy, 15*(1), 1–18. doi: 10.1080/15332691
Schore, A. (1994). *Affect regulation and the origin of the self: The neurobiology of emotional development*. Hillsdale, NJ: Erlbaum.
Seehausen, M., Kazzer, P., Bajbouja, M., Heekeren, H. R., Jacobs, A. M., Klan-Deliusae, G., Mennignhausa, W., & Prehn, K. (2014). Talking about social conflict in the MRI scanner: Neural correlates of being empathized with. *Neuroimage, 84*, 951–961.
Shilling, E. A., Baucom, D. H., Burnett, C. K., Sandlin Allen, E., & Ragland, L. (2003). Altering the course of marriage: The effect of PREP communication skills acquisition on couples' risk of becoming maritally distressed. *Journal of Family Psychology, 17*(1), 41–53.
Siegel, D. (1999). *The developing mind: Toward a neurobiology of interpersonal experience*. New York, NY: Guilford.
Siegel, D. J. (2012). *Pocket guide to interpersonal neurobiology: An integrative handbook of the mind*. New York, NY: W. W. Norton & Company.
Solomon, M. (1998). The narcissistically vulnerable couple. *Journal of Imago Relationship Therapy, 3*(1), 11–34.
Sperry, L. (2005). Case conceptualizations: The missing link between theory and practice. *The Family Journal, 13*(1), 71–76.
Sperry, L. (2010). *Core competencies in counseling and psychotherapy: Becoming a highly competent and effective therapist*. New York, NY: Routledge.
Tarlaci, S. (2012). The brain in love. Has neuroscience stolen the secret of love? *NeuroQuantology, 10*(4), 744–753.
Weiser, C., & Thomson, H. (1998). Is Imago therapy culturally relevant? Case studies with African-American couples. In W. Luquet & M. T. Hannah (Eds.), *Healing in the relational paradigm: The Imago relationship therapy casebook* (pp. 99–112). New York, NY: Routledge.
Wood, B. A. (1998). Addiction, couples and recovery. In W. Luquet & M. T. Hannah (Eds.), *Healing in the relational paradigm: The Imago relationship therapy casebook* (pp. 213–228). New York, NY: Routledge.

INDEX

acceptance 94, 96, 104, 108
Adler, A. 51, 54–5, 57–8, 66
admiration 116, 120, 123, 128, 140
Anthony, J. I. 159
Aramburu, I. 16
Aron, A. 19, 150
Aron, E. N. 19
assertion 47, 88, 103
assessments 62, 64, 67, 91–3, 97, 99, 100, 103, 105, 108, 120, 125–6, 133, 143, 154
attach 130–1
attachment 20, 22
attachment stage 154
attachment theory 20, 88, 148
atone 129
attune 129–31, 159
Aznar-Martinez, B. 16
Azrin, N. 91

Babcock, B. 115
Bain, H. 149
Bandura, A. 87–8, 93
Bank, S. 114
Barfield, G. S. 91
basic I.D. 89
basic mistakes 56
Baucom, D. 91–3, 108, 167
Beck, A. T. 89, 93
behavior change request 161–3
behavioral activation 88, 94, 108
Benjamin, J. 20
Berger, M. N. 78
Bergmann, M. S. 20
Bernhardt, E. 2
Bertoni, A. 2–3
Bettner, B. L. 56–7, 59
bid 120
birth order 56–7
Bitter, J. R. 51, 58
Blagen, M 56, 66
Blumberg, S. L. 153
Bodenmann, G. 2–3
Boisvert, M. –M. 3
Bottome, P. 51
Bowlby, J. 20, 88
Bowling T. F. 52
Bradbury, T. N. 91–2
brief self-change 93, 96, 99
Brink, R. B. 2
Brody, P. R. 32
Brok, A. ix, 15–17, 19–20, 22–4, 30–2
Brown, L. L. 57, 150
Browning, D. 52
Buehlman, K. T. 166, 169
building commitment and loyalty 124
Burbach, F. 6
Burnett, J. A. 6
Burns, D. 89
Bussod, N. 92
Butler, A. C. 92
Byczek, S. 62

Carlson, J. ix, 5, 52–4, 56–7, 59–63, 65, 70–4, 76, 78, 81–2, 160
Carns, M. R. 58, 63
Carr, L. 159

Carrere, S. 120
case transcript, 9–12, 33, 35–41, 68–70, 75, 80–1, 100–6, 132–46, 160–3, 168–74
catching oneself 71–2
Chadwick, B. 155–6
Chambers, A. L. 97
Chasseguet-Smirgel, J. 19
Chenail, R. J viii, xi-xii, 1, 7
Christensen, A. 3, 53, 96
clarification 88
Clark, A. 57
clinger-avoider couple 154
closing exits 164
cognitive distortions 88–9, 94, 100
cognitive map 17, 42
competitive/passive couple 156–7
commitment 60, 63, 96, 104, 107–8, 122–4, 126–9
concern stage 156–7
Cone, J. D. 31
conflict management 116, 127–8, 131, 143
conjoint therapy 1
contempt 73, 83, 117, 126–7, 144
Conway, E. 63
Copen, C. E. 2
Corsini, R. J. 59
couples conference 79
couples dialogue 158–9, 164, 168
creating shared meaning 120–2, 126–8, 131
criticism 73–4, 83, 117, 127, 141
crucial C's 59
Csikszentmihalyi, M. 100
current couple 23–7

daily dialogue 70–1, 79
Daniels, K. 2
Datillio, F. 93
Davins, M. 16
DeClaire, J. 127
deeper dialogues 160
defensiveness 73, 83, 105, 117, 126–7, 144
Del Rio, C. M. 2, 5
DiClemete, C. C. 67
Diffuse Physiological Arousal 118
Dinkmeyer, D. 53, 59–62, 65, 70, 72–4, 76–8, 81–2
DiPietro, R. 57
disasters of marriage 114, 119
discovering 17, 22, 39, 46
distance and isolation cascade 122, 134
Dobson, K. S. 92
Doherty, W. J. 52, 67
Doss, B. D. 3
dream sharing 19, 29–30
dreams within conflict technique 127
Dreikurs, R. 53, 57, 65–6
Driver, J. 120, 125
Duba Sauerheber, J. 58
Duffy, T. H. 58, 63

Eaker-Weil, B.164
early divorcers 122, 131
early recollections, 57
Ekman, P. 115
Ellenberger, H. F. 16
Ellis, A. 89, 91, 99
empathic bridge 35
encouragement 61, 68–70, 76, 84
encouragement meeting 70
encouraging days exercise 70
England, J. T. 53
Englar-Carlson, M. 53, 61, 70–1, 82
Epstein, N. 91–3, 108
equality 52–6, 59
Erikson, E. 156
evenly hovering involvement 30
exploration stage 155
exposure 88

family of origin 2, 12–14, 55, 67, 69, 97
Fein, J. M. 154
field relevant behavior 31, 47
Figenbaum, N. 52
Fincham, F. D. 91–2
finding 17
first session 29, 32–3, 68–70, 100, 125–6, 168–74
Fisher, H. E. 150
fondness 120, 123, 128, 140
four horsemen of the apocalypse 117–18, 127, 135–6, 141, 144
Fraenkel, P. 5
Freud, S. 15, 19
Friendship 120, 127–8
functional assessment of behavior 93
fuser-isolator couple 155

Gallagher, M. 52
Garcia, L.J. 58, 63
games of probabilities 67
Gedo, J. 30–1
Gehlert, N. 149
genetic history 24, 27, 42
genogram 14
Giordano, J. 92
Goldberg, M. 3
Goldklank, S. 34

Goldstein, M. A. 159
Goleman, D. 159
Gotlib, I. 91–2
Gottman, J. 6, 71, 73–4, 77, 91, 95, 97, 113–30, 132, 159, 166, 169
gridlocked perpetual problems 116–17, 141
Griffith, J. 56
Guevremont, D. C. 88
guided discovery, 89
Gurman A. S. 5–6

Halford, W. K. 90, 93–4, 96, 99
Hannah, M. T. 148–9, 153, 156
Hawkins, M. 120
Hawley, D. W. 53
Hawes, E. C. 65, 67, 79
Hayes, S. C. 95
Helms, K. M. 72
Hendrix, H. 74, 148–51, 154, 157, 160–2, 164, 167
Henry, R. G. 3
Hess, E. K. 159
hidden reason 81
Hill, C. M. 53
historical couple 23–5
history of the couple 9–14, 24–8, 64–5, 153–4
history of the model: Psychodynamic Couples Counseling 15–20; Alderian Couples Counseling 51–3; Cognitive Behavioral 87–91; Gottman Method 113–16; Imago Relationship Therapy 148–9
Hoffman, E. 51
holism 57
Holliman, R. 149
horizontal communication 64–5, 73
horizontal movement 55
Hoyt, M. F. 6
Hunt, H. 74, 148–9, 160, 167

I messages 74
identity stage 155
imago 149–50
the imago workup 151–2
infidelity 72, 128–32, 137, 164–5
intimacy 20, 25, 104, 107, 130
involved witness 19, 21, 29, 34, 42
involvement 22, 28
involvement theory 17, 20

Jacobson, N. 91–3, 95–6, 104, 108, 115
Jencius, M. 53
Johnson-Migalski, L. ix
Johnson, S. 6, 161

Katz, L. F. 166, 169
Kelly, A. B. 90
Kilroy, M. C. 159
Kleinberg, S. 149

late divorcers 122
Lazarus, A. 89, 91, 99
Lebow, J. 6, 92
Leggett, D. G. 62
Levenson, R. 113
Lew, A. 57, 59
Lewandowski, G. 19
Lewis, J. 71
Liberman, R. 91
life tasks 54, 62
lifestyle 55–7, 62–3
lifestyle assessment 61–3
limerence 122
loner-caretaker couple 157
Long, L. 3, 6
Lorelle, S. 54
Losoncy, L. E. 77
Love Lab 114
love map 120, 140
Luo, Y. 52
Luquet, W. x, 74, 148–51, 154–7, 160, 162

MacIntosh, H. 62–3, 77
Mahoney, M. 89
making life dreams come true 121, 131
Manaster, G. J. 59
Maniacci, M. P. 52, 67
Margolin, G. 91–3, 95, 104, 108
Markman, H. 114–15
Markman, H. J. 153
marriage inventories 97
marriage meeting 78
marriage mission statement 76
Mason, R. C. 153
Mason, M. 153
masters of marriage 114
Matteson, D. L. 53
maximizing 157, 170
McCabe, M. P. 2
McCurdy, K. G. 74, 82
McDuff, P. 3
McGoldrick, M 92
Meichenbaum, D. 89, 93
Mendelsohn, R. 29, 31–2

Meunier, V. x
Mieling, G. G. 2, 5
Miller R. B. 3, 4
Milliren, A. 56, 66
minimizing 157, 170
minorities, 58
mirroring 39, 41, 48, 75
Mitchell, S. 23
Moore K. A. 2
Mores, D. T. 62
Mosak, H. H. 56–7, 67
Mosher, W. D. 2
movement *see* psychological movement, vertical movement, horizontal movement
Muro, L. 149

Navarra, R. J. 114
negative sentiment override 94, 98, 101, 121, 125
negativity bias 166–7
Neisser, U. 88
Nelson, T. 164–5
Noack, T. 2
Norcross, J. C. 67, 170
Norman, C. 19
Notarius, C. 114

object relations theory, 15, 17, 47
Oles, K. 52
Olson D. H. 53, 67
oral history interview 125, 137–8, 141

paradoxical intervention 82
Patterson, T. x, 100
Pavlov, I. 87
Peluso, P. R. 5, 52, 62–3, 77
Perez-Testor, C. 16
Pinsof, W. M. 2
platinum rule 77
play 20, 23
play discovery states 23
Poland, W. 20
Poluso, P. 115
positive perspective 120
positive sentiment override 120
potential couple 23–4, 26
power 52–3, 66, 153
power and competence stage 156
Powers, R. L. 56
present 74
private logic 56
Prochaska, J. O. 67
problem formation: Psychodynamic 24–9; Adlerian 59; CBT 92–99; Imago Relationship Therapy 149–50, 153–4
problem resolution: Psychodynamic 29–32; Adlerian 59; CBT 99–100; Gottman Method 125; Imago Relational Therapy 158–159
prompting 88, 103
proximal change studies 115
psychoeducation, 52, 54, 94
psychological movement 55
purpose of relationships 151

reciprocal inhibition 87
refinement, extension, diversification, and integration, 6–7
reflecting as if 71, 82
reframe 69, 88, 169
Reibstein, J. 6
reinforcement 87–8, 91, 93, 158
Reiter, M. D viii, xi-xii, 1, 7, 149
relapse prevention 131–32
the relationship nightmare 153
reorientation 61, 63
repair attempts 118, 145
repetition compulsion 26–7, 36
research 1–2, 52–3, 62, 92, 113–120, 122, 149–51, 159, 166–7, 169
responsibility 54, 68, 81, 129, 135
rigid-diffuse couple 155
Roberts-Pittman, B. 62
Rogers, C. 91
role of the therapist 31, 152
Ross, D. 88
Rubin, M. E. 114
Ruscher, S.M. 92
Russell, C. S. 67

Sandberg, J. G. 3–4
schemas 56
Schmidt, C. 149
Schore, A. 159
Schwartz-Gottman, J. 115–16, 126–7, 130, 132
Seehaussen, M. 159
self management 89
Seligman, M. 100
shared meaning dimension 121
Shilling, E. A.167
Sholevar, G. P. 4, 6
Shulman, B. 56
Siegel, D. J. 159, 166
Silver, N. 117, 120, 125, 127–8, 130

Simpson, L. E. 3
Skinner, B. F. 87
social interest 58–9, 66, 77
social learning theory 88, 91, 93, 97–8, 100, 108
soft start-up 77
Solomon, M. 155
sound relationship house 116, 119
Spiegel, M. D. 88
Sprenkle, D. H. 67
Spriggs, E. x
Sperry, L. 5, 71, 149–50
Stanley, S. M. 52
Stanley, S. M. 153
stonewalling 73, 83, 117–8, 127, 136
Strosahl, K. D. 95–6
Stuart, R. 91, 107
Sue, D. 92
systematic desensitization 87–8

Tabares, A. 125, 131
Tarlaci, S. 150
temperature 62, 166
termination 31–2, 83, 108–9, 167–8
Thomson, H. 149
Thoresen, C. E. 89
Training in Marriage Enrichment 53
transitional object 22–3, 47
transitional relationships 23, 25, 27, 37–8
treatment plan 66, 120, 126–8, 162
Tremblay, M. 3
trust 72, 104, 106, 123–4, 128–9, 131, 135, 143
turn 120
turning towards 95, 120
Tuttle, L. K. 164

unconsciously collusive relationship 17

validate 35, 88, 102–3, 136, 156, 158, 160, 171
Van de Voort, D. 159
Vespa, J. 2
vertical communication 64–5, 73
vertical movement 55

Waite, L. J. 52
Waring, E. M. 92
Watson, J. B. 87
Watts, R. E. 52, 83
Weinstock, L. M. 92
Weiser, C. 149
Weiss, R. 91, 94, 108, 120
Welwood, J. 53
Whisman, M. A. 92
White, M. B. 3–4
Wiik, K. 2
Wills, 92
Wilson, K. G. 95–6
Winnicott D.W. 22
witnessing 20–1, 29, 36, 42, 45–6
Wolpe, J. 87–8
Wood, B. 165
Writght, J. 3

Yang, J. 56, 66
Yoppi, B. 114
Yorgason, J. B. 3–4
Young, M. 3

zero negativity contract 167
Zorn, P. 149